Dead Pledges

Post·45 Kate Marshall and Loren Glass, Editors
Post•45 Group, Editorial Committee

Dead Pledges

Debt, Crisis, and Twenty-First-Century Culture

Annie McClanahan

Stanford University Press
Stanford, California

Stanford University Press
Stanford, California

©2017 by the Board of Trustees of the Leland Stanford Junior University. All rights reserved.

This book has been published with the assistance of the University of Wisconsin–Milwaukee.

A previous version of Chapter 2 appeared as "Bad Credit: The Character of Credit Scoring," *Representations* (Spring 2014), © 2014 by the Regents of the University of California. Published by University of California Press. Reprinted with permission. A previous version of Chapter 4 appeared as "Dead Pledges: Debt, Horror, and the Credit Crisis," *Post45 Peer Reviewed* (May 7, 2012), http://post45.research.yale.edu/2012/05/dead-pledges-debt-horror-and-the-credit-crisis/. A previous version of the Coda appeared as "The Living Indebted: Student Militancy and the Financialization of Debt," in *Qui Parle* © 2011, University of Nebraska Press. Reprinted with permission.

No part of this book may be reproduced or transmitted in any form or by any means, electronic or mechanical, including photocopying and recording, or in any information storage or retrieval system without the prior written permission of Stanford University Press.

Printed in the United States of America on acid-free, archival-quality paper

Library of Congress Cataloging-in-Publication Data available upon request.

ISBN 978-0-8047-9905-8 (cloth)
ISBN 978-1-5036-0069-0 (electronic)
ISBN 978-1-5036-0658-6 (paper)

Cover art: Cassie Thornton. "CRED," 2014. Neon, argon. 16" × 22" × 5".
Typeset by Bruce Lundquist in 10/15 Minion

Table of Contents

Acknowledgments — vii

Introduction: Dead Pledges — 1

Part One: Social Persons

1   Behavioral Economics and the Credit-Crisis Novel — 21

2   Credit, Characterization, Personification — 55

Part Two: Home Economics

3   Photography and Foreclosure — 99

4   Houses of Horror — 143

Coda: The Living Indebted (on Students and Sabotage) — 185

Notes — 199

Index — 231

Acknowledgments

This book suggests throughout that the language of debt is inadequate to the many forms of solidarity—emotional and social, personal and collective, intellectual and intimate—on which our survival under capitalism depends. I feel doubly aware of this inadequacy as I attempt to name and thank those who have supported me during the writing of this book.

I want first to thank Stanford University Press, especially Emily-Jane Cohen, Marthine Satris, and Emily Smith, and the Post•45 series editors Kate Marshall and Loren Glass for their help and patience in the publishing process. Former Post•45 editor Michael Szalay believed in this project even in its infancy. Alberto Toscano and an anonymous reviewer were incredibly generous and perceptive readers of my manuscript. This book would not be the lovely physical object it is without the generosity and incalculable creativity of Cassie Thornton, who allowed me to use an image of her piece "CRED," originally produced for the SPACES Gallery in Cleveland, Ohio, on the cover. And I want most of all to express my deep gratitude to my dear friend Steven Blevins, whose brilliant and attentive editorial work made this book better beyond measure.

For both material support and vital conversations, I am grateful to the Mahindra Humanities Center at Harvard University, the Society for the Humanities at Cornell University, the Center for 21st Century Studies at University of Wisconsin–Milwaukee, and the Institute for Research in the Humanities at University of Wisconsin–Madison for their support of this project. I especially want to thank Tim Murray and my fellow SHC fellows for their encouragement and engagement. I feel extraordinarily lucky to have had UWM as my professional home for five years, and I am thankful for the support and kindness of the UWM English Department, particularly its former and current chairs Liam Callanan and Mark Netzlof. For comradeship in the wilds of new and unknown institutions, I am inexpressibly grateful to Julie Orlemanski,

Will Baldwin, Tom McEnaney, Amanda Goldsmith, Anna Fischer, and Antoine Traisnel, friends of the heart as well as the mind.

This book has benefited incalculably from the opportunities I have had to present it to a range of generous, critical, and thoughtful listeners and readers. I'm grateful to Chris Wike, Jeff Williams, and the graduate students and faculty at Carnegie Mellon University; Joel Burges and the University of Rochester Humanities Center; Jeff Di Leo and the Society for Critical Exchange at the University of Houston–Victoria; the dialecticians and Americanists at Harvard; Namwali Serpell and Christopher Miller at University of California, Berkeley; the Post•45 Collective and the remarkable participants of its workshops in Chapel Hill and London; and especially Don Pease, Elizabeth Maddox Dillon, and the indefatigable students of the Futures of American Studies Institute who were the first audiences for much of this book. Finally, to my students at UWM, especially the participants in my late capitalism class: you taught me a lot about what it means to live in a period of crisis that I wouldn't have known without your honesty and critical intelligence. Thank you.

I have been incredibly fortunate to have had inestimable teachers of my own. My work as a young scholar was profoundly influenced first by the writing, and then by the support, of the late Randy Martin. Chris Nealon and Neil Larsen were remarkable teachers then and are dear friends now. At UWM, Richard Grusin, Jane Gallop, and Dick Blau have been models of engaged, good-humored, and deeply compassionate mentorship. Most especially, I express my gratitude for the support of Colleen Lye, who from the day I walked into her grad seminar has always challenged and inspired me in equal measure. Her keen vision and intellectual energy are without equivalent.

My intellectual life has been defined most by an amazing group of colleagues, confidants, and co-conspirators. Margaret Ronda and Tobias Meneley have long been and will always be the sine qua non. At Milwaukee, dear friends Nick Fleisher, Rick Popp, Shannon Popp, Aline Lo, Patrick Mundt, David DiValerio, Jason Puskar, Erin O'Donnell, Rebekah Sheldon, Jocelyn Szczpeniak-Gillece, Richard Leson, Ivan Ascher, Kennan Ferguson, Carolyn Eichner, and especially my untiring writing companion Christine Evans helped me survive cold winters and long working days. Finally, my profound gratitude goes to my comrades in Marxist theory: Tim Kreiner, Chris Chen, Sarah Brouillette, and especially Jasper Bernes and Joshua Clover have shared their inimitable critical capacities, political solidarity, and friendship.

Despite this book's critique of domestic space, I am impossibly fortunate to have the families I do. The Martins have provided much laughter and kindness over the years; I consider joining their ranks one of the best decisions of my life. The McClanaclan has always been loving and supportive. My dad, Ed McClanahan, taught me to love the nineteenth-century novel of wills and bills, for which I will always be grateful. Kristina McGrath has long been a source of deep love. Anne Huntington has been caring and hospitable beyond measure. Bill McClanahan will always be my favorite person to talk to about neoliberalism and cops. Most important, to my mom, Cia White: you were my first and are still my best model of intellectual curiosity, teacherly passion, and political commitment. Thank you more than words can say.

Lulu Batya McClanahan wasn't around for the entirety of this book's writing, but her dear smile and joyous hilarity have provided pleasures beyond reckoning. Finally, this book is dedicated to Ted Martin, without whose brilliant mind and endless good humor not a page of it would be possible. Incredible, inestimable, and unrepayable, his support and love can only be counted as gifts.

Dead Pledges

Introduction
Dead Pledges

What is a "dead pledge"? Despite its gothic connotations, it actually names something that is probably quite familiar to many readers: a mortgage contract. The name for a contract on a real estate loan comes from the French *mort gage*. From this surprising etymology, we might exhume any number of meaningful lessons: about the terrifying nature of debt; the strange ontology of property; the uncanniness of ownership; the implicit threat at the heart of the credit contract. *Dead Pledges* is an attempt to show how these and other difficult lessons about debt are encrypted across contemporary culture. Looking at how debt has been represented aesthetically and conceptually in a period of crisis, this book aims to connect debt's cultural representations to its material and political consequences. Casting credit's certainty into doubt, reckoning with the problem of unpayable debts, and revealing the hidden violence of the credit economy, credit-crisis culture reminds us that debt is a matter of life and death: not just for individual borrowers but also for the economy as a whole.

Debt has certainly become the defining feature of economic life today. Since the mid-1970s, US consumers have been using credit to pay not only for housing and automobiles but also, and historically unprecedentedly, for education, health care, groceries, clothes, and all manner of other daily necessities. By the third quarter of 2008, when US and global markets suffered their worst crisis since the Great Depression, US households held $13 trillion in debt, more than thirty times what they held in the mid-1970s.[1] Meanwhile, the US economy had grown increasingly dependent on the borrowing of households, corporations, and the federal government. This borrowing not only funded consumption but also provided opportunities for the financialization of debt-based assets. When this financial market collapsed—when a vicious cycle of falling wages and increasing debt led to a rise in debt defaults, causing a decline in the value of the assets backed by those debts, causing in turn more defaults—the results were catastrophic. From the beginning of 2007 to the end of 2011, more than four million foreclosures were completed; by 2011, nearly one in ten borrowers was defaulting on a credit card or student loan.[2] In the US economy of the twenty-first century, the "dead pledge" of the capitalist system thus appears in all its horror, bringing us face-to-face with everything that is strange and violent about the most taken-for-granted aspects of our economic system: investments and liabilities, owing and ownership, repayment and default.

Dead Pledges is a study of our contemporary culture of debt. Examining novels, poems, conceptual artworks, photographs, and films, this book shows how cultural texts have grappled with the consequences of the rise and fall of the financialized consumer credit economy. As a study of cultural representations of the economy, *Dead Pledges* does not argue that the economy itself is representational—it does not argue that the debt economy can be reduced to our collective belief in it. Rather, my claim is that debt is such a ubiquitous yet elusive social form that we can most clearly and carefully understand it by looking at how our culture has sought to represent it. The chapters that follow seek to show how cultural texts from popular entertainment to avant-garde art allow us to map the landscape of contemporary debt: foreclosure and credit scoring, student debt and securitized risk, microeconomic theory and anti-eviction activism. Across this range of sites, this book offers a history and an aesthetics of contemporary indebtedness as well as an account of the theoretical and political consequences of debt: how it affects our ideas of personhood and moral character; how it changes our understanding of rationality and responsibility; how it transforms our relationship to property and possession. Bringing together economic history, debt theory, and cultural analysis, *Dead Pledges* demonstrates how our understanding of the economy can be illuminated by culture. What is at stake in our contemporary culture of debt, I argue, is not just our measures of economic credibility but also the limits of our imaginative credulity; not just our account of economic character but also our literary characters; not just the money we see but also the way we see money; not just how we pay but also how we imagine getting payback.

Debt, Credit, Culture

Since 2008, a number of theorists have provided much-needed critical accounts of the relationship between debt, sociality, and political subjectivity, including David Graeber (*Debt: The First 5000 Years*), Mauricio Lazzarato (*The Making of the Indebted Man: An Essay on the Neoliberal Condition*, originally published in French as *La fabrique de l'homme endetté*), Richard Dienst (*The Bonds of Debt: Borrowing against the Common Good*), Angela Mitropoulos (*Contract and Contagion: From Biopolitics to Oikonomia*), Fred Moten and Stefano Harney (*The Undercommons: Fugitive Planning and Black Study*), Miranda Joseph (*Debt to Society: Accounting for Life under Capitalism*), and Andrew Ross (*Creditocracy and the Case for Debt Refusal*).[3] *Dead Pledges* owes much to this scholarship, from Graeber's claim that debt turns sociality "into a matter of impersonal arithmetic," to Dienst's more historically situated argument about the relationship between contemporary debt and other forms of exploitation, to Mitropoulos's evocative treatment of the domestic economy of contracts.[4] But it is also an attempt to connect debt theory back to questions of cultural form—a sphere these works rarely address. For an account of the relation between the credit economy and culture, one would have to turn to a now canonical body of historicist literary scholarship—yet this scholarship is almost exclusively focused on credit relations rather than debt. This is largely because there has long seemed to be an intimate connection between credit and culture: more than any other economic relation, credit relies on the systems of naturalization and faith that culture provides. As Marc Shell puts it in *Money, Language, and Thought*, "Credit, or belief, involves the very ground of aesthetic experience, and the same medium that seems to confer belief in [credit] money ... also seems to confer it in literature."[5] Shell argues that to speak of "credit" was, from the beginning, to speak of faith—the faith required to lend money out and expect to receive it back with interest—and that the realist novel provided a model for faith in such paper fictions. Later New Historicist scholarship on literary and economic form—scholarship not incidentally produced in the boom period for contemporary credit—also focuses primarily on credit and the novel. In *Genres of the Credit Economy: Mediating Value in Eighteenth- and Nineteenth-Century Britain*, Mary Poovey argues that the novel taught readers how to believe in things that couldn't be proved, making possible the leaps of faith necessary to the capitalist economy and "mak[ing] the system of credit and debt usable and the market model of value familiar."[6] Deidre Lynch (*The Economy of Character: Novels, Market Culture, and the Business of Inner Meaning*), Margot Finn (*The Character of Credit: Personal Debt in English Culture*), and Ian Baucom (*Specters of the Atlantic: Finance Capital, Slavery, and the Philosophy of History*) have likewise suggested that the realist novel humanized an unfamiliar marketplace and produced a confidence that both the fiction of paper money and the fiction of novelistic character could "go without saying."[7] Descriptions of the relationship between literary form and the credit economy have also underwritten broader claims about the way that credit ostensibly creates a sense of social community. Thus Jennifer Baker argues in *Securing the Commonwealth: Debt, Speculation, and Writing in the Making of Early America*, for instance, that seventeenth-century credit fostered a "sanguine . . . view of capitalism's promise to promote simultaneously both individual opportunity and communal cohesion."[8]

We thus find in the rich landscape of recent interdisciplinary scholarship either criticism that explores debt but not culture or criticism that explores culture but not debt. In our own twenty-first-century moment, however, the smooth circulation of credit has demonstrated its ability to stall out, and the riskiness of an economy fueled by debt has become apparent. Such a moment requires us to take stock of an entirely new relationship between economic and cultural form. *Dead Pledges* contends that in a moment of debt crisis—in a moment in which the fantasy of credit as a salutary cultural and social form has been abandoned—the standard modes for representing credit and debt have likewise been altered. The credit-crisis texts analyzed in this book reveal the overt risks, phantasmatic realities, and incalculable debts that a debt economy can no longer redeem.

In *Dead Pledges*, cultural texts perform the urgent work of mediation. The economic and social history this book tells alternates between two different scales. On the one hand is the scale of the visible, the experienced, and the everyday: the strange experience of receiving a "personalized" credit card offer; the fear of housing insecurity; the public scene of eviction. On the other hand is the scale of the economic system as a whole and of the complex global financial markets that have driven world economic growth for the last four decades. *Dead Pledges* argues, first, that what connects these two scales is consumer debt; and second, that what illuminates this connection is cultural form. This book focuses on consumer debt rather than national or corporate debt because consumer debt, I suggest, is uniquely situated between our everyday experience of the economy and the economy's larger structural dynamics, which function far beyond our agency, knowledge, or control. Consumer debt's dual face—at once specific and systemic, everyday and epochal—is mirrored by cultural forms (literature, art, poetry, film) that, as this book reads them, similarly work to connect our daily lives of indebtedness to the systemic totality of the credit economy.

Debt: A Contemporary History

In order to understand the two scales of this book's analysis, it is necessary to tell the history of our contemporary debt economy. Beginning in early 2007, the first signs of an emerging crisis in US credit markets were becoming obvious. Declining real estate value and an increase in the consumer credit default rate were the first signals of the coming contagion; they were followed by a crash in securities backed by risky debt, then by defaults among the institutions that had bet on or insured those securities, and eventually by the failure or near failure of banks connected to other financial institutions who had invested in debt. By the late summer of 2008 the devastation was no longer containable, and in the fall of that year it became apparent that the entire global economy was swept up not simply in a crisis of liquidity (banks unwilling to lend) but in a crisis of solvency: the banks themselves were bankrupt. Dozens of major international financial institutions failed or were bailed out; almost unimaginably large amounts of money were infused into collapsing markets by both federal governments and the International Monetary Fund (IMF)/World Bank; a looming sovereign-debt crisis in Europe was exacerbated by the contagion in financial markets, eventually leading to a seemingly permanent state of imposed austerity; and a downturn in global economic activity overall, including productive investment and state investment, caused a global recession whose consequences (both in and outside the United States) included massive unemployment, food crises, and increased rates of eviction, bankruptcy, homelessness, and suicide.[9]

The crisis of 2007–8 was particularly destructive because by the end of the twentieth century, consumer financing had moved from the margins to the center of the US economy. The development of debt securitization (which allowed debt to function as a tradable financial instrument) meant that consumer credit was no longer simply an aid to consumption but an industry in itself. Technological improvements in data collection and processing made it possible to both evaluate and price credit risk to a fine level of quantifiable detail. Retailers began tracking consumer behavior and relying more heavily on information collected by credit bureaus. Following the passage of the Equal Credit Opportunity Act in 1974, which prohibited discrimination on the basis of race, religion, nationality, sex, marital status, or age, lenders sought out new statistical and behavioral models that used standardized data and credit-monitoring systems.[10] This science of consumer credit rating made it possible for banks to hedge credit risk in new ways by measuring a wide range of calculable risks and creating an equally wide range of chargeable rates.[11] Very low federal borrowing rates in the early 1990s and through most of the 2000s, which made the banks' own borrowing cheap, and the deregulation of caps on interest rates and fees, which allowed them to raise prices on consumer loans, made consumer lending an even more attractive industry.

The story in the market for housing debt is similar. In housing, even more than in credit card lending, securitization, which makes debt a fungible commodity by creating a secondary market for its sale, fueled the supply of consumer credit. Investors looking for profitable investment opportunities were confident that housing prices would continue the unprecedented rise they had made over the second half of the twentieth century and thus invested heavily in a financial instrument called a mortgage-backed security (MBS). The MBS was not an entirely new invention—it was originally created by the Federal Housing Administration (FHA) as a means to improve the liquidity of the mortgage-lending market after the Great Depression—but legislation passed in 1970 permitting the Federal National Mortgage Association (FNMA, or Fannie Mae) to purchase private, non–federally insured mortgages, as well as the deregulation of the savings and loan industry in the 1980s, gave more investors access to these increasingly complex financial products. The result was that whereas once most mortgages were "deposit financed"—one bank customer's debt was funded by another's savings—increasingly mortgages were funded through the sale of speculative financial instruments that turned a borrower's mortgage payment into a revenue stream by grouping many mortgages together and selling them as an investment. Those bundled mortgages were typically "tranched" into different risk categories, with the low-risk loans offering the lowest rate of return but also the least uncertainty. Many of those loans, however, were not as low risk as investors might have convinced themselves they were. As in the consumer credit industry, the repeal of ceilings on mortgage interest rates had opened up more and more markets for credit and made "adjustable-rate" mortgages (ARMs) increasingly common: ARMs are home loans whose monthly payments steadily increase over time, often well beyond the borrower's ability to pay them.[12] Demand for credit securities also produced ever-greater demand for the debt that underwrote them, which meant that soon lenders had to relax their lending requirements for mortgage credit to meet this demand. By the early 2000s, the so-called subprime market—the market in the riskiest debt—

had gone from 5 percent of all lending to 30 percent.[13] Eventually, demand for housing-debt securities threatened to outpace demand for housing itself, and lenders had to attract entirely new categories of borrowers by ceasing to even conduct background, income, and credit-history checks.[14]

The change from deposit-funded lending to the use of capital and securities markets—from mortgages funded directly by banks to mortgages funded by far-flung investors—greatly increased market liquidity: the value of a "fixed" asset like a house, or the value of mortgage payments on that house, could suddenly flow across the country in a single keystroke.[15] Or across the globe: in his excellent history of personal credit in the United States, Louis Hyman writes that securitization made it possible for "oil money from the Middle East [to] finance housing developments in the [US] Mid-west."[16] Everyone from financial investors to the Federal Reserve believed that this kind of global securitization created a virtuous cycle, through which banks could lend to previously unqualified buyers and dilute the risk by reselling those loans as securities to speculative investors around the world. But enhanced liquidity had also radically altered the use of structured finance techniques by creating opportunities for high-risk practices like arbitrage (the practice of taking advantage of small price differences) and leverage (the practice of borrowing to fund investments).[17] Commercial banks took on massive amounts of debt to buy financial instruments based on the risky loans made by other lenders, and creditors increasingly became more indebted than those to whom they were lending. Consequently, a single default could trigger a chain reaction that would spread swiftly and virally through the whole economy. The increased liquidity of money, hailed as the singular achievement of securitization, meant that a crisis in the system spread like a virus—hence the description of financial derivatives as "toxic assets." Because lenders had either passed the loans they made on to other investors or invested in instruments like credit-default swaps, it was no longer always in their interest to prevent debtors from defaulting, tearing asunder the fantasy of a socially salutary creditor/debtor relation.

Technological developments in data monitoring and analysis, alongside institutional, regulatory, and technocratic transformations in the ability of financial institutions to create, price, and trade increasingly complex financial instruments, also made it possible for creditors to lend more money than ever before. The outstanding consumer debt of households more than doubled as a percentage of disposable income (from 62 percent to 127 percent) between 1975 and 2005.[18] As of 2015, Americans owed more than $12 trillion in debt: $8.2 trillion in mortgages, $1.3 trillion in student loans, and around $890 billion in credit card debt.[19] Although default risk was increasingly easy to quantify and predict, which opened up the market to new borrowers, and although low federal interest rates made it cheap for banks to lend money, debt was not always more affordable for the borrowers themselves. So-called affordability products—loans that did not require borrowers to document their income, interest-only loans, no-down-payment loans, and loans that allowed lenders to borrow twice the value of the house—proliferated during the last years of the twentieth century and the beginning of the twenty-first. But for many borrowers, this "affordable" credit was actually coming at a very high price: credit card interest rates peaked in the 1980s during Reagan's "Volcker shock" and then steadily fell over the next few decades, but increases in fees, penalties, and membership charges—as well as the ubiquity of variable-rate cards, which add a fixed percentage to the prime rate based on a borrower's perceived credit risk—ultimately made borrowing more expensive for most debtors, especially for those who "rolled over" their debt from month to month.[20] Meanwhile, for those still trapped in the "alternative-financing industry"—the vast, unregulated, and largely undocumented system of payday loans, check-cashing services, and pawn shops that has boomed in the last few decades—the economic, social, psychological, and even physiological costs of debt have been even higher. Payday loans typically charge interest rates of well over 100 percent, often as high as 1,000 percent. In 2008 payday lenders charged their customers a collective $7 billion in fees, and if one combines payday lenders, rent-to-own shops, check-cashing services, and pawnbrokers, the alternative-financing industry robs the poor, low-credit-scored, and "unbanked" in the United States of more than $25 billion every year.[21]

Some of the most significant changes in regulated consumer lending have been in the education loan sector. In the early 1990s, only around 30 percent of students borrowed to pay for college; today, more than 65 percent of students take out loans, and more than forty million Americans currently hold at least one student loan. Having increased by more than 160 percent over the last decade, student loan debt is still on the rise, and the average graduate of a four-year institution leaves with her diploma in one hand and a bill for $29,000 of debt in the other.[22] While most student loans continue to be provided through the federal lending system, unmet financial need has increased far faster than the maximum borrowable amount, allowing a multi-billion-dollar private student loan market to emerge to fill in the gap. According to the College Board, in 1997–98 private education loans totaled $2.5 billion; ten years later, they totaled $17.9 billion, a nearly 800 percent increase.[23] These companies market their loans very aggressively, although the loans often have very high interest and much stricter rules on repayment than federal loans do. Exploited by the marketing efforts of private lenders, many borrowers take out private loans even when they are still eligible for lower-interest-rate federal loans: half of those taking out private bank loans have not used up their full federal loan eligibility, a figure almost precisely the same as the number of prime-qualified mortgage borrowers who unnecessarily ended up with subprime home loans.[24]

Because the amount of consumer lending across all these sectors (mortgages, credit cards, student loans) far outpaced other economic gains (especially wages) between the 1980s and the early 2000s, default on all these risky loans eventually became widespread. When it did, the interconnectedness of credit markets—once seen as a model for the interdependence of the social order—threatened to destroy the economy. The effects on the indebted were especially catastrophic. In the United States following the crisis, unemployment rose by more than 5 percent, while home values fell by as much as 60 percent in some regions.[25] In a single year between 2008 and 2009, credit card default rates nearly doubled.[26] In early 2009, households who had some retirement savings reported that those savings had dropped in value by around 30 percent.[27] Personal bankruptcies went up dramatically as well: the rate in 2004 (before the crash) was more than four times as high as the rate in 1980 and nearly eighty times as high as the rate in 1920.[28] At the beginning of 2011, three years after the collapse of credit markets, nationwide one in ten homeowners was ninety days or more late on her mortgage, and one in seven was ninety days or more late on a credit card payment.[29] In the first four years of the recession, 8.2 million foreclosures were begun.[30] Losses in wealth were worst within communities of color: every cent of the wealth accumulated by African American households in the post–civil rights era was lost as a result of the collapse of home and investment values.[31] Post-crisis immiseration also had a ripple effect, impacting even those too poor for mortgage debt: foreclosure significantly increased the rate of family homelessness, since many of those evicted were renters who lived in buildings owned by landlords or property developers who had defaulted on their mortgages.[32] In short, far from being sustained by collective confidence and the technocratic management of uncertainty, the financial markets of the early twenty-first century were in fact predicated on the selective deployment of uncontrollable risk and on the transfer of much of this risk to the most vulnerable economic subjects.

This history emphasizes a series of economic, social, and historical transformations in the management of consumer debt in the US economy, explaining the institutional, regulatory, and technological changes that allowed US consumers to go into more debt than they could repay. By attending to the shift from bank deposit–financed lending to speculative securitization, it also explains where the money they were borrowing came from. Yet two questions remain. First, why did borrowers go into so much debt: What explains the growing *demand* for credit, especially given that it was more available but less affordable than ever? Second, what explains the ready *supply* of liquid money: Why were capitalists so desperate for places to put their money that they were willing to divert ever more of it into financial instruments and risky speculation, spheres of the economy that had for most of the twentieth century been secondary to safer, more profitable forms of investment?

We begin with the question of demand. Here too we find that consumer and housing debt in the twenty-first century had a markedly different function than it had in the past. Historically, consumer debt was a tool to enable the purchase of expensive or luxury goods and to "smooth" consumption, allowing for a more regular and predictable quality of life over the course of a consumer's lifetime. In the last few decades, however, consumer debt has become a means for the reproduction of households and a stopgap to compensate for wage stagnation. As Hyman notes, "In the face of uncertainty and declining real wages, Americans indebted themselves to maintain the life they had once been able to afford."[33] Over a thirty-year period between 1980 and 2010, housing prices increased 50 points above the Consumer Price Index (CPI) of inflation.[34] Annual per capita health-care spending in the United States rose (in inflation-adjusted dollars) from $350 in 1970 to $7,500 in 2008.[35] Child-related costs also increased significantly in the same period: child-care spending increased from $84 to $143 per week between 1985 and 2011, and between 2000 and 2010 the overall cost of raising a child to age seventeen jumped 8.5 percent, not including college costs.[36] Not surprisingly, the cost of higher education has climbed the most vertiginously of all: since 1975 the average price of tuition at US colleges has increased 900 percent, or 650 points above the CPI.[37]

During the same period that prices for basic goods and reproductive needs climbed, wages stagnated. If one compares the CPI to increases in the minimum wage between 1970 and 2011, for every $1.00 increase in the minimum wage since 1970, the price of the average consumer good has gone up $1.36.[38] Even after the collapse of housing prices in 2008, a house today costs approximately three times as much as it did in 1970 compared to the average wage earned. The Economic Policy Institute puts the story of wage stagnation clearly and starkly: "Over the entire 34-year period between 1979 and 2013, the hourly wages of middle-wage workers (median-wage workers who earned more than half the workforce but less than the other half) were stagnant, rising just 6 percent—less than 0.2 percent per year. . . . The wages of middle-wage workers were totally flat or in decline over the 1980s, 1990s and 2000s, except for the late 1990s. The wages of low-wage workers fared even worse, falling 5 percent from 1979 to 2013."[39] And while the cost of higher education has been outpacing inflation almost exponentially, the wages of young college graduates have been stagnating, and fewer college graduates have been able to find jobs that provide health insurance, meaning that the total income of these workers, including benefits, is not simply stagnating but falling.[40] Unemployment numbers tell a similar story, particularly if we use data on "employment as a percentage of population" (which, unlike the commonly referenced "unemployment rate," takes into account workers no longer seeking employment, the underemployed, and those who do not enter or reenter the workforce because they cannot earn enough to pay for child care or transportation): as of 2013, employment as a percentage of population was at its lowest rate in thirty years.[41]

This history of declining wages and rising costs of reproduction explains much of why US workers and the unemployed were so willing to go into debt: there were not a lot of other options for them. Put simply, the availability of cheap credit, along with the effort to prop up real estate value as a form of middle-class wealth, was the means through which both capital and workers themselves compensated for declining wages and the decimation of the social safety net once funded by a high rate of profit and growth. No longer simply a means to enhance "discretionary" spending, debt became the means through which many working- and middle-class families, as well as households experiencing persistent unemployment or underemployment, were able to continue to survive.[42]

So what about supply? Why were investors willing to take on more risk than ever to make more credit available? Here again we need to take a step backward to think about the role credit typically plays in the economy. Historically, credit serves as the means through which capital extends itself in periods of growth and renews itself in moments of crisis. The first way it does so is through spatial expansion. Marx describes this succinctly in *Capital*: "The credit system ... accelerates the material development of the productive forces and the establishment of the world-market, which it is the historical task of the capitalist system of production to bring to a certain level of development, as material foundations for the new form of production."[43] Much as credit allowed seventeenth-century merchant capitalists to create a vast export market, making possible some of the "primitive accumulations" that led to fully developed capitalism, it also enabled the globalization of the postwar twentieth-century economy. As a result of competitive pressures, high oil prices, and the rising cost of labor in developed countries, by the early 1970s capital desperately needed what David Harvey has influentially termed a "spatial fix": it needed new markets for its goods and less expensive labor to produce them. Capitalists who were invested in industry, agriculture, and transportation thus struck out for new territory, seeking the cheaper labor markets and other resources of the developing world. Credit fueled all this motion and expansion, allowing capitalists to invest in new places; to speed up the turnover time between production, circulation, and sale; and to mitigate the costs and risks of moving between national currencies. The result in the United States and other developed countries was rapid deindustrialization, which caused pressure on wages and led to lower rates of industrial employment—the very things that caused the boom in demand for consumer credit described previously.[44]

Yet even globalization's spatial fix wasn't enough of a remedy for the postwar slowdown. As a result of the so-called microelectronic revolution, investments in fixed capital (machines and technology) had grown far faster than investments in the labor force, and the rate of industrial profit began to fall precipitously.[45] As political economist Norbert Trenkle puts it, "The self-supporting thrust of post-war growth came to an end. There was no increased investment in the means of production, factories, buildings etc., because these could no longer produce sufficient profit."[46] Put simply, then, those capitalists who did not move their money out of US industrial production moved it out of production altogether. Instead, they turned to financial markets, newly empowered and newly flexibilized by deregulation (itself a response to structural transformations like the rise of the multinational corporation and the boom in offshore banking).⁴⁷ Contemporary financial investments—what Peter Gowan describes as "money-dealing money"—mostly allow investors to trade on anticipated future profits (their own or other capitalists'), to insure against risk, or to provide credit to everyone from corporations and nations to individuals.⁴⁸ The financial markets that began to drive capital accumulation in the 1970s are thus different from the shares or bonds that have long funded productive investment directly. Contemporary financial speculation increasingly takes place in secondary markets such as the derivatives markets that, by the 1990s, were briskly funding mortgage and credit card debt. Whereas globalization is a spatial fix that increases the space over which commodities can be produced and circulated, this kind of financialization makes possible a kind of "temporal fix": it allows capital to treat an anticipated realization of value as if it has already happened. Thus while some of the return on this money-dealing money was the result of interest and fees siphoned off from the present profits of global manufacturing, the main source was the anticipated profits of a perpetually deferred future: money-dealing money depends on the assumption that all that corporate, or national, or personal debt will eventually be repaid when everyone has the money to do so. The rapid growth of financial markets in the 1970s was therefore not the effect of pure ideology. Rather, capital was invested in financial markets simply because they provided a higher rate of return on investment than production did: financialization allowed capitalists to supplement the declining profitability of investment in present production with money borrowed from the profits of a hoped-for future production.

Crisis and Culture

In 2008, however, all those hopes came to a grinding halt. No longer could capital convincingly promise to make good on its speculative obligations. When financial markets fell apart, the resulting crisis revealed the earlier, more intractable problem that capital had temporarily deferred: the absence of any real productive opportunities in the wake of deindustrialization. The events of 2008 were, as Gopal Balakrishnan persuasively argues, "the inexorable resurfacing of the pressure for a system-wide shake-out that was never allowed to happen over the course of the last three decades."⁴⁹

One way to view the contemporary crisis is as yet another in the series of repeating, intensifying "shakeouts" that have characterized capitalism since its inception. The most influential account of this view appears in Giovanni

Arrighi's *The Long Twentieth Century*, which describes "a recurrent pattern" in capitalism between epochs of material expansion (investment in production and manufacturing) and phases of financial expansion (investment in the stock and capital markets).[50] Reading this oscillatory history through world systems theory, Arrighi argues that each of these phases corresponded to a different imperial power. As each hegemon enters its final stage of financialization, it comes into crisis and is forced to cede control of the global economy to a new, rising hegemon: from the seventeenth to the mid-twentieth century, Italian rule gives way to Dutch, Dutch to British, and finally British to US. As Arrighi's account suggests, the current crisis is thus a crisis not only in financial markets and the global economy but also in US hegemony. Decisively the superpower of the productive economy in the postwar period, the United States entered its own phase of financialization in the mid-1970s, and this epoch of US financial and state domination arguably came to an end with the crisis of 2008. According to Balakrishnan, "We are now at the end of an Indian summer of American imperial power."[51] In his reference to the closing of US hegemony as an "Indian summer," Balakrishnan intentionally echoes Arrighi's description (itself borrowed from Fernand Braudel) of the "signs of autumn" that precede a crisis. For Arrighi, the signs of autumn are the evidence—registered culturally, socially, and politically—that a crisis is nigh and that a hegemon is at the end of its economic and political reign. It is thus in the United States where we can most clearly see both the effects and the aesthetics, both the material signs and the ideological signals, of the global crisis that came to the surface in 2008.

Yet as Balakrishnan also reminds us, the crisis that began in the 1970s and came to full, manifest expression in 2008 is a different kind of crisis from those that heralded the ends of the Italian, Dutch, and British financial empires. In this crisis, there is neither a new rising hegemon to take the reins nor an immanent resolution available within the current regime of capital accumulation: winter is coming, but not spring. As political economist Claus Peter Ortlieb puts it, "The capitalist process of accumulation and expansion [has] come up against absolute material limits, the observance of which must lead to the burning-out of the capitalist logic of valorization, and the disregard for which to the destruction of its material foundations and the possibility of human life as such."[52] Balakrishnan and Ortlieb's arguments exemplify an important strain of thought in contemporary Marxist political economy known as "value critique," which contends that the massive improvements in labor productivity made possible by the technological and computing revolutions of the late twentieth century herald not the perfection of capitalism but its end. The shift from productive enterprises to financial markets that these revolutions required allowed capital to sustain itself a little longer, but the contemporary collapse of those markets suggests the exhaustion of all other sources of profit. According to value critique, the current crisis will not lead to the emergence of a new regime of capitalist accumulation under a different imperial superpower. Instead, it heralds something akin to a "terminal crisis" in which no renewal of capital profitability is possible.[53]

Although *Dead Pledges* is not a work of political economy, the theory of terminal crisis is of profound importance to this book's understanding of debt and culture. Credit is the economic form of the boom time; it is a temporal fix when it is still possible to fix things. But debt—as a figure for credit that is unpaid, defaulted, foreclosed, bankrupted, written off, unredeemed—is the economic form of crisis: of a period in which no one can pay. For our contemporary era of debt, crisis is an invaluable historical hermeneutic, compelling us to anticipate limits, to imagine alternatives, to welcome collapse, and thus to resist the "end of history" triumphalism characteristic of late capitalist ideology in boom times. As I articulate in *Dead Pledges*, this sense of crisis has become both the ambient context and the manifest content of cultural production, social experience, and economic life in the United States.[54] You can see it in the scenes of foreclosure that occur in our neighborhoods, in the volatile stock market whose ups and downs have become a part of the daily news, in the collapsing bridges and empty housing developments that signal the effects of vanishing social surpluses, and in the reactionary and often violent economic protectionism that characterizes the social politics of a declining empire. Crisis, you could say, allows us to glimpse the owl of Minerva in the autumnal afternoon instead of only at dusk. The historical glimpse made possible in a time of crisis is afforded us, finally, by cultural form. The aesthetic forms surveyed in *Dead Pledges* are the cultural expression of our shared autumnal condition. They thus allow us to reckon with the ways crisis has transformed our sense of personhood, our understanding of property, and our experience of social belonging. While economic ideology attempts to explain away catastrophic failures of market self-regulation, capital renewal, and social connection, the cultural texts explored here expose these contradictions for what they are. The texts studied in this book do not, as in Claude Levi-Strauss's famous description, provide imaginary attempts to overcome real social contradictions.[55] Instead, they offer their own unresolved and overdetermined responses to the unique social and economic contradictions of debt. At the limit of what can be represented about debt, we confront not only the ongoing crisis that is capitalism but also the terminal crisis now stirring within it.

Overview

Dead Pledges is organized into two parts. Part One takes up the problem of subjectivity as it manifests within contemporary conditions of credit and debt. More specifically, this half of the book explores the changing relationship between the individual person and the social totality in the contexts of behavioral economics and credit scoring. Part Two focuses on the social form that most explicitly mediates our relationship to debt, property. In considering the effect of foreclosure and eviction not just on our view of the home but on our imagination of private possession itself, I suggest that the housing crisis has revealed the "dead pledge" of the mortgage to be a radically antisocial form.

Chapter 1 analyzes novelistic representations of the credit crisis. Focusing on Jonathan Dee's *The Privileges*, Adam Haslett's *Union Atlantic*, and Martha McPhee's *Dear Money*, I read the credit-crisis novel's interest in individual psychology alongside and against the rise of behavioral economics. Behavioral economists understood the financial crisis as a consequence of individual choices and cultural climates, seeing it variously as an effect of social or familial values, individual "taste" and "preference," or collective "irrational exuberance." At once mirroring and refuting these explanations, the credit-crisis novel reveals a deep ambivalence about the model of psychological complexity that undergirds both novelistic character and the behavioral economic subject. Imagining the social world in terms familiar to microeconomic theory—as the aggregation of the free acts of private, autonomous consumers in a public marketplace—these novels struggle to represent a coherent social order, bringing to the surface the buried tension in behavioralism between belief in individual accountability and resistance to a language of individual blame. This tension, I argue, is formalized in the credit-crisis novel as a problem of narrative perspective. Taken together, these credit-crisis novels suggest that the rich, full, autonomous *homines economici* of both the realist novel and microeconomic theory are bankrupt.

Chapter 2 addresses the relationship between debt and personhood. The development of a standard practice for evaluating consumer credit in the late eighteenth and early nineteenth centuries both depended on and enabled the emergence of a realist model of literary character. In the late twentieth and early twenty-first centuries, however, credit evaluation practices turned away from subjective, qualitative, narrative forms of credit evaluation and toward objective, quantitative, data-driven models of credit scoring. Although contemporary creditors claim to translate persons into impersonal numbers—freed of the designations but replete with the marks of race and class—they import the fictions of personhood stripped from human subjects into the scores themselves. To understand the perduring presence of the person, this chapter considers both characterization—the ways in which the novel produces socially legible fictional figures—and personification—the ways in which conceptual art and conceptual poetry offer mediating forms through which the subject is made or made to speak. Gary Shytengart's novel *Super Sad True Love Story* attests to the persistence of racial discrimination as the secret behind seemingly objective methods of credit evaluation, while conceptual art by Cassie Thornton and poetry by Mathew Timmons and Timothy Donnelly register debt as not simply as a personal experience but also as a material and historical force.

Chapters 3 and 4 turn from the individual and consumer credit to the larger social order and to securitized debt, specifically in the form of the mortgage. In Chapter 3, I bring together a wide range of photographs—including photojournalism, conceptual photography, and satellite images—that document the economic crisis with images of abandoned homes and evicted families. These photographs reveal the effects of the boom and bust of the mortgage market on our cultural or ideological view of the home: the difference between inside and outside, private and public, architecture and nature, inhabited and empty. But they also raise questions about the politics of representation. The ability to visualize the economic crisis by photographing a home in the process of eviction or foreclosure depends not only on technical and artistic conditions but also on legal and material forces. Photographs of the housing crisis are thus compelled to draw on what I describe as an *unheimlich* aesthetic. Rather than read the uncanny simply as the psychic and aesthetic correlative of debt in general and foreclosure in particular, I argue that the uncanny conjures a kind of historical temporality. Images of abandoned industrial landscapes and empty housing developments register the uncanny power property holds over the social order. These photographs also glimpse the foreshadowed crisis in capitalism, such that the uncanny temporality of debt becomes both the reappearance of the past and the promise of a coming future.

Chapter 4 begins by asking why the language of horror characterizes so much contemporary discourse on the economic crisis, from the ubiquitous "zombie banks" to the description of Goldman Sachs as a "great, blood-sucking vampire squid." To understand this, I turn to four credit-crisis horror films that explicitly link fear, foreclosure, and financialized credit: *Drag Me to Hell* (dir. Sam Raimi), *Dream Home* (*Wai dor lei ah yut ho*, dir. Pang Ho-cheung), *Mother's Day* (dir. Darren Lynn Bousman), and *Crawlspace* (dir. Josh Stolberg). All four films explicitly take up real estate lending, mortgage speculation, and foreclosure risk, locating horror not just in the "gothic economy" of high finance but also in the "dead pledge" of the mortgage contract. In them, the formal mechanisms of suspense become an index of the somatic tolls of risk; the visual excesses of gore become the signs of financial contagion and toxicity. Using horror and the home-invasion genre to explore not only the risks of foreclosure but also the shifting understandings of property and ownership consequent to the housing crisis, these films horrifically literalize the doctrine of caveat emptor. Exploring the relationship between "paying back" as a seemingly salutary structure of social obligation and "payback" as the logic of revenge, they suggest that the introduction of speculative risk has shifted the social force of credit contracts from the promise of trust to the threat of revenge.

As I have already suggested, the credit contract's presumption of free and equal exchange, its confidence in social judgments of moral character, and its reliance on collective belief have led many scholars to see it as the basis for social mutuality in a dispersed modern world. In the 2008 crisis, however, credit was exposed as an antagonistic rather than reciprocal relationship. The Coda to *Dead Pledges* thus explores an emerging antidebt politics. I argue that "debt strikes" and the occupation or sabotage of domestic space are forms of protest that attempt to block capital at the point of circulation. Such movements also offer a new view of sociality—one that lies outside the realm of both economic rationality and social "debts." They suggest the emergence of what I describe—against the commonplace descriptions of our illusioned belief in the defaulted promises of capitalism—as a kind of crisis subjectivity, a demystified condition of radical percipience and canny knowing.

Part One Social Persons

1 Behavioral Economics and the Credit-Crisis Novel

Following the collapse of the dot-com economy in the early years of the twenty-first century, private investment in US assets began wane. Fearful of recession, the US Federal Reserve reduced interest rates, lowering the cost of borrowing to banks and, by extension, consumers. Credit became cheaper than ever. Spurred on by high demand, housing prices rose an astonishing 68 percent. By early 2007, however, investors were beginning to recognize the profoundly high risk inherent in securitized debt. As interest rates began to tick up and housing prices began to fall, a wave of bankruptcies hit the subprime mortgage-lending sector first, then highly leveraged investment banks like Bear Stearns. From July 2007 to March 2008, investment banks and brokerages lost $175 billion of capital. In the fall of 2008, global financial services firm Lehman Brothers filed for the largest bankruptcy in US history; American Insurance Group (AIG), which had insured high-risk MBSs, and wealth-management firm Merrill Lynch were "saved" by being sold for pennies on the dollar. Although the world's central banks pumped immense amounts of liquidity into the global financial system—$150 billion in stimulus from the United States alone and $200 billion from international central banks—banks were unwilling to lend to one another, paralyzing credit markets across the United States and around the world. Between 2007 and 2008 nearly a hundred mortgage lenders failed. In October 2008, as the head of the IMF declared the global economy "on the brink" of total meltdown, many countries were forced to close markets or halt trading lest the wave of failures lead panicked depositors to run on their banks.[1]

In the immediate aftermath of this crisis, it seemed a matter of great urgency to decide who was responsible for the crash. In early 2009, *Time* magazine ran a poll identifying the "Top 25 People to Blame for the Financial Crisis." The list was noteworthy for its emphasis on individuals. There were no institutions on this list—no AIG, no Lehman Brothers, no Securities and Exchange

Commission. The subtitle of the article ("The Good Intentions, Bad Managers, and Greed behind the Meltdown") stressed personal moral failures and individual malfeasance. In a rhetorical move intended to delegitimize a handful of market players, the profiles themselves highlighted biographical details of the purported miscreants, even when such details seemed of little relevance. The profile for Countrywide CEO Angelo Mozilo, "King of the Subprime," opens by describing him as "the son of a butcher," while Bear Stearns's CEO Jimmy Cayne, who presided over the company's collapse, resulting in nearly twenty thousand layoffs, "reportedly smoked pot."[2]

Why, at the same time we frequently described the global financial system as impossibly complex, massive, and impenetrable, did we also want to insist on the causal power of personal failings or individual folly?[3] We can begin to answer this question, I believe, by reflecting on the relationship between two genres that each had a rather remarkable boom in the wake of the 2008 bust: the behavioral economic account of financial crisis and the credit-crisis realist novel.

Behavioral economics first emerged in the 1980s but had a surge in popularity in the wake of 2008. According to contemporary behavioralists George Akerlof and Robert Shiller, authors of the influential 2009 book *Animal Spirits: How Human Psychology Drives the Economy and Why It Matters for Global Capitalism*, economic events like the crash of 2008 are not "driven by inscrutable technical factors or erratic government action" but by "variations in individual feelings, impressions, and passions." Emphasizing the decisive force of "individual thought patterns: changing confidence, temptations, envy, resentment, and illusions," Akerlof and Shiller hew closely to the premises of *Time*'s list: economic crises are caused by greed and folly, and thus the way to prevent them is to change individual behavior.[4] The influence of behavioralism affected more than just economists and journalists in the wake of the crisis: novelists, invested by virtue of their own trade in the relationship between individuals and sociohistorical forces, also wanted to explore the idea that "individual feelings" were the key to understanding economic collapse. In 2010 alone, a slew of US credit-crisis novels appeared to critical acclaim: Sam Lypsyte's *The Ask* and Jonathan Dee's *The Privileges*, both *New York Times* notable books of the year; Adam Haslett's *Union Atlantic*, praised by the *New Yorker*'s famously hard-to-please reviewer James Wood; National Book Award winner Jess Walter's *The Financial Lives of the Poets*; Eric Puchner's *Model Home*, a PEN/Faulkner Award finalist and a *New York Times Book Review* "Editor's Choice" selection; and

National Book Award finalist Martha McPhee's *Dear Money*.[5] Like behavioral-economic scholarship and behavioralist economic journalism, these novels are all concerned with individual financial misconduct—everything from insider trading and money laundering to real estate disclosure fraud—and with the irrationality or greed, the false optimism or failures of will, that cause individuals to invest or manage money badly. Although no one on *Time*'s list was ever prosecuted for malfeasance (in fact, many either kept their jobs or left with tidy severance packages), the credit-crisis novel very much wanted to mount a fictional perp walk.

Neither the behavioralist op-eds nor the realist novels that appeared in the wake of 2008 put the blame exclusively on heavy hitters like Angelo Mozilo and Alan Greenspan. The idea that the crisis was also, even primarily, the fault of irresponsible American shoppers was equally ubiquitous: in journalism and op-eds, and by politicians across the political spectrum, we were told again and again that American homeowners had been all too willing to mortgage their futures to satisfy short-term desires. Indeed, the "American Consumer" appears as the single aggregate blame holder on *Time*'s list: "We've been borrowing, borrowing, borrowing," the article announces, because "we enjoyed living beyond our means." We see this same desire to blame profligate, overindebted consumers for the crisis in Walters's *Financial Lives*, Lypsyte's *The Ask*, and Puchner's *Model Home*. All of these novels are about middle-class fathers who have made bad financial decisions, lost their jobs, and gone heavily into debt. All three track the moral education of these irresponsible consumers, and each one ends as its head-of-household protagonist comes to accept full responsibility for his fate. All three also feature an adultery plot and treat marital betrayal as an analogue to financial infidelity, suggesting that these adulterous debtors must atone for both sexual and economic trespasses.[6] In turn, the language of pathological excess, promiscuity, and addiction—and subsequently the possibility of "recovery"—allows all three novels to propose that the causes of both domestic strife and burdensome debt lie in a fiscal irresponsibility that reflects a failure of moral character as much as an economic miscalculation. As *Financial Lives* puts it, "It's all connected, these crises ... they are interrelated, like ... [our] own decline, like the housing market and the stock market and the credit market. We can try to separate them, but these are interrelated systems, reliant upon one another, broken, fucked up, ruined systems."[7] Taking two very different economic scales—the domestic economy of individual mortgage holders and complex economic processes like the global demand for particular investment vehicles—and treating them as identical, the novel here unselfconsciously echoes former Treasury Secretary (and Goldman Sachs CEO) Henry Paulson's claim that "any homeowner who can afford his mortgage payment but chooses to walk away from an underwater property is simply a speculator."[8]

In fact, of course, the economic and historical relationship between domestic debt and the speculative market in debt backed by that debt—and, by extension, the conceptual relationship between the individual and the whole, between the micro- and the macroeconomic—is vastly more complicated than either these credit-crisis novels, or the behavioral economics they adopt, allow. Such entanglements become clearer, however, in the other three novels named previously: Haslett's *Union Atlantic*, McPhee's *Dear Money*, and Dee's *The Privileges*, which explore the personal lives and motivations of more powerful and institutionally situated economic actors. This chapter argues that although these works also appear to subscribe to a behavioralist account of individual economic action—suggesting that the economic crisis was brought on by the greed and hubris of individual bankers—they are ultimately ambivalent about both the narrative and political consequences of such an explanation. Although focused on the actions of individual protagonists, they also seek to capture the reality of a structural, even impersonal, economic and social whole. That is, these credit-crisis novels attempt to offer a historical rather than simply a psychological explanation for what happened in and to the early twenty-first-century economy. In this way, I argue, all three novels put pressure on the behavioralist explanation of economic volatility as the consequence of moral failure and excessive feeling. In their moments of hesitation, inconsistency, or contradiction, Haslett's, McPhee's, and Dee's novels suggest an uncertainty about the behavioralist (and, more provocatively, the novelistic) belief that the way to understand systems is to look at individuals.

Focusing on the formal modes of narrative perspective or voice that appear in each of these novels—first person, omniscient, and free-indirect style, respectively—I contend that McPhee, Haslett, and Dee confront an urgent and fundamental challenge: given the realist novel's constitutive individualism, how does one narrate an economic crisis that even the behavioralist might admit was inconceivably complex, impenetrably global, and intractably structural? Centered on the actions of a few individuals, these novels nevertheless gesture toward larger social and economic forces, and the challenges to narrative form they confront mirror impasses to grasping the totality of the contemporary global economy. As a result, they not only provide a fleeting vision of the "whole" of the social totality but also limn the contours of what the individual subject, the "part," really experiences in a post-crisis cultural landscape. Far from being the sovereign, autonomous agent of economic change—as either a full, rich, literary self or an all-powerful *homo economicus*—the individual in these credit-crisis novels epitomizes an empty and impoverished personhood, hollowed out by the material predations of unpayable debt and the conceptual vacuity of economic psychology.

Behaving Badly

To address the role of behavioralism in post-crisis discourse, we must first understand the economic theory from which it emerged. Although some behavioralists identify as macroeconomists (even as neo-Keynesians), the principles of behavioralism derive from microeconomics. As Regina Gagnier puts it, microeconomics substitutes "the social relations central to political economy" with "a theory of the individual consumer and his wants," replacing the focus on production that had made economics a political and social science with a "depoliticized" interest in consumption.[9] No longer interested in the social production of wealth but simply in individual consumer desires, microeconomics imagined the social order as, according to Daniel Rodgers, "a myriad of anonymous, disaggregated sellers and purchasers" and refused to distinguish between "aggregate, social economic behavior" and "individually modeled economic action."[10] Microeconomics, in short, presumes that the whole of society can be dissolved into its individual parts.[11] Even a large-scale and complex event like a financial crisis is understood as no more than the consequence of aggregated individual choices. This tendency to eschew structural or macroeconomic explanations in favor of arguments about poor decision making, weak cultural values, mistaken preferences, bad taste, or excessive optimism reached its apogee with the development of behavioral economics as a subfield of microeconomics.

Behavioral economics first emerged in the 1980s, as extreme market volatility began to cause economists to doubt the rationality of *homo economicus*. This volatility did not seem to threaten the foundational microeconomic belief that individual consumers were the drivers of the economy as a whole, but it did cause economists to question certain neoclassical assumptions about those individuals' fundamental rationality. The behavioralists argued that although we should retain the neoclassical idea of *homo economicus* as an autonomous actor, we should abandon the supposition that individual economic choices were consistently rational. Confronted with what economic historian Philip Mirowski describes as the "cognitively thin and emotionally deprived" agent of neoclassical rationality, economic behavioralists, like good novelists, developed *homo economicus* into a slightly more interesting character, "introducing some amendments from narrow subsets of psychology" as an "'enrichment' of simpler concepts of rationality."[12] The first such enrichment drew from decision and prospect theory, particularly the work of Amos Tversky and Daniel Kahneman, who brought psychological theories of choice into the economic mainstream.[13] Economist Richard Thaler added to their work, arguing that Tversky and Kahneman's insights necessitated a complete rethinking of rationality. Thaler contended that by assuming that economic actors behave rationally, economists themselves "make systematic, predictable errors in describing or forecasting consumer choices."[14] Thaler's approach was based in cognitive psychology and heralded complementary work in neuropsychology. Later research in behavioral economics, such as that popularized by Dan Ariely, focused less on poor decision making and more on consumer affect. Economic decisions, Ariely claimed, are a result of the relative strength of immediate positive or negative responses—or, to cite the startlingly simplistic language of affect that characterizes such scholarship, "good or bad feelings."[15]

As they turned their attention to the problem of collective "irrationality" that ostensibly led to market crises, behavioralists argued that the psychology of "human interactions" rather than structural, institutional, or historical factors is the "essential cause" both of bubbles (driven by overconfidence and irrational exuberance) and busts (driven by pessimism and crises of confidence).[16] The behavioralist account of individual economic psychology is concerned with more than just obviously economic desires. Indeed, as Akerlof and Shiller insist, crises are triggered by all manner of personal feelings, including "temptations, envy, resentment, and illusions."[17] And yet because economics has long sought to distance itself from the discipline of psychology—preferring instead to align itself with more supposedly empirical research in the sciences—the behavioralists' theory of individual behavior is psychologically thin: Mirowski argues that lay economic behavioralists rely on an "arbitrary set of folk psychological mental categories," while academic economists eschew depth psychology in favor of reductive psychological behaviorist or cognitive approaches.[18]

Thus, writing on the so-called affective approach to choice, economist Robert Zajonc insists that subjective taste (liking things) and aesthetic judgment (finding things attractive) enter into economic decision making as affective reactions masquerading as a form of rationality. In an apposite example, Zajonc explains economic judgment as follows: "We do not just see 'a house': We see a handsome house, an ugly house, or a pretentious house. . . . We sometimes delude ourselves that we proceed in a rational manner and weigh all the pros and cons of the various alternatives. But this is probably seldom the actual case. Quite often 'I decided in favor of X' is no more than 'I liked X.'"[19] Zajonc's example makes it clear that behavioral economics is not committed to psychology as such but rather to explaining how decisions made on the basis of psychological preference can ultimately be the "wrong" ones—that is, how they can turn out to be economically irrational.

Affective approaches like Zajonc's are profoundly uninterested, however, in capturing the complexities of subjective preference: *why* we like the things we like, have the preferences we do, or make the aesthetic judgments we make. For the behavioral economists, only decisions (and not the interior states of feeling they emerge from) are observable, modelable, and therefore legitimate as the object of economic analysis. Affect, in other words, is meaningful not in its concrete specificity (in discovering why a house is regarded as handsome or pretentious) but simply as a foil for economic rationality. Moreover, despite its interest in the individual, behavioral economics represents the desires that motivate that individual in entirely generic ways. While behavioralists claim to enrich our understanding of economic psychology, in the end they offer little more than *homo economicus* deprived of whatever depth and power he once possessed: compared to his classical counterpart, the contemporary behavioralist's isolated economic Robinson Crusoe is weaker as an agent, more arbitrary in his motivations, and significantly less discerning about himself and the world around him.[20]

In the wake of the 2008 financial crisis, journalists and politicians alike drew on this theory to offer a simplified account of a crisis that otherwise may have seemed beyond comprehension by suggesting that it was caused by greedy or irrational bankers.[21] Two post-crisis best sellers, John Cassidy's *How Markets Fail* and Justin Fox's *Myth of the Rational Market*, popularized this behavioralist argument for lay readers, while economists like Robert Shiller piled on by claiming that the crisis was the result of the cognitive weakness of *all* economic actors, consumers as well as bankers.[22] Shiller's *Subprime Solution: How Today's Global Financial Crisis Happened and What to Do about It* argues that the reasons typically given for the crisis, including those proffered in most mainstream macroeconomic accounts—the Fed's interest rate cuts; the growth in adjustable rate mortgages; regulatory failure; the inability of rating agencies to predict a drop in home prices—are effects of the bubble rather than its cause. For Shiller, "the ultimate cause of the global financial crisis is the *psychology* of the real estate bubble." Although Shiller's account of causality emphasizes collective feeling (an "irrational public enthusiasm for housing investments"), it nonetheless rests on the assumption that the market is driven not by structural fundamentals but by positive or negative affect.[23] Whether such feelings are held discretely (by a single homeowner or CEO) or shared collectively (by American consumers as a whole), they shape the market in essentially the same way: as individuals, we choose our homes based on subjective preferences, and between 2002 and 2007 we apparently all tended to prefer heavily mortgaged houses.

Despite their emphasis on the irrationality of individual economic decision making, however, behavioralists have proven highly reluctant to appeal to individual accountability. Thus the near-universal insistence that individual greed and human folly led to the crisis failed to produce the political will or even desire to punish the institutional power players like those identified by *Time*. To follow the logic of behavioral economics, if we are all basically irrational and if the spirited demand for big houses is identical to the exuberant desire for high-risk speculation backed by those houses, then, as MIT economist Andrew Lo puts it, "all of us participated to some extent in the crisis."[24] Because we are thus all responsible, none of us is. The result is that the economic behavioralist's remedy for financial crises tends to reflect the easy solutions offered by the contemporary psychological behaviorist: market makers and state actors should "nudge" individuals toward more rational decisions.[25] Whereas earlier, more radical behaviorist psychologists like B. F. Skinner saw such conditioning mostly as a matter of social control—and thus tended to favor "managed capitalism" and governmental regulation—today's economic behavioralists largely reject proposals to regulate markets and market actors, thus limiting potential avenues for either restraint or accountability.

To understand the behavioralists' antagonism to market regulation, it is worth exploring the ways in which the psychological foundations of behavioral economics recall an older historical discourse in which the tangible, objective rationality of the "real economy" was contrasted with the fanciful, subjective volatility of the speculative economy. Historian J. G. A. Pocock, for example, has influentially described the fear, as old as financial speculation itself, that financial markets are based solely on "imagination, fantasy, or passion."[26] Indeed, the belief that financial markets are dangerously insubstantial and subject to the errancy and error of public opinion has characterized economic culture from Daniel Defoe's fickle "Lady Credit" to Frank Norris's mesmeric market forces.[27] Yet for behavioralists like Shiller, financial markets are effective precisely *because* they are highly sensitive to changes in public opinion, including those of speculators. More speculation, not less, is thus Shiller's solution to market crisis: because the market is the only way for skeptical observers to "express [their] opinions" about the value of an asset, further securitization and greater liquidity would have ensured that "any skeptic anywhere in the world ... [could] reduce a speculative bubble" by betting against the increase in prices.[28] Rather than reduce the market's dependence on the intuitions of market actors, Shiller insists, we simply need to allow those intuitions to express themselves more forcefully. Whereas the eighteenth-century economic observers that Pocock describes worried that the speculative market's reliance on mere opinion made finance capital a threat to economic stability, contemporary economists like Shiller believe that opinion provides a hedge against volatility, since the hunches of smart, intuitive investors can correct the misperceptions and excesses of the crowd. Thus, Shiller sometimes represents the individual economic actor as an irrational market optimist and sometimes as a savvy skeptic: *homo speculator* is the cause but also the remedy for financial crises, and the power of markets lies in their capacity to express the opinions of such individuals, despite their occasional irrationality.

While economic behavioralists continue to believe, in Shiller's phrase, that "the subprime crisis was essentially psychological in origin," they struggle to provide an adequately persuasive historical account of why the economic crisis happened when and how it did.[29] The first reason for this is, once again, a problem of scale: how to account for the fact that many individuals must make exactly the same erroneous calculation at exactly the same time for a bubble (or a bust) to happen. In attempting to move between the microeconomics of individual behavior and the macroeconomics of the economy as a whole, behavioralist accounts run aground on a kind of fallacy of composition: the (mis)perception that aggregate, social economic events follow exactly the same laws as individually modeled economic behavior.[30] Moreover, their reductive understanding of human psychology renders the problem of irrationality so natural and universal that economic behavioralists cannot possibly explain the historical specificity of any given crisis. Why, we are left to wonder, were markets more volatile in this period than in others? Why did investors choose these kinds of investments in this particular moment? The incompatibility between a concern with individual psychology and the need for a historical account of structural causality thus remains manifestly a problem for behavioralist approaches to the crisis.

It is also a problem, I argue, for the credit-crisis realist novel, but here it is a more productive problem. The credit-crisis novel has served as a kind of literary laboratory for working out the problems of scale and historical causality that haunt behavioral economics. At once exploiting and miscarrying the realist novel's capacity to perform complex acts of mediation—between interiority and historical consciousness, between the private self and the public self, between subjective interiority and objective judgment—these texts expose the contradictions inherent in the behavioralist tendency. In attempting to recode behavioral economic theory to fit the formal requirements of the novel, I argue, the credit-crisis novel not only rewrites but also fundamentally destabilizes that theory.

Humanizing the Crisis

Whereas *Financial Lives of the Poets*, *The Ask*, and *Model Home* lodge primary responsibility for the financial crisis in the psychological, moral, and marital failings of American middle-class consumers, *Dear Money*, *Union Atlantic*, and *The Privileges* explore the greed, incompetence, or irrational exuberance of (respectively) an MBS trader, an investment banker, and a hedge fund manager and the illegal or unethical activities they participate in: excessive risk seeking, accounting fraud, and insider trading. Although they incorporate a lot of detail about the economy itself, all three novels are primarily committed to mining their characters' inner lives for psychological material and thus were repeatedly praised by reviewers for their ability to "humanize" the economy. Reviewing *Union Atlantic* in the *New York Times*, for instance, Liesl Schillinger commends it for thinking about "big historical forces" in terms of "tiny, intricate, cumulatively powerful personal impulses" and for revealing that "businesses become too big to fail . . . because individuals fail one another." Indeed, Schillinger's review concludes with a phrase that might appear in a behavioral economic account of the crisis with not a word of revision: the "core" of the financial crisis, she suggests, was "a knot of ineluctable yearnings and individual need."[31] To "reveal the core" of the financial crisis, in short, requires attention not to what Shiller dismisses as "inscrutable technical factors" but to what novelist John Lanchester describes in an essay on financial fiction as "the human truths which don't need explaining."[32]

To "humanize" the financial crisis thus requires attending to "human truths" rather than "technical factors." But it also means refusing to scapegoat one's Wall Street protagonists. In his aptly titled review of credit-crisis fiction, "It's Not All Rotten Apples," Arne De Boever lauds novels that "humanize Wall Street" instead of "highlight[ing] the psychotic element of the world of finance and the people in it," insisting that "while there may be plenty of rotten apples on Wall Street, not all money comes from evil, and not everything that comes from money is evil."[33] Reviewer Joseph Peschel likewise admires McPhee's *Dear Money* for being "generous" in its creation of characters who are "amusingly ... human," noting that McPhee "genuinely cares" about her banker protagonist.[34] Writing on Dee's *The Privileges*, Marco Roth asserts that "a conscientious novelist invariably humanizes the characters created" and praises Dee for "challeng[ing] readers to experience sympathy" for his characters, thus conveying a "sense that the very rich are, for the most part, moral agents like you and me."[35] Like Roth, *Book Forum*'s Christian Lorentzen applauds financial novels that avoid the "traps ... of writing about bankers" by making them "genuinely sympathetic" and notes appreciatively that credit-crisis fiction indicates that "sentimental impulses still outstrip financial imperatives as the moving forces of our fictions."[36] Meanwhile, a *Wall Street Journal* review of *The Privileges* not surprisingly commends Dee for avoiding "a moralistic take-down of Wall Street" and for instead casting his protagonists' ambitions "in a sympathetic light."[37]

Although I argue later that the question of sympathy in the credit-crisis novel is more complicated than these reviews allow, it is clear that McPhee's, Haslett's, and Dee's novels all suggest that individual investors' "personal impulses"—their hubris, irrationality, greed, lack of a social conscience—were the cause of the crisis.[38] Committed to behavioralism's emphasis on the individual both formally and at the level of content, these novels adopt a first-person or focalized point of view as a way of explaining the crash in terms of human decisions, preferences, desires, and obsessions. Because they share behavioral economics' assertion that the difference between individuals and the market as a whole is merely a matter of scale, these novels treat underwater homeowners and risk-seeking bankers as equivalently situated economic agents. As a result, they are haunted by what I earlier identified as behavioralism's fallacy of composition: the assumption that aggregate economic behavior follows the same laws as individual economic choices, a claim made in the absence of any account of how to move from one scale to the other. Dependent on behavioral economic accounts of individual action and formally trapped in their own first-person or focalized narration, credit-crisis realist novels struggle to formalize the relationship between individual actors and the broader social field those actors occupy and shape.

Yet these are novels, not economic treatises or op-eds. They are also novels that are undeniably self-conscious about their status as novels and, more specifically, about their place in a long tradition of American realist fiction about the economy. McPhee's central character is a novelist, and both *Dear Money* and Haslett's *Union Atlantic* make explicit (sometimes even heavy-handed) references to the American naturalist novel. The very title of Dee's *The Privileges* is doubly referential of literary history, echoing Jonathan Franzen's *The Corrections*, which itself intentionally evoked William Gaddis's *The Recognitions*. These affiliations and commitments complicate the relationship between these credit-crisis novels and the behavioralist positions they appear to avow. Whereas behavioral economics imagines itself as a sui generis science and, in a manner consistent with the presentism of economics as a discipline, tends to represent its own assumptions as indisputable, universal, and ahistorical, these novels engage their own literary genealogy in a manner that complicates their embrace of economic ideology. This is true not simply because of their palimpsestic relationship to the history of the economic novel but also because of their concern with the history of the contemporary economic crisis itself. Not content merely with "the human truths that remain true," as Lanchester would have it, these credit-crisis novels try to articulate, however inadequately, the broader social—and, emphatically, historical—world that their characters inhabit. To do so, they attempt to produce a psychological model that could function both individually and collectively; they seek to imagine, through the work of literary form itself, the kinds of social totality that behavioral microeconomics' aggregative account of shared cultural beliefs or collective feelings cannot envision. That they often fail in these attempts is itself revelatory, first of the conceptual incoherence that likewise fractures behavioral economics. In proving unable to reconcile the potentially privatizing work of focalized narration with the desire to provide an objective account of what happened in the economy as a whole—in remaining unwilling either to forgo or embrace the formal strategies of narrative omniscience that might allow them to move between scales—these credit-crisis novels suggest equivalent inconsistencies in behavioral economics itself. That is, the credit-crisis novel reveals behavioralism's fallacy of composition to be a problem of mediation: a problem of how to do more than simply combine individuals into a contingent aggregation and instead negotiate both the particular and the general, both the individual and the social totality. In these novels, moreover, this problem of mediation appears as a problem of narrative perspective, as each one attempts to obtain, precisely and paradoxically through the subjective consciousness of a singular protagonist, a distanced, more historical, and less individualizing view.

These credit-crisis novels' failures also reveal what may be most interesting about the behavioralist treatment of the economic subject: its tendency to reduce, flatten, and generalize individual psychology. Both behavioral economics and the credit-crisis novel indicate a deep anxiety about the consequences of this reduction. The behavioralists ultimately want to rescue the import of subjective experience and the meaningfulness of *being* a subject, to preserve the irreducibility of passion and desire even while generalizing them into near meaninglessness, and to protect a belief in deep interiority even while diminishing it to no more than cognition or observable action. The credit-crisis novel, by contrast, proves ultimately incapable of saving the individuals at the center of its narrative from a kind of ontological attenuation or even annulment and thus ends up utterly bereft of the kinds of full, unique, authentic characters—and the ideological individualism—typically ascribed to the contemporary realist novel.[39] Despite their apparent commitment to what is often described as "rich characterization," these three credit-crisis novels ultimately cannot help registering the ways in which the economic subject in a post-crisis era is, in more ways than one, poorer than ever.

First-Person Behavioral

Dear Money is written from the perspective of India Palmer, a successful literary novelist living with her family in Manhattan. India's financial situation is precarious, and when she meets the dashing Win Johns, a successful trader in high-risk mortgage securities, he seduces her into a bet of sorts, which, in one of many references to George Bernard Shaw's 1912 play, he describes as "Pygmalion Ltd.": he will train India to become an MBS trader and see whether the business can be taught to a novice. Entranced by working as a market player, India finds that she loves the excitement of being a risk taker as well as the lifestyle it affords.

Real estate permeates the book. In the novel's opening sentence—"It all began with real estate"—the "It" that begins with real estate is not only the novel's plot but equally the historical period in which the novel is set, a period in which it is precisely the household that is the object of financial speculation. Or as India later observes, "Real estate was in the air, like tech stocks in the late 1990s, like all stocks in the late 1920s when even the shoeshine boys offered tips, famously forecasting the end.... Everyone had discovered the golden-egg-laying goose called real estate. It had, in its very name, a kind of commanding authority that was solid, unsexy, and it rang true: it was real."[40] India's description suggests that property, and by extension property value, is paradoxically ethereal ("in the air") and substantial ("solid" and "real"), aligned with the irrational speculative economy of the stock market and the rumors ("shoeshine boys offered tips") and fairy tales ("the golden-egg-laying goose") that sustain it, but also with the prosaic world of real (if "unsexy") assets that simply "rang true." Elsewhere real estate is figured the stuff of dreams: "One didn't bet against the galaxy. And what mattered in the galaxy we'd created—the substance of our dreams, our deals, and the fabulously spinning non-correlated assets we'd invented, those curious cycles and epicycles derived from dreams—was something that had always mattered. It was something beyond logic or reckoning.... Real estate" (338). The market, now "beyond reckoning," is imagined as a celestial formation that is both made up of and driven by dreams. Domestic property is not the opposite of financial speculation but merely a star in the same vast constellation of wealth.

This understanding of real estate as no longer the stolid *oikonomia* to speculation's sexy *chrematistike* (as Aristotle and centuries of his economic antecedents would have had it) is very contemporary. Yet, as I have already suggested, *Dear Money* is also a novel with a strong awareness of its literary prehistory. In addition to borrowing from Shaw's *Pygmalion*, the novel makes repeated reference to the early twentieth-century naturalist novel of economy: India is forever rereading Thomas Hardy's *The Mayor of Casterbridge* and at one point describes "want[ing] to be a poor girl in a [Theodor] Dreiser novel"

(125). In a winking nod to Edith Wharton's *House of Mirth*, the novel even features a minor character named Lily Star, a beautiful social climber who meets a tragic end. It is thus not surprising that *Dear Money*'s description of the market draws on metaphors that would have been familiar to these naturalist writers: debt, "assembled and gathered," is "a bracing chasm"; mortgages are "a massive revenue river"; and market forces are likened to "a beautiful wild storm . . . a wonderful whipping blizzard" (46, 194). Although Frank Norris is not among the writers explicitly cited in the novel, McPhee's naturalist motifs particularly recall Norris's portrayal of the powerful wheat market in *The Pit*—in Norris's text, as David Zimmerman has influentially noted, tropes of water and wind, storms and floods, "figur[e] the market as a mechanism through which nature and its laws speak."[41] Following in Norris's footsteps, *Dear Money* often figures the market as a kind of sublime force—the "bracing chasm" whose vastness surpasses the individual and whose power can be neither understood nor controlled: "Across it we walked even if we had no idea of the depths of this dream" (46), the novel rhapsodizes.

Yet the novel also insists that individual economic actors control and shape the market. Whereas Norris described the market as a force of nature precisely to refute the fantasy of economic mastery—as Zimmerman puts it, *The Pit*'s Curtis Jadwin ultimately "surrenders control of, and is finally surrendered to" the market—*Dear Money* vacillates uneasily between naturalist tropes that characterize the economy as an implacably material force of nature and a rather different language of dreams and imagination.[42] Thus, in one of the novel's most telling passages, India asks herself what she finds most compelling about her new work as a trader compared to her former profession as a fiction writer and muses that she is most taken with

> the idea of pooling people, trying to understand how they operated psychologically (all the yous and all the mes with our various styles of spending and saving, our susceptibility to trends, our ridiculous hopes that place all our bets on tomorrow) as a collective lot, reading them and translating their likely actions into the amassing of money on a colossal scale. . . . This was better than the plot of any story I'd read in a while. . . . This was imagination at work, imagination with consequences—nothing less. (47)

This is a curious passage for a number of reasons. It is a passage in a novel, spoken by a character who is herself a novelist, about how inadequate novels are, and this self-abolishing position is never refuted by *Dear Money* itself, as India happily abandons writing for investing without a regret or a look back. More important, the passage associates finance with a kind of fictionality to be "read" or "translated" or "plot[ted]." This clearly echoes the centuries-old representation of financial markets as a kind of collective delusion. Yet in *Dear Money* the idea that financial speculation is based on nothing more than "imagination, fantasy, or passion," in Pocock's phrase, is not a source of anxiety but rather expresses a sanguine belief in the transformative power of the individual imagination. Fanciful and intuitive, speculation is not the antithesis of reality but the very "putting to work" of it, such that the realist literary imagination (represented both by the novels India writes and by *Dear Money* itself) is continuous with the "real-world" imagination of speculative finance. In *Dear Money*, economic speculation offers the fanciful mind a kind of reality principle, affording the imagination a sense of consequence.

Moreover, this passage suggests not that the market is an implacable force of nature, as the previous passages implied, but that it is an ephemeral and effervescent social force: to study the market is not to succumb to the noise of the crowd (as, again, in Norris's novel, with its images of cacophonous and dangerously mesmerizing sound) but to "tune in" to it. The market, in short, can in *Dear Money* do the very thing fiction (including *Dear Money* itself) apparently no longer can: give expression, meaning, and organization to a diverse sociality. *Dear Money* is thus remarkably untroubled by the idea that the market is driven by mass psychology. Because the market can record a wide variety of psychological responses and reactions, it can also translate those desires into rational investments. The fact that the market is subject to irrational mass opinion is therefore no longer something to fear—instead, such determinations render it available to control by those individuals sufficiently attuned to expressions of collective affect within the market's chaotic din. As a trader, India participates in an "Appolonian quest for the purest signal" as she attempts "to filter out the noise . . . and to seize the signal, the trend, the very flow of history itself" (172). *Dear Money*'s language here plainly echoes the claims of behavioralists that rational "signal traders" (unlike irrational "noise traders") can steer the market back to sanity.[43] At the same time, however, the uneasy proximity of Dionysian chaos (the poetics of the sublime, the language of imagination and fancy) alongside Appolonian rational action also registers a fundamental tension between behavioralism's descriptive claim that markets are chaotic because individual investors are generally irrational and its prescriptive remedy for market volatility: that markets should remain unregulated to allow savvy investors to administer their guiding influence.

In describing the ways and means of real estate investing, *Dear Money* produces a flourish of mixed and contradictory metaphors of quality and quantity, the earthly and the ethereal. When it describes the commodity objects that successful investment affords, however, the novel offers a more straightforward fantasy of fulfillment, proliferating the details of purchases such as a "dark blue wool dress, fitted, falling to just above the knee, three-quarter-inch sleeves, mother-of-pearl buttons running down the back—Cuban-born designer" (306–7). As this passage suggests, India's consumer purchases are far more richly detailed in the novel than her work as a trader is: for example, we are told of a "sharp black bikini" with "a halter top and square cut brief" (81); a "chocolate-brown wool [skirt], a loose weave of lace at the hemline, an ivory satin shirt, chocolate slingbacks, a gold wire wrapping pink jasper" (291); an "elegant and decadent . . . Scalamandré chenille, picturing prancing tigers" (125); "a cream linen with the thinnest border of silk organza" (228). Despite its interest in the work of mortgage brokers and MBS speculators, *Dear Money* appears more committed to representing—in intricate but scarcely intimate detail—India's private purchases than in describing the securities she sells to fund them. Consumption, the fulfillment of subjective desires, appears to have more explanatory power than any other economic transaction, but what precisely it explains is never really made clear. For Dreiser's Sister Carrie, Walter Benn Michaels observes, money "is never simply a means of getting what you want, it is itself the thing you want," and since "money, by definition, is the desire for money, then money can never quite be itself."[44] India, in contrast, is a more untroubled microeconomist: for her, money decisively *is* the means of getting what you want, and because money is merely a means rather than a meaningful end, her desire for money does not undermine her autonomy or existential coherence (as it does in *Sister Carrie*). In fact, money in *Dear Money* becomes even more satisfying the more one has: "It's a lie," India blithely proclaims, "that money is more interesting for those who don't have any than for those who do. It's too fun to spend" (306). Because *Dear Money* presents the satisfaction of individual desires as the economy's driving force, the money of the novel's title appears especially apt, since it is always money, annulled and fulfilled in each act of consumption, and never capital itself, extended indefinitely toward future gains, that India expends.

The novel thus follows microeconomics in converting a theory of individual consumption into an account of social totality. Like the behavioralists, *Dear Money* suggests that the economy fell into crisis circa 2008 not so much because individual investors did not *know enough* to speculate successfully but rather because individual consumers *wanted too much* to be rational when it came to satisfying their desires. That in the novel, as in popular discourse, this particular form of wanting too much is feminized should come as no surprise. Associated with market irrationality, excessive desire, and overconsumption, the female shopaholic appears as the handiest scapegoat available: thus *Time*'s image of American consumers is represented in the singular by a young woman, head cocked in ditzy oblivion, holding shopping bags and looking suspiciously like the character depicted on the poster for the film *Confessions of a Shopaholic* (tagline: "All she ever wanted was a little credit") released the same week the *Time* poll was published. Signifying inconstancy and excess, the feminized shopper echoes what Marieke de Goede has described, in her analysis of the historical figure of "Lady Credit," as the "personification of . . . all the irrational, fantastical, passionate, and irresponsible elements" of the speculative economy.[45] *Dear Money* thus explains the housing crisis in almost exactly the same way it explained India's desire for slingback shoes: "Want, want, want. Need, need, need. The wish for a piece of America, your own home, was a noble desire" (19). Whereas critics of credit-based speculation in the eighteenth century of de Goede's account would have seen individual (and specifically female) consumer desire as a potentially dangerous threat to the rational world of political economy, here there is no such counterposition: always and everywhere, for good or for ill, the thing that drives the economy is the fluctuation of individual consumer desires. The more we presume that *homo economicus* is irrational by nature, the more the female consumer and feminized credit become not the economy's Other but its most obvious representative.

Dear Money extends its account of individual consumer *desire* as a powerful economic force into a story of collective *demand* as the source of the crisis. As a result, it treats the irrational exuberance of homeowners as a desire analogous to India's desire for beautiful dresses but unrelated to India's work as a seller of securitized mortgage debt. The desire to own a home is presented as self-evident ("owning a home was something I longed for"), while "the intricacies of high finance" are merely the historically particular way that demand is met (47). Although *Dear Money* suggests that the desire for real estate exerts extraordinary power over the economy, because the novel has gone to such lengths to naturalize and personalize this longing, it cannot explain where desire originates nor why everyone happened to experience the same longing at the same time. It is far easier to account for India's desire for shoes than the entire country's sudden demand for real estate (and debt). As a result, *Dear Money* sometimes makes the historically situated (if still amorphous) claim that real estate was simply "in the air" between 2002 and 2007 but at other times implies that the desire for home ownership is natural and transhistorical, fueled "by an ethos first inscribed in our nation's birth document" or even by the imperatives of the Old Testament itself (192–94). Later, in an extended passage detailing the emergence of the securities market, India imagines the intersection of consumerism and home ownership as so many historical "roads converging," beginning with the first road, "our national belief in homeownership" and ending in "the fourth road ... the need for capital—the money to be loaned to finance all those dreams." Where, she asks herself, did that money come from?

> It came from those investors in China and France and Germany and Waco. Here the roads begin to intersect, an elaborate freeway with exit ramps and on-ramps and cloverleafs. And there you have it: home values rose, homeowners tapped into their newfound wealth, squeezing every last drop of value from their houses. Houses became ATM machines, allowing us the means to fund our desires. Appliances became fancier, trips more exotic, children more numerous—three was the new two, four the new three, credit the new savings. (199)

The passage makes a number of strange turns as it attempts to contort itself around its own assumptions. India's attempt at historical explanation falters in its spatial metaphor of intersecting byways connecting past (money "came" from investors) and present (roads "begin" to intersect). The failure of the temporal logic of causality also manifests itself as a crisis of scale. While India tries to bring a global perspective to her account of the global constitution of financial markets (adding "China and France and Germany"), this broader view quickly recedes as the passage retreats back into the naturalized "our" of American homeowners and to a portrayal of those homeowners as too greedy, too shortsighted, and too irrational in their desire to consume.

Self-consciously limited by its own first-person perspective, McPhee's novel makes it clear that this limitation is not simply a problem of method (looking at the individual versus looking at the economic whole) but also of mediation:

how to move between one scale and another. The novel embraces the individual particularity of the first-person voice as a way to humanize the economic crisis, yet by its own logic—according to which markets themselves are better at connecting people and places than fiction could ever be—it cannot convert this into an explanation of the relationship between "China and France and Germany" and the American homeowner, any more than Shiller can explain why everyone became so individually irrational about houses all at the same time.

So how do the credit-crisis novel and the behavioral economist resolve this problem? What do they offer as the mediating term between the micro and macro, the individual and the totality? In *Dear Money*, the answer to the problem of perspective and representation is something McPhee refers to as "our national belief," a generalized and naturalized articulation of individual desire: "We all wanted the money, believed so invincibly in ourselves that we mortgaged our futures for the Mercedes today, the new kitchen, the addition, the trip to Europe. Isn't that what America has done?" (332). Cultural "belief" thus serves as the mediating term between the micro and macro, the individual and the totality, but only by reducing the totality to a mere aggregation: the contingently combined behavior of isolated self-interested individuals. The limitation of first-person perspective demands something as vague and unexplanatory as "culture," and culture's fuzziness as a category reminds us that it is really only a stand-in for a kind of hidden first-person perspective—"We *all* wanted," India asserts, certain that her own desires are both sui generis (they are, after all, the economy's cause and never its effect) and universal, and equally certain that there is no "we" beyond the shared natural desire to own a Mercedes.

Not surprisingly, culture is also the answer offered by behavioral economics. In his nonfiction account of the crisis, *IOU: Or Why Everyone Owes Everyone and No One Can Pay*, novelist John Lanchester locates the blame for the crisis in both moral lapses—individual malfeasance and personal greed—and institutional failures. Like McPhee, Lanchester moves from the problem of moral character to the social category of institutions through the language of culture: "all the funny smells, the missed warning signals, the misaligned incentives, the distorted attitudes to risk, the arrogance of the masters of the universe, the complicity of regulators, the doziness of legislators—symptomized a culture, *and also constituted one*."[46] Here again, as in *Dear Money*, recourse to an abstract and vitiated idea of "national culture" is hustled, tautologically, into the place of causality: culture is both the cause of economic behavior ("symptomatized") and the effect of it ("constituted"). Likewise, the property boom is explained away by observing that "our risky, long-term, innovative (sometimes recklessly so) mortgages came into existence because the market set out to find ways to let us fulfill our heart's deepest desire, to own our own property. The appetite created the product and not the other way round."[47] As in *Dear Money*, only consumer demand (here, tellingly, "appetite") creates bubbles. For another example of this kind of nonexplanation, consider Shiller's claim that "the changing zeitgeist drives common opinion among the members of society at any point in time and place," which effectively maintains that the zeitgeist is the cause of the zeitgeist.[48] Such vacuous tautologies emerge from the conceptual and methodological lacuna around which behavioralism circles: an assertion, as in Walters's novel, that "it's all connected." The nature of this connection, however, is constantly displaced. By focusing exclusively on the micro-decisions of the individual, whose relationship to the social whole is purely homological, behavioral economics suggests less that it's all connected than that it's all the same thing.

In the end, McPhee's novel returns to more naturalist images of the market, and it does so because it cannot find another way to describe a crisis that even the novel itself must admit had a logic in excess of any individual: thus, India describes herself "walk[ing] as if on a mighty earthen levee" that "[holds] the waters ... at bay." She goes on,

> But riding out across the ever narrowing asymptote of chance, at the far periphery of thought, at the remotest end of possibility, a cold dark number was ever so occasionally rumored to exist. This was the one percent chance that the levee would break, that the supercollider experiment would somehow form antimatter that would fuse everything ... into a solid, ever-expanding ball of destruction. The one percent was Kali, destroyer goddess, riding on a theoretical comet of the apocalypse. ... [But] the only way you understand is after the fact. (337)

This passage eschews the behavioralist representation of the economy as controllable in favor of a rather wildly mixed metaphor of natural catastrophe, nuclear disaster, and apocalyptic reckoning. It also conjures Nassim Taleb's oft-quoted characterization of the 2008 crisis as a "black swan": an event so unexpected it can be understood only in retrospect. It thus reflects the volte-face of the language of personal responsibility: the language of unrepresentable complexity and historical unpredictability. Leigh Claire la Berge usefully critiques this discourse of complexity, suggesting that it both obscures and exculpates, functioning as "a placeholder for a process that cannot be represented in its entirety for some unknown, and perhaps unknowable, reason."[49] Yet in the context of *Dear Money*, this language does something critically useful too, putting pressure both on the novel's own formal premise (that the market can be understood and represented through and as the actions of certain powerful individual traders) and on its ideological affiliations. There is no sense here that some magical shared "belief" either caused or could prevent the collapse, as if the economy were in the last instance as fully imaginary as *Dear Money* earlier suggested, as if mere suspension of narrative disbelief could protect us against falling home prices or rising unemployment. Nor is there a sense of faith in what Christopher Nealon usefully terms "the equilibrium to come"—the belief that every act of capital destruction heralds a later moment of capital creation, the faith that crises are extrinsic (the fault of foolish individuals or bad institutions).[50] Rather, crisis is something simultaneously natural and monstrous, the new status quo of capitalism but also an immanent condition that threatens at every moment to destroy it. Indeed, despite this passage's manifest refusal of any kind of historical narrative—its treatment of the economy as a more-than-human, cosmic, even metaphysical entity—it concludes with a rather remarkable moment of historicist uncertainty. "But you only understand after the fact," India muses, then adding, as if in explicit compensation for her momentary flight of apocalyptic fancy, "unless you're Win Johns" (337). Here, a moment of epistemological modesty (the impossibility of prospective understanding) confronts the novel's idealized view of individual knowledge (the fantasy of individual percipience) head-on: the idea that even someone as attuned as Win could somehow grasp a "theoretical comet" sits uneasily, even impossibly, next to images of metaphysical chaos. Crisis here is at once the black swan—the singularity that comes like a lightning bolt from outside the system—and the owl of Minerva, the moment of dusk at which one can glimpse, fleetingly, a historical totality otherwise out of view.

Too Omniscient to Fail

The problem of gaining a historical view vexes Haslett's *Union Atlantic* too, where it is yoked to the aforementioned problem of mediation: how to move between the small scale of the individual and the larger scale of the social and historical whole. The novel offers an explicit meditation on the relationship of parts to wholes, one voiced by one of its central characters, Henry Graves, president of the New York State Federal Reserve. Henry, we are told, "disliked the use of personal anecdotes to illustrate the workings of the economy. They were almost always a distortion, a falsely simple story of cause and effect. Truth lay in the aggregate numbers, not in the images of citizens the media alighted upon for a minute or two and then quickly left behind."[51] While Henry's attention to the difference between the qualitative nature of the anecdote and the quantifiable truth of numbers suggests one problem of mediation, ultimately the novel as a whole stages another: the gap between the personal and the aggregate, or the individual and the social. As this passage suggests, *Union Atlantic* cannot help acknowledging the inadequacy of using personal experience as a synecdoche for the totality of economic forces. Yet Haslett's novel is also premised on this very synecdochic transfer, since its account is thoroughly routed through the credit-crisis novel's principal concern with individual psychology as both the cause and most visible effect of the crisis. Dissatisfied with its own constricting particularity, the novel repeatedly attempts to access a more impersonal collective. Thus, Henry sees the crowds of workers leaving for the weekend and imagines the flow of bodies as an allegory for the circulation of money itself:

> Henry looked down at the crowds rushing westward . . . toward the buses and subways that would drain them from the city by the tens of thousands, emptying them into Jersey, Westchester, and Long Island, where supermarket inventories had already dropped a few points and the local banks had balanced their sheets for the week and sent their people home.
>
> Downstairs, the Open Market Desk would trade T-bills for another half hour but the volume would be light. Soon Fedwire would settle, clearing everything from corporate bond sales to the credit card purchases of the secretaries and mutual fund salesmen hurrying now along the street below. Over the weekend when these people went to the movies or the mall they would swipe their cards through magnetic strips and thus do what for centuries had been the sole province of kings and parliaments: they would create money. Short money to be sure, but money nonetheless, which until that moment had never appeared on a balance sheet or been deposited with a bank, that was nothing but a permission for indebtedness, the final improvisation in a long chain of governed promises. And as they slept, the merchant's computers would upload their purchases and into the river of commerce another drop of

liquidity would flow, reversing their commute, heading back into the city to collect in the big, money-center banks, which in the quiet of night would distribute news of the final score: a billion a day shipped to Asia and the petro states. (231–32)

Here *Union Atlantic* attempts to represent an aggregate social body irreducible to any particular individual part: to depict the disbursal of money from banks to consumers is to give us a view of the economy as a whole. Yet the curious economic omniscience rendered by this passage is itself focalized through a strikingly *literal* bird's-eye view: Henry's meditations on the unseen motion of money is made possible by the perspective afforded by "the window of his office on the 10th floor of the Federal Reserve Bank of NY" (231). Henry's apparently formal omniscience thus depends on his actually ascending to the top of a tall building. Thus despite offering a rather striking view of an economic system in motion, this passage does not illustrate the ease with which novelistic form itself can provide an impersonal view of the whole. Rather, like the aforementioned passage about the anecdotal versus the numerical, it highlights the various obstacles to gaining perspective on an opaque economic totality by way of an individual perspective. What results cannot help erasing the differences between the microeconomic and the macroeconomic. Thus, when Henry imagines consumers "swip[ing] their cards through magnetic strips" at stores and ATMs as an act that "for centuries had been the sole province of kings and parliaments: . . . creat[ing] money" (232), he mistakes the microeconomic ways individual consumers *access* money (using a card to withdraw cash held in a personal account) with decidedly macroeconomic forms of *creating* money (the generation of fiat money or through federal monetary policy).

The formal vacillation between the structural and the personal in *Union Atlantic*—one that becomes most obvious when the novel attempts to represent an aggregate totality that is irreducible either to the individual "anecdote" or to the limited focalized perspective of an individual character—speaks to the novel's treatment of the federal bank bail outs. In the end, Henry must decide whether or not to save Union Atlantic, a bank that has gotten itself into trouble with heavily leveraged off-balance-sheet investments. In its treatment of this institutional dilemma *Union Atlantic* follows the moral arc of melodrama, with all the attendant clichés expected of the genre: Evelyn, a midlevel compliance officer at Union Atlantic, discovers that a banker (not coincidentally) named McTeague has been hiding off-the-books losses by secreting them away in structured investment vehicles; her boss, Doug Fanning, first encourages her to keep it quiet and then attempts to bribe her into doing so. Evelyn thus faces an ethical dilemma: say nothing or risk losing her job in order to do the right thing. She then remembers hearing Henry give a speech to a group of compliance officers "reminding them that while the business of keeping money flowing was a technical one, it supported and allowed millions of daily activities from the purchase of food to the paying of rent or salaries or medical bills," and enjoining them to recognize that "all of it relies on you. You're the invisible medium. Not the hand of the market but the conduit. You touch virtually everything you see. Most of you work for private corporations. But the trust, it's public" (189). Inspired by this memory and hoping, apparently, to find in Henry the one honest man who will indicate the continued existence of economic virtue, she visits him in his office, where he eventually compels her to tell him what's been going on at Union Atlantic.

Henry persuades Evelyn to expose the bad actors at the bank by using the language of personal moral obligation and by suggesting that individual actions remain decisive: "all of it relies on you." At the same time, his invocation of the vast and invisible public trust conjures a far larger, more impersonal, economic system. As in the passage narrated from the top of the Federal Reserve building, here Henry himself is the hinge between these two perspective: he is the one individual who can save the system precisely because he can see—figuratively as well as literally—the larger social whole the market both constitutes and depends on. Henry's strangely individualized omniscience, a point of view we might characterize as Too Big to Fail, is thus the device through which the novel attempts to reconcile not only the formal tension between focalization and omniscience but also the ideological tension between private and public interest. In a sense, Henry himself operates as something like Adam Smith's "invisible hand,"[52] mediating between the public interest and private enterprise. Formally, likewise, he literally gazes down on the social totality in a manner similar to Smith's "impartial spectator,"[53] the imagined moral arbiter whose projected objectivity teaches us how to reconcile individual self-interest (the first-person economic) with the public good (panoramic omniscience).

However, the capacity of the market to self-regulate through the invisible hand of self-interest seems an odd idea to evoke in the midst of a financial crisis, a crisis *Union Atlantic* itself suggests was caused by unfettered individual pursuit of profit. Moreover, for Smith, the power of the invisible hand was precisely not located in any individual (or any institution), and the impartial spectator was a conceptual fiction, not a real individual—the butcher he imagines acting not out of "benevolence" but rather out of "self-love" quite emphatically does not know he is serving the public good when he expresses his self-interest.[54] *Union Atlantic*'s decisively un-Smithian treatment of the invisible hand as an individual—its representation of Henry as a uniquely benevolent technocrat with an equally unique (narrative) capacity to see the system as a complex whole—is thus an attempt to resolve a problem the behavioralists also faced as they attempted to defend governmental bail outs: how to claim that individuals were the cause of the crisis while simultaneously seeking to protect those individuals from the consequences of their actions. To save private self-interest as a principle, *Union Atlantic* must imagine a private individual interested only in the public good. To justify protecting irrational economic actors from the consequences of their self-interested decisions, the novel, like post-crisis ideologues across the political spectrum, must counterintuitively suggest that doing so is in the public interest.

To perform this latter ideological maneuver, however, the novel must equate the public with the economy: "Dry up the lending system," Henry avers, "and the losses would no longer redound to the investor class alone" (262). The market becomes both the image and the origin of sociality as such, a contingent aggregation of individual spenders whose simultaneous participation in a consumer economy constitutes them as a whole. *Union Atlantic* presents this consumer market as a domain that must be protected at all costs and insists that what is at stake is not simply the solvency of particular banks but the overall stability of a vast moral economy of consumption. The functioning of the economy, Henry says, is "all anchored to nothing but trust. Cooperation. You could even say faith. . . . Without it you couldn't buy a loaf of bread. . . . There are conditions of possibility for doing any of these things. Whichever choices we make, the system has to work. People have to trust the paper in their wallets. And that starts somewhere. It starts with the banks" (236–37). The novel imagines the movement of capital as a kind of sympathetic social connection, an unseen but powerful world of promises and trust—language not incidentally tied to the economic ideology of credit. Thus, at the precise instant (historical as well as narrative) that we are reminded that the financial economy requires an immense amount of highly technical management, as well as state intervention, to prevent it from collapsing at the slightest tremor, *Union Atlantic*'s description of currency as social cohesion reinforces the idea that the economy is an organic form of human cooperation. The work of managing the money economy becomes a moral labor not only because it *depends on* trust and cooperation but also because it *produces* it. As if to realize some utopian content at the heart of late capitalist ideology, *Union Atlantic* sees circulating money—money designed specifically to fund the purchase of consumer goods, whether movie tickets or a loaf of bread—as the expression of social relationships and the vehicle for sympathetic attachment. Henry imagines monetary liquidity not as an "anti-social fetish," in John Maynard Keynes's famous phrase, but rather as the very condition of sociability itself.[55] (I return to some rather different treatments of liquidity in Chapter 4.)

The novel's portrayal of a moral economy of trust in currency depends on representing financial markets as a kind of domestic economy. The state must step in to bail out the financial sector not because it wants to protect the stock market or the banks but because the liquidity of financial and credit markets "allow[s] millions of daily activities from the purchase of food to the paying of rent or salaries or medical bills" (262). Henry's language of the domestic, and his emphasis on the relationship between money and social trust, echoes the self-exculpating explanations of federal officials when explaining the necessity of bank bail outs and asset-purchasing programs: "We could not separate what was happening in the corridors of our financial institutions from what was happening on the factory floors and around the kitchen tables," Barack Obama remarked in a 2009 speech about the financial "rescue" package, "[so] we helped restore the availability of two things that had been in short supply: capital and confidence." Like *Union Atlantic*, Obama yokes money and trust. And like the behavioralists, he puts the blame for the crisis squarely on the psychology of Wall Street: "We will not go back to the days of reckless behavior and unchecked excess that was at the heart of this crisis, where too many were motivated only by the appetite for quick kills and bloated bonuses," he avers.[56]

Yet much as Henry is ultimately unwilling to send Fanning and McTeague to jail and let the bankrupt Union Atlantic collapse, the Obama administration was distinctly uninterested in prosecuting all those quick-killing, greedy bankers. Curiously, given their emphasis on the behavior of individuals, so were the behavioralists. Thus in *Subprime Solution*, Shiller writes, "The aftermath of the subprime crisis has involved considerable finger-pointing. . . . It is natural to want to blame what has happened on some combination of evil-doers. [But] the danger is that the emphasis on placing blame may cause us to lose sight of the real solution."[57] At first glance, this seems perplexing: If bubbles are not caused by "inscrutable technical factors" but by "variations in individual feelings, impressions, and passions," why wouldn't we blame what has happened on a combination of individuals—if not on evil-doers, then at least on bankers with overly emotional, impressionable, passionate feelings about MBSs?[58] For Shiller, the answer to this question is that "we do not want to let our desire for retribution go . . . to the punishment of the institutions themselves and their principles."[59] Blame must be lodged in individuals and their failures precisely to protect the institutions those individuals represent. This reveals a fundamental confusion at the heart of behavioralism, one inherited from Hayekian microeconomics: behavioral economists retain neoclassical ideas about the fundamental rationality of the markets while still holding on to a belief that humans are typically foolish, greedy, and excessively emotional. For Smith, self-interest was both enlightened and prudent, and these characteristics of individual psychology created the conditions for a society in which the market was ostensibly a social good. For Shiller, on the other hand, humans are both unscrupulous and irrational, and it is the market—both its institutions and its principles—that saves us.

However, much as *Dear Money* could not help turning to the metaphysical and the cosmic when confronted with crisis, in *Union Atlantic* even Haslett's wise technocrat has a moment of peering into the existential economic void: "These days much of the world seemed drained of present to him . . . because objects, even people sometimes, seemed to dissipate into their causes, their own being crowded out by what had made them so" (62). This passage, with its flash of ontological dread and fear, appears to be at odds with Henry's earlier fantasy that exchange and the economy offer a form of social being and social connection—and with his deep faith in the "invisible architecture of [economic] confidence." But of course Henry's glimpse of drained, dissipating subjects is not the opposite of his faith in money but rather the product of it: as Karl Marx evocatively puts it in the 1844 manuscripts, "Only through . . . the medium of private property does the ontological essence of human passion come into being. . . . [But] if *money* is the bond binding me to *human* life, binding society to me, connecting me with nature and man . . . can it not [also] dissolve and bind all ties? Is it not, therefore, also the universal *agent of separation*?" Here, Marx clarifies the relationship between the reduction of sociality to exchange—

the belief that social cooperation is the same as market credibility—and the destruction of sociality as such: once money becomes the "bond of all bonds," it causes all other bonds to break. Marx also reveals the connection between this breaking and Henry's image of people themselves "dissipating": once "money is the real brain of things," Marx writes, it causes the "distort[ion] of individuality" as such.[60] It is to that very distortion that my final section turns.

Free Indirect Money

Jonathan Dee's *The Privileges* tells the story of Adam and Cynthia Morey, a young couple married fresh out of college (sometime, we are lead to surmise, in the mid-1980s) with two children, April and Jonas. Adam starts out as a broker at Morgan Stanley but quickly feels a "toxic stasis" in the position and joins Perini Capital, a small private-equity firm "with a shitload of money behind it."[61] Adam is successful at the firm, where he is tasked with evaluating companies the firm is considering investing in (or, more pertinently, hoping to demolish for parts). Once again, however, he starts to chafe at the position's limitations and at how long he will have to wait to make big money. Impatient, Adam concocts an insider-trading scheme with Devon, a young trader he meets at a charity gala, and using information he obtains through his work at Perini Capital, he begins making highly lucrative investments for himself, socking the profits away in multiple offshore accounts. When he is later fired from Perini (though, strikingly, not for his insider trading, which is never discovered), Adam closes down the insider scheme and founds his own private-equity fund, which eventually "put[s] up numbers that pushed him into shamanistic territory, where people earnestly believed that he was performing a kind of magic" (203).

Although it makes no reference to the events of 2008 and concerns insider trading rather than MBSs and collateralized debt obligations (CDOs), *The Privileges* has been read as a clear morality tale about the crisis. As Marco Roth puts it, the novel "challenges readers to experience sympathy for those apparently lacking in ordinary compassion." In terms that will now be familiar to us, Roth praises the novel for its "humanization" of "the inner lives of America's latest aristocracy."[62] But Roth's characterization of Dee's novel as humanizing its wealthy characters ignores its consistent use of ironic distance. As James Wood observes, the narrative "at every moment is subtly undermining" its characters, rendering Adam and Cynthia so thoroughly unlikable that we cannot possibly experience moral sympathy with them.[63] In the end, however, neither Roth nor

Wood quite gets it right: precisely by vacillating between the intimacy of focalized narration and the remove produced by the forcefully ironic third person, *The Privileges* is ultimately a self-reflexive meditation on the formal limits of sympathetic identification (and thus, I suggest, on the behavioralist individualism it seems to promote). At one point in the novel, Devon, the young man whom Adam has drawn in to his insider-trading scheme, admits to Adam, "I'm just not a stone cold killer like you are.... I know that you are one of those guys, those guys who are like missing a part of their brain or something. No conscience. No memory for losses" (143–44). Here the novel appears to stand outside Adam's perspective on his actions to give voice to the reader's own desire to blame Adam for being one of the greedy bankers who caused the economic crisis. Yet we also realize that Devon's pathologization of Adam as a sociopath overshoots its mark: the point is that Adam is not a stone cold killer, just a canny investor like all the other canny investors around him. Further, after this moment of distanced perspective on Adam, we are thrust back into Adam's consciousness as he reckons with this account. Adam himself sees Devon's as a kind of false characterization: he doesn't recognize this description of himself and muses,

> Still, when he did consider the life his family was living now, a life in which literally anything was possible, every desire was in reach, no potential was allowed to wither, and they had all seen so much of the world; when he thought back to the moment he had gone for it, to his own fearlessness when threatened with the unhappiness of those he loved, and how readily ... he had cleared the hurdle that most men would never have the fortitude to clear; and how all this was accomplished by his taking all the risk onto himself, so much so that they would never even have a clue that there was risk involved; the only reasonable conclusion, he felt, was that it was the noblest thing he had ever done in his life. It was humility, really, that made him so uncomfortable reminiscing about it. (144)

Adam's self-congratulatory account of his own humility indicates that the very perspective we are inhabiting, through the novel's focalization, lacks not simply conscience but self-consciousness. In this way, *The Privileges* registers the desire to understand the psychology of the people whose decisions supposedly drive the economy but also the ultimate failure of such knowledge to illuminate anything in the face of a psychology that is nothing more than flat, mindless, economic calculation. Thus, far from deploying what Roth calls "psychological realism," the novel ultimately acknowledges that it is not so much about economic psychology as about the economy's own psychology—that its bildungsroman is ultimately not the Moreys' but money's.[64] It is money that makes things happen and money that propels the novel's human subjects to acquire more money. Rather than suggest that human psychology drives the desire to accumulate, as the behavioralists do, *The Privileges* insists that such desires originate in money itself, which thus displaces human psychology as the source of character motivation. Adam's sense of himself as a kind of epic figure ("He felt invincible, like a martyr, a holy warrior" [172]) is tellingly misdirected, since the "invincible" hero of the novel is, in the end, money.

The substitution of money's self-moving liquidity for the concretion of the human subject solidly rooted in psychology is made possible through subtle use of free indirect style in *The Privileges*. This technique produces what Steven Shaviro, writing in the context of cinema, describes as "a sort of double consciousness" in which the character's inner voice is channeled through the third-person, omniscient point of view. The result, writes Shaviro, is a reflection on the condition of being suspended within the motion of global capital itself: "What action can still be meaningfully accomplished in the new 'world space' of endless circulation and modulation? What sort of subjectivity can remain true to itself, in a world where body and mind are measured and defined as flexible investments?"[65] Behavioralism, I have suggested, attempts to compensate for the substitution of a locatable, individual, autonomous consciousness with the placeless, expanding agency of money by suggesting that money is nothing more than the desire of individuals. *The Privileges*, however, implies the inverse: not that value depends on the psychology of individual subjects but that what appears to be a psychological subject is in fact nothing more than the animation or ventriloquization of value itself. Consider the following passage, which pretends to get us inside Adam's consciousness: "He was perfectly aware that what he was doing here affected many more fortunes than just his own. Money was its own system, its own language, its own governing principle. You introduced money into a situation and it released the potential in everybody. Maybe you got rich, maybe others around you got rich while you didn't, but either way it had to be better to learn the truth about your own nature" (243). Why, one might ask, doesn't Adam care about whether or not he personally gets rich? The answer is that by the end of this passage, it is not Adam but capital itself that is stating "the truth about [its] own nature"; capital, after all, cares only for the infinite, impersonal "potential" represented by money as "its own governing principle," money referring to nothing outside itself.

In this sense, money in *The Privileges* provides something like what Brian Richardson describes, in his narratological account of contemporary literary perspectives, as a "permeable" narration, marked by the intrusion of an "uncanny and inexplicable" narrative voice that does not come from any of the given characters. Stepping between the reader and Adam's interior consciousness, this narrative intruder makes any real understanding of or identification with Adam utterly impossible.[66] In *The Privileges,* this voice is the voice of investment itself, which Adam subsumes and is subsumed by: "The momentum of the business world was one-way only, a principle that should not be rationalized. He and Cynthia had a vivid faith in their own future, not as a variable but as a destination" (41). Dee's use of indirect voice absorbs Adam into the particularly reflexive self-consciousness of money in a way that (in Richardson's description) "violate[s] the principle of an autonomous individual consciousness" by "tak[ing] over and permeat[ing]" Adam's voice with "a voice that is not his own."[67] Thus Adam's psychology is not merely shaped by the principle of investment; rather, Adam is himself a cipher through which this principle speaks.

In the end, Adam does not represent "human capital" in the Foucauldian sense developed by theorists like Wendy Brown, for whom financialization produces individuals who "think and act like contemporary market subjects even where monetary wealth generation is not the immediate issue."[68] Rather, *The Privileges* imagines a more uncanny kind of characterization: capital remade in the image of the human. Like the novel's narrative voice, this speaking, self-animated human capital is both free and indirect: abstract, impersonal, taking no shape, and possessed of no content beyond its own drive to increase. As Adam describes it, "You create wealth where there was no wealth before, and if you [do] it well enough there [is] no end to it" (123). Adam's representation of investment as creating wealth from wealth recalls Aristotle's description of finance as an unnatural form of reproduction: "the birth of money from money," he argues, is "the most unnatural" form of wealth generation there is.[69] However whereas Aristotle's description of finance as perversely autochthonous was a means of separating it from the more "natural" economy of the *oikos*, Adam and Cynthia repeatedly embrace their status as self-made, Adamic, representing their marriage as "Year Zero" and their very existence as sui generis: at one revelatory moment, Cynthia struggles to recall the word "parthogenesis," a Freudian lapse that calls attention to the way the couple imagine themselves as parthenogenic, without origins, without history, and thus without responsibility for anyone else. Indeed, in their self-styled freedom from both history and liability, Adam and Cynthia's personhood in the novel is no more than a "legal fiction" akin to the personhood of the corporation—no surprise, then, that Cynthia, reassuring Adam of the strength of their marriage, tells him, "We're a fucking multinational, baby" (235).

Walter Benn Michaels has influentially argued that what he terms "the neoliberal novel" is the formal correlative of Margaret Thatcher's famous claim that "there is no such thing as society. There are individual men and women, and there are families." The contemporary novel, Michaels argues, likewise insists with "every sentence . . . that there are only individuals."[70] Certainly Thatcher's aphorism is in lockstep with the microeconomics of behavioralism and consonant too with the credit-crisis novel's attempt to treat the crash as the result of foolish, or greedy, or overly optimistic individuals. Yet if we read *The Privileges* as narrated not by a man or a woman but by money itself, we find that it registers not simply the foreclosure of "society" but the liquidation of "individual men and women" themselves. Consider the following passage in which Adam reveals that he doesn't simply want to wait around for his boss to die and leave him the company in his will:

> It wasn't enough to trust in your future, you had to seize your future. . . . As for Adam, when he was lying speechless in some hospital bed after his third coronary, everybody would think he was thinking about one thing, but he would be thinking about something else. (98)

Remarkably, we are never told what that something else might be, so that at the precise moment the narrative device of indirect speech seems prepared to enter Adam's real interiority—to give him the conscience as well as the self-consciousness he otherwise totally lacks—*The Privileges* instead withholds the most crucial information: what he is thinking. Reading for the novel's insistent irony, we find that we are not in the ideological terrain of the free, autonomous, particular individual. Rather, the individual of Dee's novel has no agency, and he is all automaton, no autonomy. He has no interiority (he does not speak; money speaks through him) and no capacity to act or decide (he does not move; money moves through him).

For the behavioralists, money has value because of the individuals whose subjective desires it expresses; investment moves at the whim of individuals' relative folly or rationality; and the economy is driven by individuals' exuberant optimism or lack of confidence. For Marx, in the passage quoted earlier, money subsumes and replaces those individual subjects, seizing their desires and their cognition, stealing their autonomy and making it its own. Whether money is subjective or whether it is what becomes of subjectivity under capitalism, a question remains: What happens to this subject when money ceases to flow, when possession is subject to the uncertainty of debt, and when the vast social aggregation created by exchange and credit actually does fall apart? *Dear Money, Union Atlantic,* and *The Privileges* suggest that the kinds of confident individualism so often ascribed to both contemporary ideology and the contemporary novel can really be accommodated only in (and by) boom times, since this is a form of characterization we often describe in terms of profit and plenitude, as in the commonplace expression "rich characterization" or what Slavoj Žižek terms "the wealth of human personality."[71] The unique, autonomous, psychological self—the "rich" forms of both political and aesthetic personhood, the *homines economici* of both economics and the economic novel—is, to use postcrisis parlance, underwater: present only as an absence of value, as a kind of hollow shell attesting to its missing content. It is this emptiness that the credit-crisis novel, unlike behavioral economic theory, formalizes and mediates.

These credit-crisis novels suggest that the subject of crisis founders in the gap between assumptions of rationality and descriptions of irrational folly; in the distance between naked self-interest and "personal responsibility"; and in the indeterminacy of accounts of large-scale economic structures driven by an inchoate model of consumer demand. And they suggest a still more intractable contradiction between the consolidation of subjects defined by their desires and the subjection of those subjects to insurmountable debt. The credit-crisis novel reminds us of the difficulty of representing the individual as an autonomous market actor endowed with infinite consumer freedom while also burdening that individual with full responsibility for his own reproduction in an economy fueled by consumer debt. The radical contradictions that fracture this individual's representation in a period of financial volatility underscore the fact that it is the economic subject's ideological and material maintenance, as much as the economy as a whole, that is in profound crisis. In the next chapter, I turn to what remains of such a subject under the conditions of indebtedness.

2 Credit, Characterization, Personification

A 2010 ad campaign for FreeScore.com, a website selling credit reports and credit monitoring, presents a sequence of strange but resonant images.[1] Titled "The Three Score Guys," the series emphasizes the importance of getting one's score from all three major credit bureaus. The ads in the campaign all feature a variation on a theme: A young, male consumer is seeking credit to make a major purchase. Suddenly he finds himself shadowed by personifications of all three of his credit scores. Two are good (in the upper 700s, of a possible 850) and are represented by attractive, athletic white men in black bodysuits emblazoned with the score being personified. But when a third, lower score of 583 appears in the form of a shorter, balding guy with a paunch and wearing a hockey mask, his presence threatens to prevent the young man from getting credit for his purchase (Figure 2.1). By ad's end, the low score has been replaced with another high-700s score, now represented by a third athletic white guy.

In one sense, the ideology behind these images is not surprising. As the previous chapter made clear, contemporary behavioralist thought insists on a link between personal behavior and economic rationality. Here, the idea of "fitness"—implied by the youthful athleticism of the high-score figurations and contrasted to the apparently older, weaker, fatter physique of the low score— registers the association between personal responsibility and fiscal credibility. Being obese and being in debt are linked, by "The Three Score Guys," within what Lauren Berlant calls the "shaming sickness of sovereignty," as "cris[es] of choosing and antiwill." These ads suggest that much as a seemingly objective, impartial piece of biophysical data like the Body Mass Index can become the site of biopolitical norms—regulating and managing both the individual body and the species body of the population—the credit score makes it possible, as Berlant puts it, to "link the political administration of life to ... the care of the monadic self."[2]

Figure 2.1. From Free Score.com advertising campaign, "The Three Score Guys," 2010

Yet the suggestion in "The Three Score Guys" that there is something inevitably personal about the credit score also runs counter to the credit scorers' insistence that contemporary credit evaluation is scientific, technical, objective, and profoundly impersonal. Indeed, banks and other credit institutions typically describe the objectivity of modern credit scoring and the technocracy of contemporary credit relationships as a progressive transformation away from the qualitative nature of prior regimes of credit evaluation, which tended to dally in subjective judgments and personal relationships. Fair Isaac Corporation (FICO), the producer of a proprietary credit-scoring algorithm, thus claims that because of these technological improvements, today's lenders "focus only on the facts related to credit risk, rather than their personal feelings." Since the individual's credit rating is simply a fact, it tells us, lenders are incapable of discriminating and barred from rendering moral judgments. As the major consumer credit-reporting agency Experian puts it, "No matter who you are as a person, your credit score only reflects your likelihood to repay debt responsibly."[3]

Against these claims to impersonal objectivity, however, "The Three Score Guys" campaign indicates the persistence of the personal. If credit scores are an objective measurement of risk, why does this borrower have three different scores attached to him? If there is no such thing as inherently good credit, why represent the low score as simultaneously embarrassing (his slumped shoulders and beer belly are clearly meant to contrast with the stalwart hands-on-hips poses of the high scores) and frightening (wearing a style of hockey mask famously associated with a horror-film serial killer)? What do the algorithms and facts invoked by credit scorers have to do with the highly subjective personifications appearing in the ads and with Experian's language of "responsibility"? In short, if credit is not a judgment of "who you are as a person," why personify it in the first place?

Credit evaluation is objective and scientific, and credit relationships are impersonal and anonymous; debt is personal and moral, and repaying it is a matter of individual and social responsibility. These contradictory assumptions are what this chapter seeks to challenge. While the credit scorers insist on objectivity and quantification, they make it clear that both the person (in ads like "The Three Score Guys") and the personal (in the language of responsibility) continue to haunt both the practice and discourse of credit evaluation. Yet an emergent body of post-crisis critical theory on debt often makes the opposite mistake, insisting on the personal, affective, and subjective aspects of contemporary credit and debt but failing to address either the turn in credit evaluation toward quantification or the return in debt collection to material coercion rather than moral suasion. The truth, this chapter argues, lies somewhere between these two positions: debt persistently and simultaneously occupies the logic of quantitative, scientific objectivity and of qualitative, even moral, subjectivity. This paradox presents an impasse for both the ideology of credit and the critical study of debt, since it means that the personal can never be a corrective for credit's impersonality nor objectivity a solution to the problem of debt's personalization.

Contemporary literature and conceptual art have found in this oscillation between the personal and the impersonal not a problem to be resolved but a compelling set of questions to be pursued. I suggested in the previous chapter that the autonomous, sovereign, desiring individual often thought to characterize economic ideology is actually a psychologically thin subject to whom neither robust agency nor moral accountability can be attributed. This chapter seeks to understand what kinds of personhood emerge as alternatives to this defaulted individual subjectivity in a range of post-crisis creative works that explore the link between credit, debt, and personhood and provide new ways of figuring the social person in light of contemporary modes of credit evaluation. How has the emergence of new forms of credit scoring and new ways of tracking economic personhood transformed characterization (the production of socially legible fictional characters) and personification (the production of mediating figures through which subjects are made or made to speak)?

I begin by exploring the way the credit economy and the realist novel once worked as mutually constituted forms, each lending its narrative economy, its epistemology of credibility, and especially its use of the character "type" to the other. As new modes of credit rating and scoring emerge, new types of literary characters adequate to those modes arise in turn. Thus, I read Gary Shteyngart's 2010 farcical novel *Super Sad True Love Story* as an effort to limn the relationship between contemporary credit and anti-realist characterization.[4] Through Shteyngart's novel, I explore the problem of relating the individual to the population, and the typical to the stereotypical, in the context of transformations in contemporary credit and debt. *Super Sad True Love Story* does more than simply register these historical shifts at the level of its content; it brings them to bear on its own mode of characterization, providing one way of intervening between the rhetoric of moral character and the practice of quantitative credit evaluation. Shteyngart's adoption of antirealist modes of characterization, I argue, attests to both an anxiety and an excess present even in the reductive simplicity of the credit score. His use of stereotype and caricature also suggests the persistence of racial and gender discrimination as the blackboxed, "subprime" secret behind seemingly systematized, "objective" methods of credit evaluation.

The second section of the chapter turns from characterization to what I describe as personification: the ways conceptual art and poetry offer mediating forms or figures through which the subject can be represented or produced. To show how experimental practices in poetry and visual art reveal new links between debt and the personal, I explore three formal devices characteristic of post-crisis personification: portraiture in the work of artist Cassie Thornton and debtor selfies from the Occupy Wall Street movement; impersonality in conceptual poet Mathew Timmons's book-length project *CREDIT*; and prosopopoeia in Timothy Donnelly's apostrophic poem "To His Debt." These works allow us to think both critically and historically about the material condition of indebtedness, conjuring debt not simply as a personal experience, an affective disposition, or an ideological construction but also as a material and historical structure, one profoundly indifferent to the particular persons it affects.

Characterization and Credit

I begin by considering the relationship between credit scoring and what Marcel Mauss influentially termed the "social person." Mauss suggests that persons are "categories of the human mind" rather than sui generis entities—they are as much personae as *personnes*—and argues that these constructed social persons "not only sustain the life of things and of the gods, but the [social] propriety of things" in the context of social and economic exchange.[5] Literary critic Elizabeth Fowler takes up Mauss's term to define social persons as "abstract figurations of the human . . . that attain recognizable, conventional status through use": the social person marks the way that fictional characters are actively interpreted and measured by readers according to a set of social conventions through which the character is made legible.[6] Drawing on these two accounts, I suggest that the social person is at once an economic and a literary category and explore the ways in which changes in the credit economy redound formally, aesthetically, and politically on the production of social personhood.

As a number of literary critics and economic historians have argued, the development of a standard practice for evaluating consumer credit in the late eighteenth and early nineteenth centuries depended on but also enabled the emergence of a realist model of literary character. That is, the practice of credit evaluation borrowed the realist novel's ways of describing fictional persons as well as the formal habits of reading and interpretation the novel demanded. In turn, the realist novel drew on the credit economy's models of typification—the representation of a social class on the basis of its individual representatives—to produce socially legible characters. The salutary link between the practice of credit evaluation and the production of credible literary characters made it possible for economic creditworthiness to appear as a matter of both moral character and social context.

By the end of the eighteenth century, the market economy was fully dependent on consumer credit to extend the temporality of circulation and exchange.[7] However, despite rising demand for loans to purchase new types of consumer goods, consumer credit was not rendered formal and contractual until the early twentieth century.[8] Nineteenth-century creditors thus lacked the kinds of institutional standards adequate to an increasingly dispersed and anonymous economy. In the absence of quantitative or systematized instruments for evaluating the fiscal soundness of those to whom they leant, creditors in this period relied instead on subjective evaluations of personal character as a kind of proxy measurement for a borrower's economic riskiness.[9] According to historian Kenneth Lipartito, these subjective evaluations were rendered in a very specific form: "The genre of communication about credit in the nineteenth century," Lipartito explains, "was largely a narrative one."[10] Thus the first successful commercial credit-reporting agency in the United States, R. G. Dun, opened its guide to assessors by noting, "The report is a story." By "shap[ing] field reports into compelling narratives," early credit-reporting agencies transformed information into a salable commodity.[11] While allowing the reporter to sort and contextualize detail, such narratives also required that readers make their own judgments. More descriptive than prescriptive, credit "stories" necessarily demanded subjective interpretation. The use of narrative form also allowed the continual revision of credit histories, as customers' changing circumstances forced the reporting agency to update its evaluations frequently.[12]

The narrativity of credit reports was especially important as the credit economy became increasingly delocalized, such that lenders often lacked longstanding personal knowledge of borrowers. Under these conditions, creditors needed a way to feel confident in their ability to immediately judge the personal character of strangers. Credit bureaus thus required face-to-face interviews, which they saw as an opportunity to evaluate—indeed, to read—the applicant's appearance and demeanor. As one credit bureau interviewer of the period put it, a "prospective customer may strike [one] very forcibly as being 'shifty,' 'evasive,' 'argumentative,' 'seedy appearance,' 'flashy,' 'wife looks as if she might be extravagant,' and the like."[13] Evaluators were called on to make interpretive judgments based on a range of seemingly superficial observations, from fashion to physiognomy. Much as fictional narrative provided a form for writing the credit report, it also taught creditors how to read these details evaluatively: Deirdre Lynch and Margo Finn have demonstrated persuasively that novel reading provided models for how trivial observations might provide meaningful pieces of information suitable for inferring an unknown person's credibility.[14] Realist fiction taught readers to interpret literary characters on the basis of their dress, manners, and appearance; certainty that such novelistic details could prompt accurate literary judgments produced, in turn, confidence in their economic equivalents. The novel showed economic actors how to deduce the intrinsic character of the strangers whose promises to pay they needed to appraise.

To do this, both novelistic character and credit assessment depended on a balance of specificity and generality. Although they were defined largely by their particularity, the fictional characters of the realist novel also had to be recognizable as familiar social types. As in a credit file, the need for sufficient detail had to be weighed against the hazard of superfluous information. Too little detail might render a character too generic, while too much might make generalization impossible.[15] By establishing a set of fictional character types—convincingly specific but familiar enough to be recognized as "that kind of person"—the novel thus provided an emergent credit economy not only with a way to collect information and a heuristic for interpreting it but also with a model for generalizing that information. Since the details gained in a face-to-face interview were often not explicitly economic, characteristics such as an individual's argumentative manner or flashy demeanor had to be converted into a measure of creditworthiness through the imaginative calculus of typification: other similarly flashy borrowers have turned out to be unreliable, so this borrower might also be unreliable. Carefully elaborated descriptions, along with highly interpretive judgments, could thus be made to signify according to a subtle logic of social classification.

The social type thus not only regulated particularity and generality; it also mediated the relationship between individuals and their social and historical contexts. If, as Fredric Jameson maintains, the typifying imagination assumes that individual figures "stand . . . for something larger and more meaningful than themselves," in both the realist novel and the credit economy of the nineteenth and early twentieth centuries that "something" was the individual's economic and social class.[16] The realist novel's seemingly paradoxical commitment to both psychological interiority (depth) and social interconnection (breadth) yoked private psychological character to public credibility.[17] The typifying practices of credit agents depended on this same association between individual character and social credibility. Thus, it was deemed necessary to interview a borrower in the privacy of the credit agency office—to plumb the depths of his moral character in an institutional space resonant of a doctor's office or church confessional—but it was equally important to pay a visit to his lived environment—to observe him in the context of his social class.[18] A store executive of the 1920s, for instance, describes sending staff investigators to "visit the neighborhood of the applicant's residence, size up the appearance of the house and question local shopkeepers regarding his standing."[19] The effect of this emphasis on social credibility did more than just reassure lenders that their money would be repaid. It also allowed credit to seem both personally meaningful and socially salutary: grounded in local specificity and traditional values, the link between economic credibility and moral virtue appeared self-evident.

However the mid- to late twentieth century saw radical transformations in the nature of consumer credit, in the evaluation and commodification of credit risk, and in the theory and practice of credit scoring. Banking deregulation in the 1920s withdrew strict limitations on interest rates and allowed debt to be resold at a profit.[20] The production of new types of goods, particularly mass-produced but expensive consumer goods like the automobile, and the emergence of new kinds of retailers, particularly large department stores targeting middle-class consumers, necessitated the creation of new forms of installment-plan lending suited to a burgeoning consumer economy.[21] After World War II, consumer demand was bolstered by the shift from fixed installment plans to revolving credit, which allowed flexible payments and charged monthly interest. By the century's end, consumer finance had moved from the margins to the center of the US economy. Facilitated by the development of debt securitization (which allowed debt to function as a tradable financial instrument) and necessitated by wage stagnation, consumer credit was no longer simply an aid to consumption but an industry in itself.

As a result, creditors no longer wanted to avoid default risk entirely; instead, they wanted to be able to predict and price it—put simply, they wanted to be able to offer credit to more borrowers than ever. "Universal" credit cards, accepted by virtually any retailer, were introduced in the mid-1970s, and initially credit card companies offered these cards only to less risky borrowers: the "non-revolvers" who paid balances in full every month. But as a result of low federal borrowing rates (which allowed banks to borrow cheaply) and the deregulation of caps on interest rates and fees (which allowed banks to raise prices on consumer loans), creditors became increasingly interested in "revolvers," borrowers who accumulated debt and interest while making low monthly payments.[22] In the early 1990s, credit card companies began to target consumers who had previously been denied credit because they were considered too poor or too risky. Other consumers were inundated with aggressive direct-market campaigns: rather than require consumers to apply for a credit line directly, creditors sent "preapproved" offers, even the cards themselves, to consumers who had not requested them.[23] In short, creditors extended more and more kinds of credit, at an ever-widening range of prices, to an ever-growing group of potential borrowers.

These changes required a total reimagination of consumer credit evaluation. By the final decades of the twentieth century, creditors had fully turned away from subjective, qualitative, narrative forms of credit evaluation and accomplished what economic historians have termed a "quantitative revolution."[24]

One pithy definition, written as the practice of credit scoring first emerged in the early 1970s, makes the terms of this reimagination clear: "Credit scoring is an empirical technique that uses statistical methodology to predict the probability of repayment by credit applicants."[25] Here in a single sentence we see all the salient shifts of a contemporary credit regime: from evaluation to scoring, interpretation to empirical analysis, credible narrative to probabilistic statistics, moral judgment to impartial prediction. Drawing on developments in behavioral science, credit evaluators created an increasingly fine-tuned system for pricing credit risk that depended not on a qualitative assessment of moral character but on a quantifiable history of economic behavior. Retailers began tracking consumer behavior and relying more heavily on information collected by credit bureaus. Using standardized data and consistent credit-monitoring systems, they were able to devise rating models, replacing qualitative narrative with quantitative practices and subjectivity with science. Thus, we see FICO calling its score a "fast, objective measurement of credit risk," as if a credit score is simply a way of gauging a natural phenomenon, like the temperature.[26]

Such claims to objectivity were particularly important in the wake of the 1974 Equal Credit Opportunity Act (ECOA), which prohibited creditors from discriminating on the basis of race, religion, nationality, sex, marital status, or age. Emphasizing mathematical models and scientific data collection allowed the information-collecting credit bureaus (TransUnion, Equifax, and Experian), the analytic firms behind proprietary scoring models (FICO and VantageScore), and the score-monitoring websites (FreeCreditScore.com, FreeCreditReport.com, CreditKarma.com) to present quantitative objectivity as an improvement over the subjective—and thus potentially discriminatory—techniques used in the past.

As Donncha Marron explains, new forms of credit evaluation and new ways of managing consumer credit agreements "marked a departure ... from older focal points such as 'character.'"[27] Drawing on developments in behavioral psychology, evaluation techniques now emphasized behavior (borrowing history, habits of repayment, consumption patterns) rather than personal characteristics (marital status, age, occupation) or moral character (social status, reputation, perceived integrity). Attempting to remain in compliance with the ECOA, lenders sought less openly judgmental techniques of evaluation. These new statistical and behavioral models allowed the easy exclusion of explicit references to race and gender while retaining less obvious behavioral indicators of the same information. They also marked a shift from what Martha Poon describes as "control by screening" to "control by risk." Control by screening had created only two general classes of borrowers: creditworthy and not creditworthy. Control by risk substituted a highly segmented spectrum for this simple binary, opening a new "space of calculative possibility" by measuring a wide range of calculable risks and creating an equally wide range of chargeable rates.[28]

The spectrum approach, in turn, demanded new modes of screening—what Poon describes as "razor sharp segmentation games"—to assess the relative merits of a consumer population lacking the kind of credit and employment history once definitive of fiscal credibility.[29] A contemporary credit bureau report might contain as many as 450 discrete data points, including employment and salary history, address history, health history, and court judgments. In the 1990s, creditors (as well as employment agencies and insurance companies) began to use these reports to create lender-specific algorithms to predict delinquency risk. Large credit card firms used the immense amounts of consumer data to which they had access to study their customers' borrowing and purchasing habits in intimate detail. In so doing, they were able to produce highly particularized behavioral and psychological profiles characterized by what Poon calls an unprecedented "quantitative granularity."[30] By the early 2000s, lenders were predicting default not only on the basis of credit history and income but also through the study of seemingly trivial spending habits. They observed, for instance, that consumers who bought premium bird seed, rooftop snow rakes, and furniture-leg pads to protect floors from scratches were unlikely to miss payments, whereas those who purchased generic motor oil or "chromeskull car accessories" were highly likely to default.[31] In 2008, some American Express card members received letters explaining a drop in their credit limit: "Other customers who have used their card at establishments where you recently shopped have a poor repayment history with American Express."[32] Subprime lender CompuCredit faced Federal Trade Commission (FTC) scrutiny for basing credit limits on what the FTC described as "an undisclosed 'behavioral' scoring model that penalized consumers for using their cards for certain types of transactions: marriage counselors . . . automobile tire retreading, bars and night clubs, pool and billiard establishments, massage parlors."[33]

Credit bureaus and credit card companies consistently emphasize the purely quantitative, scientific nature of these practices, representing their scoring instruments as highly objective measurements radically different from the subjective practices of the past. Critical accounts of contemporary credit scoring have similarly claimed that the turn to scoring marks an unequivocal departure from character-based, narrative models of credit evaluation. Marron, for example, argues that the "bureaucratic administration of limited, categorical, quantified data" performed by contemporary credit scoring substitutes "the breadth and color of *detail*" with the "new depth and specificity of *data*."[34] Ingrid Jeacle and Eamonn Walsh likewise observe that "judgment based on character" has been replaced by "the systematic analysis of an archive of payment behavior," while "moral character profiles" have been replaced by "seemingly objective numbers."[35] Lipartito claims that "the FICO score ... was almost 180 degrees from the narrative in form."[36]

There is no doubt that the turn from narrative records to algorithmic scores constitutes a radical shift in the formal logic and outward appearance of credit evaluation. The qualitative narrative model of credit evaluation, which imagined consumers as socially embedded economic actors describable through a finite set of typifying characteristics, has been replaced by a system in which a vast and indefinite number of data points are fed through a quantitative algorithm and recombined into a wide range of highly individualized microassessments. Thus, the contemporary credit economy appears to do away with the category of the person entirely, substituting the individual's constancy with the scoring algorithm's contingency. Despite the contemporary credit economy's avowed preference for objective numbers, however, credit scoring cannot leave subjective personhood behind, since the very category of "creditworthiness" remains a quality of individuals rather than of data. Despite the credit bureaus' claim that their scores merely index a consumer's contingent and changing relationship to a model, the discourse of personal responsibility and moral rectitude is at least as resonant in the language of "behavior" as it was in the discourse of moral character and personal characteristics: an insurance industry analysis of risk assessment, for instance, asserts that credit scoring "provides a numerical proxy for the biopsychobehavioral makeup of the individual" and thus "tap[s] the 'responsibility and stability' component of an individual's behavior."[37] Much as the credit narrative once offered a social rendering of personal detail, today the credit score represents a social rendering of a person's data. Once calculated, this score makes the details of our personal history and individual behavior legible and functional: the credit score thus performs the work of mediation once accomplished by the narrative report.

In particular, credit scores mediate the relationship between individuals and social contexts, although not at all in the manner of the nineteenth century's typifying practices. Credit scoring displaces the credit narrative's emphasis on the generalized social type by insisting on a new kind of individualized granularity, but the score itself remains intractably social insofar as it determines an individual's relative position within the social logic of the marketplace. Although credit scoring (like the microeconomic theories discussed in Chapter 1) assumes that economic society is not a complex totality of social classes but merely an aggregate of autonomous individuals, the very act of consumer modeling imagines, indeed constructs, a working relationship between persons and populations. This relationship is far more fluid and temporary than the relatively fixed relationship between representative individuals and their generalizable social class assumed by the prior regime. But as a number that is highly responsive, heavily circulated, and perpetually recalculated, the individual score remains meaningful only insofar as it can be understood in relation to a larger collective body. The credit score also constitutes populations through discriminatory practices like subprime lending. Much as the first land enclosures dispossessed a population by first creating it *as* a population, subprime borrowers are rarely imagined as singular individuals but as a group, a neighborhood, an economic class or, most often, a race. Like the premodern enclosures, subprime debt entails an *inclusion* into the social order through a highly generalized form of discrimination operative at the level of a mass population. Thinking about the persistence of personhood in contemporary credit—the personhood of both the individual subject, whose race or class is discerned through the collection of purportedly neutral data points, and of the group or population, whose collective exploitation precedes and makes possible their incorporation into the economic processes from which they were once barred—is thus crucial to understanding the ways in which categories of class, gender, and race are reaffirmed at the very site of their disavowal.

The credit score, as much as the credit narrative, thereby creates its own version of Fowler's social persons: if literary characterization is "the collective imaginative technology" that turns words into characters, contemporary credit scoring is the empirical technology that turns persons into numbers.[38] Yet it also cannot avoid turning those numbers back into persons, as the FreeScore.com ad makes clear. Despite the thoroughgoing displacement of character by number, narration by calculation, qualities by quantities, an uncanny remainder of the social person persists whenever and wherever the credit score appears. Thus credit-scoring technicians claim to translate actual persons into impersonal numbers—freed of the designations but replete with the marks of race and class—even as they import the fictions of personhood stripped from human subjects into the scores themselves.

So what happens to literary characters when credit evaluation no longer requires fiction's socially embedded personal details but depends instead on the algorithm's socially distributed atomized data? In his work on the changing conventions of literary characterization, Raymond Williams argues that while the dominant way of producing character relies on a "known model of 'people like this'" (that is, typification), historical changes sometimes require "new articulations, new formations of 'character' and 'relationship.'"[39] Following Williams, I argue that the kinds of characters associated with contemporary credit scoring are markedly different from the typified, realist characters of credit narrative and that the contemporary novel concerned with the effect of credit on social persons must introduce precisely such "new formations" if it wants to register the concomitant emergence of quantitative credit scoring. To read for literary character in the credit-crisis novel, we must be attentive to the formal and historical differences that separate the kinds of persons produced by and for these two distinct regimes of credit evaluation.

I locate these new kinds of characters in Gary Shteyngart's 2011 *Super Sad True Love Story*, a post-crisis novel explicitly concerned with the emergence of new models of credit evaluation. *Super Sad* treats those new models not just as forms of characterization comparable to its own but also as modes of racialization likewise comparable to its self-conscious treatment of race and ethnicity. Set in a recognizable near future in which the US economy is in sharp decline and massive debt, *Super Sad* tells the story of Lenny Abramov, a middle-aged middle manager for a company called (and promising) Indefinite Life Extension. On a trip to Italy to recruit European clients, Lenny falls in love with Eunice Park, a Korean American teenager obsessed—like the novel's farcically dystopian culture as a whole—with shopping and social media, especially with her "äppärät," the novel's neologism for an omnipresent technological device similar to the iPhone but worn around the neck to project data about the wearer into the surrounding space. While fascination with the perversities of consumer culture has been a staple of the postmodern novel, *Super Sad* addresses what it means to live in an economy where all consumption is fueled by credit, or, more specifically, what it means to live in an economy that once was fueled by credit but that is now running out of steam as fewer and fewer debtors are able to pay. *Super Sad*'s fascination with the specific instruments of credit scoring emphasizes their technological mediation, their use as a way to manage and control otherwise unruly subjects, and their effectivity as a mode of social (mis)recognition. Thus the novel stages the relays between persons and credit in both its form and its content, as when the narrator describes public "Credit Poles" that involuntarily display the scores of passersby:

> My fashion friend Sandi in Rome had told me about the Credit Poles, yapping on about their cool retro design, the way the wood was intentionally gnarled in places and how the utility wire was replaced by strings of colored lights. The old-fashioned appearance of the Poles was obviously meant to evoke a sturdier time in our nation's history, except for the little LED counters at eye level that registered your Credit ranking as you walked by.... I felt the perfunctory liberal chill at seeing entire races of human beings so summarily reduced and stereotyped, but was also voyeuristically interested in seeing people's Credit rankings. The old Chinese woman had a decent 1400 but others, the young Latina mothers, even a profligate teenaged Hasid puffing down the street, were showing blinking red scores below 900, and I worried for them. I walked past one of the Poles, letting it zap the data off my äppärät and saw my own score, an impressive 1520.[40]

This passage offers a kind of allegory for the history I have just given. Credit scoring enters contemporary daily life as a variation on an older—or, here, "retro"—form of typification, celebrating its own novelty as a social technology while simultaneously claiming to be a benign improvement on a long-standing practice, and thus nothing to fear. More important, the passage begins to reveal the ways in which Shteyngart's novel formally appropriates the credit economy's constant accumulation and analysis of personal information. Declining the conventions of characterization associated with the realist novel, particularly the use of limited but meaningful qualitative detail, the novelist instead adopts two modes of characterization usually disparaged in literary fiction: caricature and stereotype. By harnessing the excesses of caricature and the reductions of the stereotype, Shteyngart creates characters emblematic of the contemporary regime of credit scoring.

Caricature

The appearance of caricatures in *Super Sad* has been read as a failure of the novel: for example, reviewer Rayyan Al-Shawaf complains that many of Shteyngart's characters are mere "caricatures," too "one-dimensional."[41] But the primary formal feature of caricature, which Al-Shawaf's assessment fails to acknowledge, is over- rather than underdescription. Historically, what makes a character a caricature is not its inadequacy but its too-much-ness, as Lynch suggests by noting that "the term caricature derives from the Italian *caricare*, to load." "One looks at a caricature," Lynch observes, "and finds oneself gazing not so much at a nose appended to a face but at a supernumerary face that has attached itself to a nose."[42] Or one might find oneself gazing at *Super Sad* protagonist Lenny Abramov's overloaded face:

> a slight man with a gray, sunken, battleship of a face, curious wet eyes, a giant gleaming forehead on which a dozen cavemen could have painted something nice, a sickle of a nose perched atop a tiny puckered mouth, and from the back a growing bald spot whose shape perfectly replicates the great state of Ohio, with its capital city, Columbus, marked by a deep-brown mole. (4–5)

This hyperbolic "battleship of a face"—with its cavernous forehead, state-shaped bald spot, and impossibly, incredibly large proboscis—perfectly echoes Lynch's description of those caricatures featuring "noses of preposterous size."[43] The caricatured face is too particular and too eccentric—its features too large, its details too many—to be recognizable or familiar, making it difficult to attach it to a credibly imaginable person. For precisely this reason caricature, as a mode of characterization cast aside by the realist novel's search for credible characters, is particularly suited to contemporary quantitative credit scoring. Indeed, sociologist Michael Curry uses the term to describe the modern digital self in an age of credit-data accumulation: "I am being treated not like 'me' but as a caricature."[44] Curry's use of this literary term to describe the social persons imagined by credit scoring implies a link between the excessive particularity of data collection under a contemporary regime of credit and the overloaded descriptions of *Super Sad*'s physical caricatures, which cease to be identifiable as well-rounded persons and can stand only as the sum of an ever-changing, ever-increasing collection of trivial details.

Unlike older modes of caricature, however, Shteyngart's descriptions feature not only an overabundance of physical details but also an overabundance of data. If Lenny's face offers us one kind of caricatured excess, characterizations such as the following, wherein Lenny describes a potential client for Indefinite Life Extension, offer another:

> Income yearly $2.24 million, pegged to the yuan; obligations, including alimony and child support, $3.12 million; investible assets (excluding real estate)—northern euro 22,000,000; real estate $5.4 million, pegged to the yuan; total debts outstanding $12.9 million, unpegged. (18)

Here the accumulation of numbers echoes the physiognomic excess in the depiction of Lenny's face; in both cases, the sum of the details never quite adds up to a recognizable person. Just as Lenny's face was too eccentric to be imagined, these data points are too numerous to be calculated or interpreted, a problem heightened by their appearance in three different currencies. Modified not by a finite number of physical characteristics but by an endless stream of data, such caricatures register the seemingly preposterous particularity of the information attached to the social persons of the contemporary credit economy.

Data offer a descriptive poetics for more than just the novel's minor characters. Indeed, the same kind of quantified information is used to introduce us to its other central character, Lenny's "beloved," Eunice—the young, beautiful, self-loathing daughter of Korean immigrants. After meeting Eunice in Rome, Lenny yearns to know more about her so he tracks her "digital footprint." Browsing online using his äppärät, he quickly gleans information on her family's wealth (examining a chart "giving the income for the last eighteen months; the yuan amounts were in steady decline since they had mistakenly left California for New Jersey—July's income after expenses was eight thousand yuan"); their purchasing behavior (learning that "the Park sisters favored extra small shirts in strict business patterns, austere grey sweaters distinguished only by their provenance and price, pearly earrings, one-hundred-dollar children's socks (their feet were that small), panties shaped like gift bows, bars of swiss chocolate at random delis, footwear, footwear, footwear"); and their health statistics (observing that "Sally, as the youngest of the Parks, was awash in [data]. . . . Her LDL cholesterol was way beneath the norm while the HDL surged ahead to form an unheard-of ratio. Even with her weight she could live to be 120 if she maintained her present diet") (37–38). This accumulation of detail is overwhelming for both the reader and for Lenny, commingling—as a contemporary credit report would—disparate and fluid information on income, consumer habits, and physical health. Unhierarchized and continually updated, these data lack the consistency of a more qualitative account of physical appearance or personality. The use of parataxis adds to the sense of quantitative aggregation generated by the moment-to-moment accumulation of data points, which then provides Lenny with "the numerical totality of the Park family" (38).

In this sense, the novel's use of data caricature elegantly registers contemporary credit scoring's treatment of individuals as bundles of information. The alienating experience of "not me" one experiences on encountering one's caricatured representation by credit data is not, counterintuitively, the anxiety of reduction but the anxiety of excess, the experience of being defined not by a carefully limited array of personal details but by an indefinite accumulation of data.[45] Under such conditions, we are left with something like what Gilles Deleuze famously called "dividuals," the divided data bodies of late capitalism, atomized persons whose lack of coherence or consistency can be registered only by caricature's excess of detail and data.[46]

Stereotype

Despite the excesses implied by the caricature's hyperparticularity, however, *Super Sad* includes another kind of character whose depiction features not the overloaded too-much-ness of the caricature but the reductive generalization of the stereotype. As the reference to "seeing entire races of human beings summarily reduced and stereotyped" by the Credit Poles suggests, the language of stereotype suffuses the novel. In the first chapter alone we encounter a slew of minor characters who are flattened and generalized rather than highly particularized or overdescribed: "coma-bound Europeans," "the Korean," "the Ukrainian," "the Neapolitan," and someone having "one of those very angry Italian äppärät chats on the couch" (14–20). This produces a kind of paradox in the novel: while its caricatures cannot represent any larger social totality, a character described simply as "the Ukrainian" can be nothing *more* than a flattened representative of her racialized nationality.

If *Super Sad*'s use of caricature captures the creation of excessively particular data-persons, its use of stereotype registers the paradox by which a contemporary credit economy also reifies generalized social categories. As we have already seen, contrary to the credit institutions' own claim that credit scoring does not discriminate by race, gender, age, or class, the allocation and price of credit in the United States are in fact stratified along precisely those lines. The data on race and subprime mortgage lending leave little doubt about the effect of race on the price and availability of mortgage credit: the findings of the 2011 case *US v. Countrywide*, for example, revealed that Bank of America and Countrywide Mortgage charged hundreds of thousands of minority borrowers higher interest rates and fees than similarly qualified and similarly rated white borrowers. They also placed nonwhite borrowers in subprime loans rather than offering the prime-quality loans for which those borrowers were qualified, a practice known as "reverse redlining," or discrimination by inclusion. By segmenting borrowers into risk classes rather than excluding them outright, mortgage borrowers could include more nonwhite borrowers while offering them far worse terms and interest rates.[47] As a study conducted jointly by the US Department of Housing and Urban Development (HUD) and the National Community Reinvestment Coalition found, "The single most utilized defense of lenders and their trade associations concerning bias is that credit scoring systems allow lenders to be colorblind in their loan decisions. [However,] African-American and elderly neighborhoods . . . receive a disproportionate amount of high cost subprime loans."[48]

Frank Pasquale thus reasons that far from eliminating bias, quantitative credit scoring "may be . . . systematizing [it] in hidden ways" by "laundering past practices of discrimination into a blackboxed score."[49] Recall, for instance, "The Three Score Guys" ad for FreeScore.com. Although the ad attempts to personify the difference between scores through the representation of body type—and the ideology of fitness it implies—we should also note its racialization. The unmarked white man in the ad appears to represent the product of objective processes of abstraction, quantification, and neutralization. Ultimately, however, the figure's very whiteness serves as a desperate attempt to disavow the link between credit and race: the scores are neutrally white precisely to avoid implying any essentialized link between particular scores and particular ethnicities. Yet this link, as well as the discrimination it produces, is the primary and intended consequence of these credit-scoring systems themselves, as an image created by comic artist Tak Toyoshima brilliantly conveys (Figure 2.2). In Toyoshima's image, the issue of the ad's all-white casting is connected, in an overdetermined way, to the material reality of economic discrimination repressed by the original "Three Score Guys." Far more than the real ad's so-called colorblind casting (or the scoring companies' so-called colorblind credit scoring), the racialization of credit scores performed by Toyoshima's parody powerfully acknowledges the way race and ethnicity determine economic relationships.

Figure 2.2. Image by Tak Toyoshima from *Secret Asian Man* blog, 2011

Super Sad trades in a similarly ironic manner on this relationship between credit scores and racial stereotypes, showing not only that the score serves as a technique of racialization but also that the score's own internal logic depends on racialization. If the credit score is a means to understand and organize an excess of data—to "reduc[e] everyone to a three-digit number," as Lenny puts it—the stereotype is the inevitable consequence of this reduction. Because it must be rendered legible in the form of a score or a ranking, a massive amount of data cannot avoid generalization. Thus, in the passage concerning the Credit Poles, as Lenny observes the difference between the credit scores of an "old Chinese woman" and those of "young Latina mothers," his own tendency to generalize according to race or nationality emerges as the necessary effect of an economy in which credit scores themselves produce racialized stereotypes. The Credit Poles that update one's data in real time are also devices that address consumers directly, hailing them according to the logic of racial control:

> In the Chinatown parts of East Broadway, the signs read in English and Chinese—"America Celebrates its Spenders!"—with a cartoon of a miserly ant happily running towards a mountain of wrapped Christmas presents. In the Latino sections on Madison

Street, they read in English and Spanish—"Save it for a Rainy Day, *Huevón*"—with a frowning grasshopper in a zoot suit showing his empty pockets. (54)

The poles display racially and ethnically specific ads on the basis of economic data, and this generalization reifies racial and ethnic difference. The fact that such generalizations can produce only flattened stereotypes rather than well-rounded, fully realized characters is highlighted by the infantilizing cartoon images: the allegorical "miserly ant" and woebegone grasshopper of children's stories.[50] Such stereotypes provide, in turn, the basis for explicit racism, as when Eunice overhears someone in the park shout, "Hey, ant, buy something or go back to China!" (162). The point here is not only that this taunt is empirically wrong (because Eunice is not Chinese and is already obsessed with shopping) but also that it assumes that Eunice is reducible to the thrifty Asian of the Credit-Pole signage. The novel's own descriptions of characters as, for instance, "a confident Filipina" or "A-level Koreans," register the same relationship between the reduction of persons to numbers and the reduction of groups to broad generalizations.

Although the stereotype's oversimplification would seem to oppose the caricature's overdescription, *Super Sad* suggests that when read through the logic of credit scoring, stereotype and caricature emerge from the same process. The contemporary credit economy depends on the capacity to attach a near-infinite amount of behavioral data to an individual, and this excess of detail is formalized through caricature. But the turn toward "control by risk" not only replaced the binaries of credit screening with the granular specificity of the risk spectrum; it also produced the stereotypical category of the "subprime population."[51] Stereotype, then, is the form of characterization appropriate to an economy in which a large group of borrowers are rendered economically vulnerable not through their exclusion but through their inclusion, an inclusion that depends in turn on their reductive constitution as a risky population. As Fred Moten argues in an essay evocatively titled "The Subprime and the Beautiful," to be subprime is to always already be part of a target population, to "consent not to be a single being," with all the vulnerability such a state of aggregation implies.[52]

Vacillating between overdescription and generalization, between intimate physical detail and strictly numerical data, between atomization and total social transparency, the novel's half-comic, half–"super sad" characters function much like what Sianne Ngai calls the "zany" figure of late capitalism: a "person/character who implodes the concept of character from within."[53] As a result, and as negative reviews of the novel suggest, *Super Sad*'s characters often don't seem like believable persons at all. Yet this is precisely Shteyngart's point, since to a risk-seeking credit regime the most profitable borrower may no longer appear as a narratively credible person. In their narrative "incredibility," Shteyngart's caricatures and stereotypes show that social personhood—once defined by its consistency, predictability, and legibility—has been transformed at a time in which one cannot necessarily keep one's promise to pay. *Super Sad*'s imploding characters index new and profoundly unstable forms of social personhood generated in a moment of credit crisis.

Personification and Debt

Whereas Shteyngart's novel locates its modes of characterization firmly within the forms of credit evaluation contemporary to it, a recent conceptual art piece by Cassie Thornton considers the history of contemporary credit scoring by casting its gaze backward. For a project called "GMC (Give Me Cred)" Thornton took over abandoned storefronts in Cleveland, Ohio, and Oakland, California, from which she disbursed what she terms "extremely alternative credit reports." "At GIVE ME CRED (GMC)," her artist statement announces, "We will look at you and ask you why we should trust you. When we believe in you, we will make you a unique PDF [Public Document of Fidelity] document that proves to landlords, employers, and creditors that you are a person with a story that expands beyond your credit score." Noting that Ohio's employment laws allow potential employers to use credit reports as part of the job applicant screening process, Thornton adds,

> The GMC offers documentation of our client's complex personal narrative as a way to represent their integrity with more than numbers, and with as much as possible. Starting with an actual meeting with a person, we will find a way to document the unique story of all persons, places, or things in search of validation, homes, work, loans, or general approval. At GIVE ME CRED (GMC) we will give you all the credit you can handle. GMC is the #1 source of extremely alternative credit scores. Our clients range from people to places and things.[54]

While cannily ironic about the way credit has long deployed the language of personal validation and social approval, the piece also underscores the difference between older forms of credit assessment and contemporary credit scoring. In this way, it maneuvers between two modes of credit evaluation, insisting that credit has long exploited social personhood but also evoking the distinctly impersonal form this exploitation takes under contemporary capitalism.

Moreover, Thornton's piece explores the impersonality of contemporary credit not simply in its content but also in the aesthetic registers it evokes. The older credit narratives to which it refers were intended to rationally ascertain credibility and were risk averse in their tendency to judge economic "integrity" with parsimonious caution. Such parsimony was as much aesthetic and formal as institutional and material. As I argued previously, realist ideas of credibility were used in narrative credit reports to prevent the problem of gratuitous and distracting detail. The idea that all credit seekers could be represented through a delimited set of characterological types hedged against the risk that credit evaluation could become too eccentrically personal. Thornton's piece, in contrast, insists on the "unique" and the "extreme" and uses this extremity to describe both the aesthetics of the reports she will produce (which will represent persons "with more than numbers, and with as much as possible") and the credit itself ("we will give you all the credit you can handle"). In this regard, "GMC" evokes the excesses of credit scoring's infinitely detailed and illegibly overloaded caricatures. More interesting still, it recalls the irrational exuberance of lending in the period of the contemporary credit boom, during which concern for objective credibility was similarly dispensed with and credit seekers were likewise offered "all the credit [they] could handle"—and often more than they could handle. By restoring the language of the person and the personal to the impersonality of credit reporting, Thornton's "GMC" does not mourn the loss of an older form of credit evaluation based on narratives and face-to-face encounters but instead suggestively invokes the complex and historically shifting relationship between the personal and the credible.

As discussed previously, new forms of credit scoring have transformed the available modes of social legibility and thus also affected how novelistic characterization mediates social personhood. So too have new ways of being in debt transformed the affective, experiential, subjective condition of debtors themselves. In the remainder of this chapter I thus explore works that explicitly connect the condition of unpayable debt and the problem of figuration to produce a theory of what I describe as "personification": the figuring or conjuring of faces, bodies, and voices, whether individual or collective. Personification registers the ways in which the subject does not precede her representation (as when one approaches a credit bureau to be evaluated or walks up to a "Credit Pole" to be scored) but instead is constituted out of or made to speak through modes of representation. In my analysis of the following works —Thornton's site-specific conceptual art, the debtor self-portraits on the "We Are the 99%" tumblr, Mathew Timmons's conceptual poetry project *CREDIT*, and Timothy Donnelly's apostrophic poem "To His Debt"—we find multiple types of personification deployed to conjoin social personhood as a historical condition, personification as a mode of figuration, and the experience of being in debt. Substituting realist characterization with more abstract, experimental, and decisively incredible ways of representing persons—modes I categorize here as portraiture, impersonality, and prosopopoeia—these works may at first appear to presume a strong relationship between debt and the personal. They do so, however, to represent debt as a historical, material, and ultimately collective condition.

Personification as I read it here is a mode of representation that exposes the mediations that produce social persons. In this sense, it shares with characterization an insistence that "persons" are not natural but rather the product of a collision between form and history. Yet personification goes even further than characterization in denaturalizing the categories of the person and the personal. In an essay on photography and unemployment, Walter Benn Michaels similarly identifies the need for a politically engaged way of representing historical agents. Identifying personification as either overly individualizing or overly focused on identity, Michaels wonders how to imagine collective agency in ways that are historical rather than merely personal. Such alternative modes, he proposes, could represent collective subjects (like classes) that "have no character" and thus enact a "de-personification" that would "represent, without personifying, not a group but a structural element."[55] Although Michaels educes the possibility of a representational mode that could capture the structural mechanisms that produce class, he fails to anticipate the radical work that personification itself might do. What the modes of personification in post-crisis art register is precisely *not* self-evident persons, or a self-evident aesthetic or affect of the personal. Rather, these works use personification to produce a simultaneously expanded and denaturalized category of the personal, representing social relations and collective subjects as if they were speaking persons and thus setting into motion a complex dialectic between the personal and the impersonal.

The relationship between subjectivity and debt has been a central theme in an emergent body of post-crisis critical theory on debt. Books like David Graeber's *DEBT: The First 5000 Years*, Richard Dienst's *Bonds of Debt*, Miranda

Joseph's *Debt to Society: Accounting for Life under Capitalism*, Angela Mitropoulos's *Contract and Contagion: From Biopolitics to Oikonomia*, and especially Mauricio Lazzarato's *The Making of the Indebted Man*, which I discuss later, as well as essays by theorists Jason Read, Jussi Parikka, Brett Neilson, Melinda Cooper, Simon Wortham, and others all explore the way new forms of credit and new experiences of debt have transformed the relationship between debt and subjectivity.[56] A striking number of these contemporary works of debt theory return to two nineteenth-century writers: Karl Marx, especially the essay "Notes on James Mill" (1844); and Friedrich Nietzsche, *On the Genealogy of Morality* (1887). As the above critics all observe, for both Marx and Nietzsche, credit's ability to appear personal makes it both powerful and alienating. In his essay, for instance, Marx notes that credit seeks to capture "man's *moral existence*, man's *social existence*, the *inmost depths of his heart*." Marx argues that credit depends on a social system of obligation and promise and on the social evaluation of another's credibility, lamenting, "One ought to consider how vile it is to *estimate* the value of a man in *money*." In the credit relation, he continues, "human morality itself" has become "the material in which money exists."[57] We find strikingly similar language in Nietzsche's *Genealogy*: in credit, Nietzsche asserts, "person met person for the first time, and *measured himself* person against person." Thus, for Nietzsche, the modern social order is imbued with violence precisely through the horrifyingly personal quality of the credit relation. Literal and material in the "primitive" period of credit and exchange, social violence becomes more reflexive and internalized in the modern era as man is "bred" into an ideological subject by way of the connection between debt and guilt (or "bad conscience").[58]

There are three clear reasons why contemporary theorists of debt have returned to these two writers: first, to account for the way that credit is simultaneously intensely personal and profoundly dehumanizing; second, to explain how credit evaluation exploits social personhood, turning one's credibility into an asset to be priced; and third, to describe the alienating experience of being in debt and debt's association with guilt and shame. However, when we consider the most influential of these recent works, Maurizio Lazzarato's 2010 *The Making of the Indebted Man*, we find that it misses much of what is specifically new in contemporary credit relations. Lazzarato argues that "debt represents an economic relationship inseparable from the production of the debtor subject and his 'morality'" and that credit "entail[s] specific forms of production and control of subjectivity—a particular form of *homo economicus*, the 'indebted man.'" For Lazzarato, debt "implies subjectivation": "the debtor affected by guilt, bad conscience, and responsibility."[59] He maintains that Marx and Nietzsche, in their emphasis on the psychic and affective dimension of credit relations, actually anticipate the intensified relationship between subjectivation and economic value demanded by late capitalism. That is, for Lazzarato not only do Marx and Nietzsche's similar accounts of the uncanny "personality" of debt remain relevant to the twenty-first century credit economy; in fact they are more relevant than ever.

However much as today's credit scoring looks radically different from the credit evaluation of the nineteenth century, so too has the nature of debt changed dramatically in the late twentieth century. No longer simply a tool to facilitate "discretionary" spending on nonessential goods, debt over the last few decades has become increasingly necessary to individual and household survival. As Louis Hyman puts it, "In the face of uncertainty and declining real wages, Americans indebted themselves to maintain the life they had once been able to afford."[60] In the first decade of the twenty-first century, wages stayed stagnant or declined for the entire bottom 70 percent of the wage distribution while the costs of residential real estate rose 60 percent and the cost of medical care for middle-income households increased 51 percent.[61] As a result, the outstanding consumer debt of households as a percentage of disposable income more than doubled between 1975 and 2005.[62] The availability of cheap mortgages and consumer credit compensated for declining wages and for reductions in the kinds of social welfare programs that once protected poor and working-class households from the rising cost of commodities like food and housing. Personal debt became the means through which middle-class families, as well as households experiencing persistent un- or underemployment, continued to survive.

The increased normalization of consumer debt—the fact that for many households it is no longer a choice but a necessity for economic survival—means that the degree of stigma attached to debt has changed apace.[63] As a result of the normalization of debt, the techniques used to ensure debt collection have not, contrary to the Foucauldian narrative Lazzarato avows, shifted from direct physical coercion to more ideological forms of self-discipline. Rather, history has arced in the opposite direction: the use of imprisonment as a punishment for failure to pay one's debts was officially outlawed in the United States in 1869, but as Adrienne Roberts notes in an article on the post-crisis recarceralization of debt, "the growing threat of imprisonment as punishment evidences the extraordinarily coercive power that wealthy creditors have been able to exert over working-class and poor debtors in the contemporary era."[64] The commodification of unpaid debt and the increased coercive power that the state has extended to banks and other debt collectors mean that the consequences of default now include more than just the social shame emphasized by Nietzsche and Lazzarato; they now also include imprisonment and other forms of impersonal structural violence that operate on the debtor's body more than on her conscience.

To understand how these historical changes necessitate a new understanding of the relationship between personal debt and social personhood, one not accounted for by Lazzarato's theory of the indebted man "affected by guilt, bad conscience, and responsibility," the remainder of this chapter takes up the problem of figurative personification in post-crisis conceptual art and poetry. Variously deploying portraiture, impersonality, and prosopopoeia as modes of formalizing a more-than-personal debt, these texts allow us to better understand the ways in which contemporary debt is and is not a truly personal condition.

Portraiture

A financial advice website begins its entry on "Credit History" with this confident assertion: "A credit history is your financial autobiography."[65] This association of the genre of autobiography with the peculiar archival texts that make up one's credit history is not surprising. Although a credit report appears to present a strictly bureaucratic account of our "history," its memory is often better than our own. Perusing the document allows one to recall forgotten addresses, be reminded of employers long past, or remember a range of life events, occasions both financial and not: a mislaid parking ticket that led to a bench warrant, a period of marital distress marked by bank overdrafts, a hospital bill turned over to a collection agency.

The intuition that there is a connection between one's debts and one's life story also appears in the aforementioned theoretical accounts of debt, where it is common to assert that there is an "affective economy of debt" or a "morality of debt" that is "individualized at the level of guilt"; that debt is a "dispositif" capable of "captur[ing] ... mutual affection"; that debt creates "new identifications, sympathies, dispositions, points of view."[66] However, I argue here that contemporary debt portraits put pressure on this apparently self-evident formal association between debt and autobiography, and on the ostensible conceptual relationship between debt and personal affect. Instead, they suggest a complex and critical connection between debt and the social person or collective historical subject.

Debt's relationship to the confessional mode and to the genre of the self-portrait became particularly apparent during the Occupy Wall Street (OWS) protests in 2011 and 2012, when it was common to see protesters bearing signs attesting to their own debt loads. It was visible as well in the "We Are the 99%" tumblr, to which hundreds of OWS participants and sympathizers sent images of themselves holding up a description of their own economic history, particularly their experience with unemployment and debt. The image in Figure 2.3 is exemplary of the genre: the person who posted this narrates his (economic) life from his teens to his fifties, describing jobs had and lost, loans borrowed and repaid, medical expenses accrued and still unpaid. In this image, as in most on the site, the face of the person is partly obscured by his sign. This act of conceal-

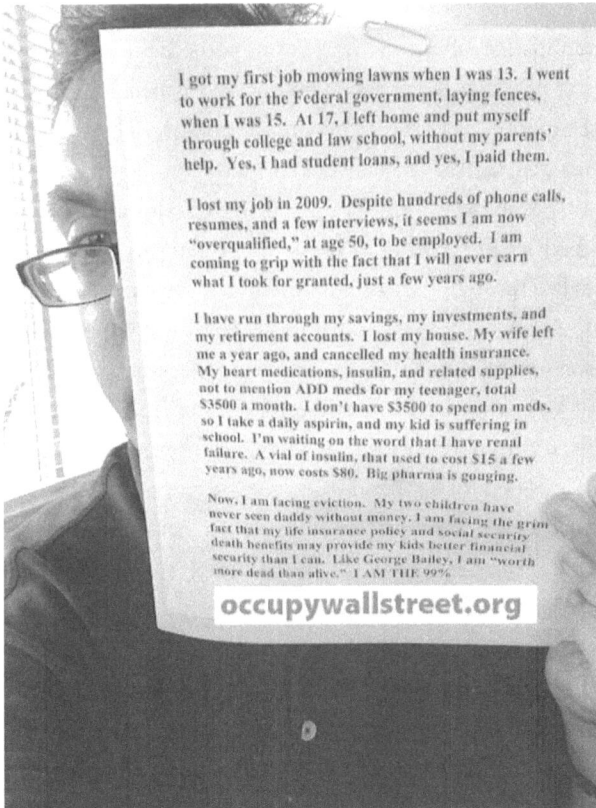

Figure 2.3. Self-portrait from "We Are the 99%" tumblr, 2010

ment is typically interpreted as an expression of shame, a public confession of private guilt. Thus, when describing the tumblr, John Protevi laments, "What's especially heartbreaking . . . is that so many people still have some shame, as they only peek out from behind their messages."[67] Read this way, the portraits are straightforward acts of self-expression, since even when hidden, the face expresses private shame as well as a "personal story."

Yet the images on "We Are the 99%" are neither self-evidently personal nor merely confessional. Rather, by partially concealing their own faces—what one would expect to be the center of the selfie, a visual genre associated with self-regard—these tumblr posters grasp precisely the nonindividuality of debt as a shared condition. Indeed, what one quickly realizes while browsing the website is the sameness of these stories—stories that, when read in sequence, register less the specificity of personal history than the impersonality of a shared systemic condition. By obscuring the face and substituting for it a narrative about dollars spent or earned or borrowed, about the large and impersonal institutions of one's economic life, about the number of years spent unemployed or in arrears, these self-portraits put pressure on the very association between debt and the personal experiences that they apparently conjure. They are often as much quantitative as qualitative. The substitution of the individual face with the impersonality of numbers and the nonspecificity of common stories is thus the aesthetic correlative of a refusal to see debt in the terms of shame or sin. Here debt operates less through the exploitation of bad conscience and more through a direct compulsion, since almost all of those "confessing" their debts emphasize that the reason for their indebtedness was brute necessity: "My fiancée works 14 hours a day, 6 days a week and we still can't pay our bills"; "I have done dozens of [job] applications, phone calls . . . and after 4 months not one call"; "I'm attending the University of MN and I depleted all my savings just so I wouldn't have to take out a loan this semester. I'm trying to get by debt-free and it seems near impossible." The debt described on the tumblr was incurred mostly to pay for the costs of self-reproduction (food, housing, health, education), which accurately attests to the fact that contemporary debt functions much like the wage: although an ideological emphasis on something like "work ethic" may usefully grease the wheels of the wage relation, to ensure that the worker will submit to exploitation, it is necessary only to rob her of the capacity to reproduce herself.

Despite drawing on the seemingly "subjectifying" imagery of portraiture, the personifications in "We Are the 99%" indicate that debt works not so much at the level of ideology and subjectivization (whether positive, as an "investment in the future," or negative, as shame) but rather as brute material force. Moreover, as the "We" in the tumblr's title implies, these portraits present debt as a shared condition, such that the differentiating details seem minor relative to the experiences shared in common. Insofar as the condition of being in debt is thus imagined to be structural rather than affective, it appears as a political and historical category akin to class: to the collective experience of a structural condition. With this in mind, I return to Thornton's debt art to explore the relationship between the individual subject of debt and the understanding of debt as a shared structural condition through which an antagonistic collective political subject might emerge.

Much of Thornton's oeuvre emphasizes the affective and embodied personal experience of debt. In a piece called *How It Feels*, for instance, Thornton personifies her own debt as a large rock she carries with her. She took the rock with her to a Sears portrait studio where she had a series of photographs taken in which she clutches the rock to her chest (Figure 2.4). Turning the apparent immateriality of debt obligation into a recalcitrantly material burden, Thornton represents how it "feels"—both emotionally and physically—to carry

Figure 2.4. From *How it Feels*, Cassie Thornton, 2012

around this weight. In this sense, her work seems to confirm the idea that debt depends on negative affect. However, by substituting the bad feelings typically associated with debt—guilt, shame, melancholy, isolation—with the campiness of kitsch (evident in the Sears portrait-studio backdrop) and the giddy mania of sheer joy (implicit in Thornton's frenzied facial expressions), *How It Feels* ultimately presents debt not as the individual experience of ideological coercion but as the structural condition of a subprime population.

Oscillating between comedy and pathos, the affective mood of Thornton's Sears portraits might be described as a kind of irrational exuberance from below, evoking what Melinda Cooper and Angela Mitropoulos, in their provocative essay "In Defense of Usura," describe as "the manic phase of credit creation."[68] Indeed, Cooper and Mitropoulos observe that while "the subprime class in the U.S. is exhorted to live within its means in a virtuous gesture of belt-tightening," the excessive borrowing of the subprime debtor is in fact a canny "strategy" for living. "The subprime class rolled over their debts and lived beyond their means," they write, "generating surplus in the most unproductive of ways."[69] Or as Fred Moten puts it, members of this subprime class "establish pockets of insurgent refuge and marronage, carrying revaluation . . . into supposedly sanitized zones."[70] It is this collective refusal of productivity, rationality, and order that appears in Thornton's campy portraits. Like Shteyngart's Lenny, they also evoke something like Ngai's idea of the "zany." If, as Ngai suggests, the style of the zany indexes an indistinction between work and play, Thornton's zany photographs evoke a similar indistinction between debt as productive investment in the self and debt as radical waste and expenditure (as, for instance, the debt incurred by the art student who knows full well that the cost of her education will in no way correlate to her future earnings). They are the immoderate subjects invoked by "Give Me Cred" as it references the "extreme," the "as much as possible." Thornton takes capital's most central personification, the rational actor, and "implod[es] it *from within*," to use Ngai's phrasing. Put simply, there is no sense—indeed, there is nutty *nonsense*—in associating debt with guilt if one knows from the outset that one has no choice or that one might never pay it back.[71]

Thornton's work puts further pressure on the ostensible relationship between debt and the personal by imagining the subject of debt as collective. The indebted subject she represents is not produced primarily through affect or ideology but is an effect of specific historical and material conditions, what Alberto Toscano describes as "the supra-personal and collective character of social subjection."⁷² Again, this supra-personal subject is mediated through a highly personal form. Thus, as part of a collaborative project called *Our Bundles Our Selves*, Thornton led a guided meditation in which participants were encouraged to visualize their debt. She then supplemented the transcripts of these visualizations with her own psychoanalytic interpretations of the imagery. Despite this seemingly individualizing frame, however, the final product of the project took the form of a mock yearbook for the "Class of 2012" (Figure 2.5), which collected visualizations from Thornton's MFA cohort and grouped them into "bundles" based on similarities of language and imagery.

While *Our Bundles* draws on the seemingly personal metaphor of debt as a psychic and affective experience, it resists the language of individual person-

Figure 2.5. Cover of *Our Bundles Our Selves*, Feminist Economic Department/ Cassie Thornton, 2012

hood by reframing the self-portrait as a group photo. The "graduating class of 2012" thus presents and preserves a historical subject, one that is collective rather than individual, invoking something more complex and critical than what Claire Bishop, in her nuanced criticism of participatory art, calls an "ethics of interpersonal interaction."[73] "Financial products like debt seem to descend from the past as hard, opaque, immutable forms," *Our Bundles* explains; "they are launched at us, blunt intergenerational weapons, totally camouflaged as a friendly part of the topography."[74] Here we see that Thornton's generational cohort is a "class" not simply because its members share a graduation year but because they constitute a collective social and historical subject with a material rather than a personal predication. Moreover, by describing their intergenerational experiences through the language of warfare, *Our Bundles* insists on the inescapability of class antagonism—recognizing that to be of a class *is* to be in a state of war—and on the political (rather than psychic or ethical) determination of this particular historical subject.

Impersonality

Despite the persistence of the personal in credit rhetoric, what most explicitly characterizes contemporary credit scoring and debt agreements is their impersonality. Mathew Timmons's conceptual writing project *CREDIT*, an eight hundred–page coffee-table book published through a print-on-demand service, both registers and problematizes this impersonality by querying its relationship to poetic subjectivity.[75] The book is divided into two sections, "Part A: Credit" and "Part 2: Debit." In the "Credit" section, Timmons reproduced (in the form of both a visual scan and an OCR [optical character recognition] text scan) the twenty-six credit card offers he received over a three-week period in 2007. In the "Debit" section, he reproduced ten overdue payment notices he received over a two-week period in 2009.[76] In both sections, specified information was "redacted" by being crossed out with black marker: in the "Credit" section Timmons removed all proper names, addresses, and numbers, while in the "Debit" section he removed everything except proper names, addresses, and numbers (Figure 2.6). Although his redactions initially had a purely practical purpose in the project, they also frame *CREDIT*'s response to the collection of personal information integral to the contemporary credit economy. As Stephen Voyce observes in a powerful essay on the poetics of redaction, redaction's "operative logic is secrecy rather than negation."[77] In other words,

Chapter 2: Credit, Characterization, Personification   87

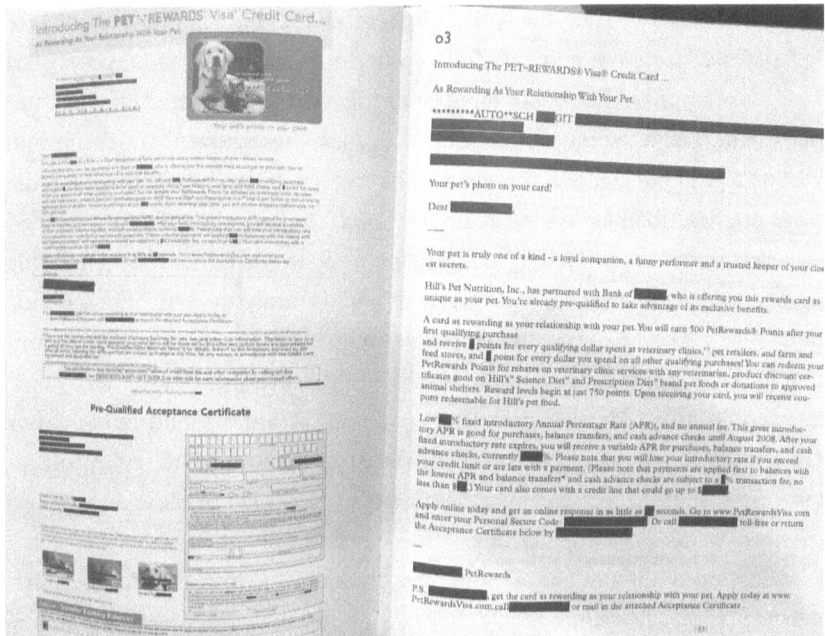

Figure 2.6. Page from *CREDIT*, Mathew Timmons, 2010

redaction does not simply remove potentially offensive or damaging information; it conceals it, suggesting that there is still one who knows, one who can decide at some later point either to reveal or to conceal more information. Although Timmons's piece is more playful and less politically engaged than the projects Voyce considers (most of which have to do with surveillance in the context of imperial warfare and military bureaucracy), we might nonetheless see *CREDIT* as an example of what Voyce compellingly describes as "a *counter-forensic* poetics of militant research, one that reverse-engineers those technologies of surveillance ... increasingly absorbed into the fabric of everyday life."[78] In this sense, the practice of strategic redaction registers the obverse of the credit scorer's acts of surveillance. The project becomes a means of control over disclosure that signals both Timmons's power over his own records (the ability to remove his own information from public view) and his vulnerability to data collection. Like the text itself, formatted as a coffee-table volume intended for display, Timmons is an open book.

CREDIT also reflects the history of twenty-first-century lending and borrowing. In the period of the boom, credit no longer had to be solicited by the potential borrower. Thus, the typical "prescreened" offers Timmons collects are rechristened "generous and gracefully worded offers of credit." Ostensibly based "on information in [his] credit report indicating that [he] meet[s] certain criteria," as one offer letter puts it, Timmons's credit is "preapproved," which sets into motion a proleptic temporality wherein the credit preexists its acceptance, as the cards are described as "reserved" for Timmons. Indeed, the offers are worded such that it appears as if failing to accept the credit would be equivalent to losing money. One letter repeatedly describes the opportunity to "earn" free gasoline by using a gas company credit card, while a solicitation from the financing arm of a local car company promises that the business has "agreed to mark down their entire new and used car inventory to keep within the guidelines of your pre-approval," rhetorically situating the would-be borrower as the epic protagonist of a vast economic narrative. Timmons's description of these preapproval letters as "generous and gracefully worded" is thus not entirely ironic. Whether representing credit as a gift or as an offer one cannot refuse, the strange solicitousness of the letters means that they take on the quality of a savvy seduction, presenting future satisfactions as fully present. Thus, the car-dealership offer includes the canny imperative, "Be prepared to accept immediate delivery of your new or used vehicle," a vehicle the recipient of the letter has not selected, purchased, borrowed for, or even expressed an interest in buying.

The "Debit" section, by contrast, consists largely of black boxes, since only numbers, proper names, and addresses are left in place. Because the book's "Appendix" also includes everything that was redacted, however, we can see all the missing text, such as this series of lines, whose repetitions take on an almost poetic syntax: "Your account will be permanently restricted. Your account will be transferred to a debt collections agency. Your account's progressing delinquency will be reported to three national credit bureaus." Appearing in the aftermath of the credit and liquidity crisis of 2008, when all that so-called easy credit came due, the promissory language of these credit offers takes on the darker cast of a threat.

My particular interest in Timmons's project concerns the relationship between the book's data aesthetic and its attempt to register and reimagine the impersonality of economic information. Although Timmons describes *CREDIT* as "a highly revealing and emotional work chronicling a personal tale of credit," the book is at first glance neither revealing nor emotional; indeed, it is not even readable in any conventional sense. This mix of unreadability and impersonality is precisely the point of both conceptual art and its more contemporary counterpart, conceptual poetry.⁷⁹ But Timmons's work eschews earlier conceptual art's concern with information as difference and suggests instead a logic of information as indifference.⁸⁰ Stubbornly antinarrative, cryptically quantitative, explicitly tedious, this collection of unmediated data is the site at which conceptual writing limns the impersonality of contemporary economic and social relationships.

Still, one is left with the sense that Timmons's claim that the book is a "personal tale" is not simply a joke but rather a canny account of what constitutes the personal in the contemporary credit economy. Timmons removed all the addresses and numbers in the "Credit" section because he initially intended to blanket his city with large-scale posters made out of the scanned images and thus wanted to protect any information that might put him at risk for fraud. The anxiety of identity theft—indeed the very phrase "identity theft"—suggestively conjures the indistinction between one's being and one's data. Furthermore, identity theft threatens to leave one vulnerable to various forms of criminal *impersonation*, which we might see as the legal correlative of personification as an aesthetic form. But for the purposes of identity theft, the way to access the truly personal—the way to gain entry into another's identity—is precisely through such seemingly impersonal information as account numbers and PINs. By attempting to keep his data private, as one might a diary or a cache of love letters, Timmons infers that what constitutes the personal is much more complicated than simply data versus detail, or qualitative versus quantitative.⁸¹ Indeed, the language that remains in the "Credit" section seems to speak directly to the individual it solicits, offering personalization services such as the ability to select the image on one's plastic credit card or a "Pet Rewards" card that promises to be "as rewarding as your relationship with your pet." By making clear that these apparently personal preferences are known by one's bank or creditor—by suggesting that what appear to be expressions of personal "taste" are in fact simply responses to the solicitations of a financial institution—*CREDIT* implies that the constitution of the "truly personal" is tenuous at best. If, as Theodor Adorno famously argued, "lyric implies a protest against a social condition which every individual experiences as hostile, alien, cold, and oppressive," Timmons's highly impersonal, even tedious, reproduction of these promises to personalize borrowing might be regarded as a protest against a social condition experienced as uncomfortably intimate, warm, and expressive.⁸² In this sense, the "Debit" section is both the formal and the ideological rebuttal to "Credit": here everything except numbers and proper names are redacted so that all that remains is the facticity of dollar amounts and the tedious, banal repetition of Timmons's own name, now attached, with all the intervening flourishes removed, solely to money due.

All of this would appear to confirm the commonplace description of conceptual poetry as "an outright rejection of what is often described as the individual poetic voice," to use conceptual poets Kenneth Goldsmith and Greg Dworkin's phrasing in *Against Expression*.[83] In the end, however, Timmons's book is not a straightforwardly reactive (or reactionary) avant-garde antilyric. Rather, *CREDIT* puts into play a more complex dialectic between subject and objectification, invoking something akin to what Virginia Jackson characterizes as a less familiar, weirder, lyricism of the "inhuman and inhumane."[84] Whereas the lyric, for Adorno, provides "the objective expression of a social antagonism," *CREDIT* offers the antagonistic expression of a social subjectification.[85] The language of personal supplication and seduction appearing in the offers of credit is undone in *CREDIT* by being intensified. The rhetoric of the personal and the "specially for you" pivots into the language of an abusive relationship: "Your account is now days past due. Maybe you've been meaning to call us, but for one reason or another you keep putting it off"; "We can't do anything to help if you don't call"; "Let's work through this together." Thus *CREDIT* plays out the oscillation between the personality of credit's ideology and the impersonality of its actual material functioning.

The book's structure also suggests the complex relationship—rather than mere opposition—between the qualitative and the quantitative. Choosing to call the second part "Debit" rather than the more familiar "Debt," Timmons evokes the conventions of double-entry bookkeeping. As Mary Poovey has influentially argued, double-entry bookkeeping provided the form through which "information was reworked from narrative to number," but this reworking was, she adds, no more straightforwardly teleological than was the transition from credit evaluating to credit scoring. Instead, the double-entry system retained a more dialectical relation between "narrative and number," one that relied on personification in order to render the fictitious categories of the account book legible without appearing subjective: "in order to write a transaction as *first* a credit and *then* a debit, the bookkeeper had to personify aspects of the business." Such fictions, Poovey concludes, meant that the double-entry account system, like Timmons's own double-entry poetic text, "purported to be, but was not, a system of total disclosure."[86] Poovey's account of the personification of purely structural categories such as profit and loss implies that personification gives us not only a form for thinking about the impersonality of subjects—as in Timmons's reproduction of the personalized credit offer, which reveals one's tastes and desires as accessible to and manipulable by the financial institution—but also a form for thinking about the uncanny personality of structures themselves. To better understand the relationship between personification and the transformation of structures or silent abstractions into speaking subjects, I now turn to a final mode of depersonalizing personification, prosopopoeia.

Prosopopoeia

Paul de Man describes the tropological figure of prosopopoeia as "the fiction of an apostrophe to an absent, deceased, or voiceless entity, which posits the possibility of the latter's reply and confers upon it the power of speech." In prosopopoeia, de Man continues, "voice assumes mouth, eye, and finally face, a chain that is manifest in the etymology of the trope's name, *prosopon poien*, to confer a mask or a face."[87] Here I look at prosopopoeia in Timothy Donnelly's powerful poem "To His Debt," an apostrophic address to the speaker's own debt that appears in Donnelly's 2010 *The Cloud Corporation*. (Although I address only this single poem here, *The Cloud Corporation* as a whole is emblematic of the post-crisis moment in its concern with unemployment and late-imperial collapse and specifically with the intrusion of the economy into personality through the granting of legal personhood to corporations.)[88] I conclude with a reading of Donnelly's poem in part because it offers a kind of "allegory of reading" for the argument that has run throughout this section that post-crisis conceptual art and poetry deploy personification in a paradoxical (or dialectical) fashion, using personification to imagine the absolute destruction of personhood. It suggests they do so as a canny response to the solicitations of personal feeling performed by the contemporary credit economy. Donnelly's poem is reproduced in full here:

> Where would I be without you, massive shadow
> dressed in numbers, when without you there
>
> behind me, I wouldn't be myself. What wealth
> could ever offer loyalty like yours, my measurement,
>
> my history, my backdrop against which every
> coffee and kerplunk, when all the giddy whoring

around abroad and after the more money money wants
is among the first things you prevent.

My phantom, my crevasse, my emphatically
unfunny hippopotamus, you take my last red cent

and drag it down into the muck of you, my
sassafras, my Timbuktu, you who put the kibosh

on fine dining and home theater, dentistry and work
my head into a lather, throw my ever-beaten

back against a mattress of intractable topography
and chew. Make death with me: my sugar

boat set loose on caustic indigo, my circumstance
dissolving, even then—how could solvency

hope to come between us, when even when I dream
I awaken in an unmarked pocket of the earth

without you there—there you are, supernaturally
doubling over my shoulder like the living

wage I never make, but whose image I will always
cling to in the negative, hanged up by the feet

among the mineral about me famished like a bat
whose custom it is to make much of my neck.

Donnelly's use of prosopopoeia does not simply personify debt—in the manner of allegory, for instance—but gives debt voice through what de Man calls "the fiction of an apostrophe."[89] By addressing debt, the poem endows debt with subjectivity indirectly but also quite thoroughly: debt is given body, face, feeling, will; debt drags, chews, sucks, and "put[s] the kibosh." Unlike the more classic prosopopoeiac odes and epitaphs that are the subject of de Man's analysis, Donnelly's poem is very much *about* the process of such personification, which appears in the poem not as a given but rather as the dialectical overcoming of a series of contradictions (as in "massive shadow"). The poem's metaphors perform exchanges in which equivalence produces an unaccountable (or uncountable) surplus: What does it mean, after all, to describe debt as an "emphatically / unfunny hippopotamus"? In this way, the poem performs Engels's "laws of the dialectic."[90] First, it stages the transformation of quality into quantity, as debt is personified yet still recalcitrantly numerical: "dressed in numbers," debt serves as the speaker's "measurement." Second, "To His Debt" elaborates Engels's second law, the interpenetration of opposites, so that the image of colossal heft (the emphatic hippopotamus) comes paratactically after two images of void and absence ("my phantom, my crevasse"). Finally, it suggests the all-important third law, the negation of the negation, since debt appears to flicker in and out of personhood—neither quality nor quantity, neither presence nor absence—and becomes a kind of suspended, ephemeral, and thus ultimately dissolvable or annihilable subject.

The poem also, of course, recalls Marx's use of the rhetorical trope of personification to describe the transformation of a mere thing, the commodity, into a speaking subject: the means by which the object as use value becomes a commodity that "stands with its feet on the ground" or even "on its head" and "evolves out of its wooden brain grotesque ideas."[91] Walter Benjamin observes that in giving to the object the characteristics of the subject, Marx implies that the commodity seductively offers us comfort, pleasure, and even recognition; that it becomes "the most empathetic [being] ever encountered in the realm of souls ... see[ing] in everyone the buyer in whose hand and house it wants to nestle."[92] We see some of this seductive intimacy in the poem's play with the apostrophic language of love: "where would I be without you ... / when without you there // behind me, I wouldn't be myself." Yet the speaker ultimately suggests—contra Benjamin—that debt doesn't need to be "empathetic" nor does it need to cuddle up to us; rather, debt approaches us not to make love but to "make death," or to steal away with the truly "living // wage" we "never make." Debt, Donnelly makes clear, works through the fully material (rather than affective or intimate) necessity of self-reproduction. Thus, the line "where would I be without you" is not simply a play on romantic cliché but a horrifying literalization of a relationship of absolute material dependence. By retracting any other means of survival, debt requires only the fact of our "circumstance / dissolving" to secure our dependence on it. It is this systemic indifference, this more fundamental impersonality, that Donnelly captures in the poem's ambiguous final lines, in which the speaker imagines himself "hanged up by the feet / /among the mineral about me famished like a bat / whose custom it is to make much of my neck," at once the body from which the bat feeds itself and the bat itself, both starved and predatory.

Donnelly's poem registers the specificity of debt in the contemporary period, in which the vanishing of a "living // wage" is the reason we depend on debt to accommodate the difference between our vital needs and our economic capacities.[93] Donnelly's personifying prosopopoeia presents debt as a relation not of intimacy but of utter indifference, a relation that has no more concern for the particularity of the subject's moral life or existence than has the wage contract. It is precisely this violent connection between the animation of the thing and the death of the subject that prosopopoeia conveys, as de Man's economic metaphor of prosopopoeia as "privative" suggests. Debt appears as a personal, subjectifying form to mask the indifference of its demands and the impersonality of its material coercion, while credit appears as a social relationship of trust to mask its actual reliance on the expedient violence of the state. Capturing this work of masking, prosopopoeia turns an object into a subject to put the subject to death. In both its content and its form, Donnelly's poem not only suggests, as Margaret Ronda puts it in a compelling reading of Donnelly's work, that "the only possibility of separation [from debt] is death," but also that debt quite literally follows one to the grave *and beyond* (which legally it often does).[94] As in de Man's account of prosopopoeia, debt's personification is a displaced figure for this death. Prosopopoeia, like debt, "deprives and disfigures to the precise extent that it restores" the personal subject.[95] Donnelly's speaking debt is the very figure of manifest horror, the fearful subprime to the fetish's seductive sublime.

What, then, do we fear, and why do we repay? Lazzarato uses Marx's essay on Mill, cited earlier, to argue that debt depends on a "'moral' judgment" of the debtor, whose "'morality,' even his 'existence' are measured as guarantees of repayment."[96] But Marx's essay makes clear that what appears as "the moral recognition of a man" is in fact the creditor's "trust in the state" as the guarantor of last resort. Marx argues that it is ultimately not "moral guarantees" but "the guarantee of *legal* compulsion and still other more or less *real* guarantees" that underwrite the credit contract.[97] When Lazzarato writes that "the creditor-debtor relationship is inextricably . . . an 'ethics,' since it presupposes, in order for the debtor to stand as 'self'-guarantor, an ethico-political process of constructing a subjectivity endowed with a memory, a conscience, and a morality that forces him to be both accountable and guilty," he misses what is most important in Marx's argument.[98] For Marx, the very fact that the debtor's body serves as the ultimate collateral for the loan means that in the end there is no need for either accountability or for guilt, let alone ethics or subjectivity. The trust on which credit claims to depend is secured not through the alienation of the debtor's morality but by the power of the state to act on her body—it emerges not from the success of the debtor's subjectivation but from capital's ability to remove the debtor's capacity to feed and educate and house herself. While we may sometimes feel accountable and guilty about our loans, we repay them primarily because we quite reasonably fear the consequences of not doing so, offering our necks to Donnelly's ravenous bat not to remain in the light of social mutuality and moral rectitude but to escape the shadow of the debtors' prison or bankruptcy court or unemployment line.

I do not mean to suggest that the debtor's experience—and her subjective condition—are not meaningful: indeed, in the Coda I discuss the ways in which they might become very important indeed, as the basis both for a canny historical consciousness and, potentially, for collective solidarity. But I do insist that even though indebtedness may be felt as an affective and psychic condition, we are mostly in debt for more impersonal reasons, like the rising costs of health care and housing and education. And though the contemporary debtor may optimistically believe, in the manner of the oft-described neoliberal logic of entrepreneurship, that some of this debt is a metaphoric "investment in her future," she is more likely to feel that she has no other option.

In Shteyngart's wild oscillations between the incredible excess of the caricature and the reductive simplifications of the subprime stereotype; in Thornton's group portraits of the materially composed "class" of the indebted; in Timmons's aesthetics of impersonality, framed against the attempt of creditors to exploit the language of personal seduction; and in Donnelly's prosopopoeiac capture of debt's privation and violence, we find a nuanced and dialectical treatment of the way in which even the most quantitative forms of credit depend on a particular formation of social personhood, while even the most seemingly personal affects of debt are ultimately based in material necessity and structural coercion. Such transformations of the person also redound on cultural form's representation of the social and its capacity to continue to mediate the relationship between the individual and the totality. The next two chapters thus turn away from the individual person and toward the social forms that characterize a period of total crisis.

Part Two Home Economics

Photography and Foreclosure

As the etymology of the word "economy"—from the Greek *oikos*, house—reminds us, homes are economic assets. Yet although domestic real estate has long been understood as a valuable commodity, and even a form of investment, it has rarely acquired the status of a high-yield, speculative venture. Historically, the growth in the value of residential real estate just barely outpaces inflation. Looking across the entire twentieth century, we find that the average annual increase in home prices was just 0.2 percent, while the average rate of return on stocks in the same period was around 9 percent.[1] In fact, according to housing economist Robert Shiller there has been only one extended period since 1900 in which the return on US real estate investment outpaced both inflation and returns on stocks and bonds: the housing bubble that ran from the late 1990s until 2007.[2] During this period, average nominal returns on residential real estate were 11 percent, and in some cities home prices appreciated by as much as 80 percent. The housing bubble thus marked a unique period in the history of US housing in which the home no longer gave refuge from the volatility of the market but instead came to symbolize the spectacular magic of speculative investment.[3] US consumers became mesmerized by houses opened to public view through a visual culture dominated by glossy architecture and design magazines and televised home shows. Entire television networks were dedicated to recasting the home as simultaneously a fetish object and a savvy investment, and to narratives in which real estate agents and house-flipping speculators were well-nigh epic heroes. The home was no longer regarded simply as a consumer good but as a financial asset imbued with an aura of erotic desirability (hence the twenty-first-century coinage "real estate porn"). The primary subject position from which we viewed these homes—as they were purchased, built, updated, remodeled, flipped, marketed, and renovated again—was as voyeurs. In much the same way that the logic of investment slipped into what was once merely a useful commodity, consumers of US culture imaginatively slipped into other people's houses.

By 2007, however, the housing bubble had reached its breaking point, as built-in rate hikes on subprime loans began to kick in and many borrowers found themselves saddled with unpayable mortgages. As credit tightened, it became harder to refinance or sell one's home; the resulting decline in demand brought about a drop in prices and the crisis began to affect non-subprime borrowers as well. From 2006 to 2008, the default rate on non-fixed-rate mortgages quadrupled, jumping from 10 percent to 40 percent.[4] In a single year between fall 2008 and fall 2009 overall foreclosure fillings increased nearly 30 percent, and in states like Nevada, Florida, Arizona, and California, one household in every eleven was facing foreclosure.[5] By the start of 2011, three years after the collapse of credit markets, one in ten US homeowners was ninety days or more late on her mortgage payment and twelve million individuals and families (nearly 30 percent of all homeowners) were termed "underwater" on their homes, meaning they owed more than the house was worth.[6] From the beginning of 2007 to the end of 2011, there were more than 4 million completed foreclosures and 8.2 million foreclosure starts.[7] Losses in wealth were worst within communities of color: every cent of the wealth accumulated by African American households in the post–civil rights era was lost in 2009 alone.[8] A large number of those evicted were renters who lived in buildings owned by landlords who could no longer pay their mortgages: women and families with children were disproportionately impacted by renter eviction, and many states saw a rapid increase in family homelessness as a result.

From the pleasurable voyeurism of real estate porn to devastating scenes of foreclosure, our understanding of home economics has been radically transformed. This chapter takes up that transformation by considering how the spectacle of eviction and foreclosure provides an urgent way to make the private domestic economies of debt public. In *The Bonds of Debt*, Richard Dienst observes that "although we should be able to find its traces everywhere . . . there is something not quite visible" about debt.[9] Yet from the "Short Sale" sign to the sheriff banging down the door, the visible signs of housing debt have, in the wake of the crisis, been nearly everywhere. Indeed, if images of lavish interiors constituted the visual culture of the housing bubble, scenes of foreclosure have defined the visual culture of the bust. Consider, for example, an image of a boarded-up house in upstate New York captured by Associated Press (AP) photographer Spencer Platt in winter 2012 (Figure 3.1). Although a largely unremarkable instance of the very populated genre of post-2008 photojournalistic images of foreclosed homes, it happened to appear on the AP wire service just days before five large banks agreed to a large settlement over fraudulent mortgage practices. As a result, this one photograph appeared alongside more than a dozen different stories and op-eds about the settlement. In the *New York Times*, Platt's photo illustrated a report on the response of the banks to the settlement; in *USA Today* it appeared in an article about the effect of the settlement on homeowners. Even for an age in which news agencies increasingly depend on AP wire photographers, Platt's photograph had an unusually wide run, notable enough to occasion a *Huffington Post* story about its ubiquity.[10] Platt was not alone in his success: photojournalists documenting the housing crisis in the United States won two Pictures of the Year International awards and the National Press Photographer's Best of Photojournalism award in 2008, and the World Press Photo of the Year in both 2009 and 2012.

Nor was fascination with images of foreclosed or abandoned houses unique to photojournalists. Between 2009 and 2015, galleries across the country curated group shows and solo exhibitions about foreclosure, eviction, and housing debt: Damon Rich's *Red Lines Housing Crisis Center* (Queens Museum of Art, 2009), Kirk Crippens's *The Great Depression: Foreclosure USA* (San Francisco MOMA, 2010), the group shows *Foreclosed: Rehousing the American Dream* (New York

Figure 3.1. Wire service photograph by Spencer Platt, New York, 2012

MoMA, 2012) and *Foreclosed: Documents from the American Housing Crisis* (Alice Austen House Museum, New York, 2012), and Olga Koumoundourous's *Dream Home Resource Center* (Hammer Museum, Los Angeles, 2013). As their titles suggest, these exhibits all centered around the image of the house as a precarious commodity, as a site of lived insecurity, as the stuff of both dream and nightmare. Not all of these shows were purely documentary, nor did they all include exclusively photographs—the installations by Koumoundourous and Rich were primarily conceptual and performative, for instance. But photography—particularly photography with a documentary impulse—has dominated post-housing-crisis visual art. For photographers like Emily Kennerk (*America's #1 Foreclosed City: Las Vegas*), David Wells (*Foreclosed Dreams*, images of Providence, RI), Douglas Smith (*Scenes from Surrendered Homes*, images of California's Central Valley region), and Kelly Creedon (*We Shall Not Be Moved*, images of Boston's Roxbury neighborhood), scenes of eviction and foreclosure have provided a vivid way to represent the local effects of national economic dispossession.

Responding to this trend in the widely discussed *New York Times* essay "Picturing the Crisis," Paul Reyes remarks that "foreclosure photography has . . . helped define an era that will mark American society for decades to come." Contrasting the relative invisibility of "the Great Recession" to Great Depression–era images of long bread lines and mournful stockbrokers, Reyes, like Dienst, acknowledges that "in a digital era, the outward signs of economic pain are often hard to capture."[11] The genre of foreclosure photography, he concludes, has filled an urgent desire to make visible, legible, and comprehensible an economic crisis whose effects might otherwise remain too complex, invisible, or latent to be easily represented in documentary art. This chapter takes up the ways that foreclosure photography—a category that here includes images of foreclosed homes and forced evictions as well as photographs of abandoned factories and uninhabited real estate—has produced varying and sometimes competing narratives of the 2008 financial crisis. I explore art photography by Bruce Gilden and James Griffioen, featuring abandoned homes overrun by nature; award-winning journalistic photographs of home evictions by Anthony Suau and John Moore; eerie images of empty domestic interiors by Todd Hido, John Francis Peters, and T. J. Proechel; photographs of abandoned industrial spaces in Detroit by Yves Marchand and Romain Meffre; and satellite images and on-the-ground photos of the "ghost cities" of rural China. I contend that these post-crisis photographs register a changing relationship between private property and personal privacy, between the status of domestic ownership and the desire to be protected from public view. They toggle uncertainly between the photojournalist's desire to give economic insecurity a local habitation and the anxious awareness that insecurity is more everywhere than ever before; between awareness of the increasingly commonplace fact of debt and the wish to disavow it; between the recognition that the commodified house has always been a site of unhomely alienation and the fear that losing its protection might be even worse.

I divide these images into four categories: feral homes, evictions, haunted houses, and uncanny landscapes. I begin with photographs in which the abandoned home is rendered "feral"—overrun by nature. These images imagine the decay of the civilized *domus* in order to treat the raced and classed subjects that are absent from the frame as abject others. I then turn to photos that document scenes of forced eviction and foreclosure to explore the ways these images indicate an anxiety about their own apparatus of mediation. In them, mediation is not just an aesthetic and technical condition of possibility but also a set of material conditions, one linked to the power of the state to invade domestic space. The third section takes up the uncanny aesthetic of "haunted" houses. Reading Freud's famous essay on the *Unheimlich* through Marx's analysis of the alienated spectrality of private property, I argue that these photographs capture the eerie uncertainty of housing debt. Besides functioning as the aesthetic correlative of debt in general and foreclosure in particular, the uncanny here also provides a canny form of historical temporality. Thus the conclusion of the chapter extends the discussion of the *Unheimlich* into photographs of architectural landscapes. Not only do these images disclose the uncanny power of commodity automatons and alienating property relations over the social order; they also eerily foreshadow a potentially terminal crisis in capitalism. In them, the uncanny temporality of debt is both the reappearance of the past and the anticipation of the future.

In his essay on foreclosure photography, Reyes appears confident in the capacity of documentary representation to depict historical events objectively through their "outward signs." His conviction that photographs can function as a "forensic study" of the economic crisis, however, implies a belief in the indexicality of historical reference not shared by most photography critics.[12] While theorists like Siegfried Kracauer argued that photography allows us to "[reconstruct] . . . events in their temporal succession without any gaps," and critics such as Alan Sekula linked the fantasy of photographic positivism to the ideology of bourgeois science, scholars tend to agree that photography provides what Kracauer himself acknowledges is only "a limited sort" of access to historical events.[13] Martha Rosler, for instance, observes that the photograph "cannot show, but can only refer to, social forces," emphasizing the fundamental incompleteness of photographic representation.[14] Ariella Azoulay similarly insists on the "essential unreliability" of photography, observing that "a photograph does not possess a single sovereign, stable point of view" but must "be grounded [in] its interpretation."[15] Geoffrey Batchen, in attempting to debunk the idea that modern digital technology has turned photography from a transparently referential medium to a more uncertain kind of representation, argues that "if we look closely . . . at photography's indexical relation to reality," we find that it affords "nothing but a play of representations."[16] Photography, these critics all agree, is always already contingent, perspectival, and incomplete.

Here I am less concerned with photography's status as a transparent reflection of reality or with its capacity to provide documentary evidence, although I later consider the relationship between photography and the power of the police. Rather, my primary concern is with the idea that the inherently partial, limited aesthetics of the photograph serves as a dialectical complement to the effort to represent the economic totality. While the photographic image neither objectively "shows" nor, to use Reyes's phrase, "captures" economic history, it can register economic history obliquely, at an angle. It usually does so by mediating the relationship between part and whole: a single image of a solitary foreclosed home is meant to stand in for housing precarity as such. Yet in these foreclosure photographs, I argue, the work of both mediation and typification becomes a problem. Mediation is complicated by the fact that it depends, in these images, not simply on apparatus, medium, and form but also on the manifestly violent power of the police or the surveillance camera to enter otherwise closed or private spaces. And typification, in turn, is problematized by the question of whether the scene being depicted is meant to be representative or unique, general or specific, a problem linked, I suggest, to anxieties about the generalization of debt in the contemporary era and to questions around whether particular places with particular histories (here, Detroit) really can stand in for the crisis as a whole. We must thus consider the kind of specifically historical, as opposed to mimetic, work photography's partial representations do: rather than move immediately from the scale of the part to that of the whole, I argue, these images produce a set of powerful historical resonances. Relying on a metonymic historicism, a logic of proximity and connection rather than typicality and substitution, post-crisis foreclosure photography folds together the longer history of late twentieth-century capitalism and the more immediate, punctual event of the twenty-first-century financial crisis.

If, as Rosler suggests, photography's suspended stillness allows it to register the motion of "social forces," the post-crisis photograph also prefigures the stilling of capital's motion—the freezing up of credit—that occasions terminal economic crisis. Walter Benjamin describes this photographic suspension as "dialectics at a standstill." "Ambiguity," Benjamin writes, "is the pictorial image of dialectics, the law of dialectics seen at a standstill. This standstill is utopia and the dialectical image is therefore a dream image. . . . [It is] both house and stars." Post-crisis photographs of lost and abandoned homes are similarly both critique and utopian "dream image." On the one hand, they represent the house as commodified property and capture the uncanny affects that attend domestic enclosure. Yet by depicting these fetishized commodities at the moment of their ruination, photos of foreclosed homes also imagine a radical opening onto freedom from real property and from the inhospitable forms of domestic life produced by it.[17]

Feral Houses and Moral Panic

The wide run of Platt's photograph of a foreclosed home is arguably attributable to the way he has cropped from the frame anything that might suggest local particularity or intimate specificity: the bareness of the house's facade and the simplicity of its shape make Platt's image of it appear less a photo of one particular house and more a depiction of the very idea of house-ness. Lacking obvious markers of geographic specificity, the photograph's subject exists in no specific place. In this section, however, I explore two series of photographs of abandoned homes that emphatically draw our attention to the exotic and the local: James Griffioen's 2009 series *Feral Houses*, shot in Detroit between 2007 and 2010, and Bruce Gilden's 2008–9 photo-essay on the housing crisis in rural southern Florida, titled simply *Foreclosures*.

Aesthetically, these two series are fairly distinct. Griffioen's photographs have a flat, snapshot aesthetic; impassively rendered, they almost resemble the purely instrumental images a city assessor or surveyor might take. Gilden's photographs, in contrast, are black and white, and his use of silver-gelatin processing produces a much more stylized aesthetic. But both Griffioen's and Gilden's photos highlight the slow decay of abandoned architecture. Griffioen documents the wooden Victorian-style houses in Detroit as they are covered—and ultimately destroyed—by organic life: in Figure 3.2, for instance, we see that the hedges that once marked the neat division between the private space of the home and the public street have now grown so large that they dwarf the house itself; in Figure 3.3, the high grass and prolific wildflowers growing up around the house mark the amount of time the lawn has gone untended. Gilden, in turn, captures the more modest houses, including many trailer homes, of the working-class communities around Fort Myers: Gilden's photographs document the way the region's fecund, tropical plant life grows over and even into the frame of the house (Figure 3.4) or pushes upward through the concrete of driveways and patios (Figure 3.5). I categorize both these series using Griffioen's

Figure 3.2. From *Feral Houses*, James Griffioen, Michigan, 2007–10

term "feral houses" to underscore how both Griffioen and Gilden draw our attention to the overtaking of abandoned homes by prodigal nature.

Although Griffioen's and Gilden's images were the most widely circulated and widely discussed instances of the "feral houses" genre, photographs of homes or buildings overrun by teeming nature have been common in the post-housing-crisis period. The trope of the abandoned house was especially ubiquitous in discussions of Detroit, where it undergirded what Sarah Safransky calls the "frontier narratives . . . that describe Detroit's postindustrial landscape as empty and underutilized." Safransky describes these references to "'urban wilderness,' 'dangerous jungle,' 'urban pioneers'" as part of a contemporary settler colonial imagery. To characterize cities hard hit by the housing crisis as "awaiting inhabitants and transformation," she argues, is to demand an intensification rather than

Figure 3.3. From *Feral Houses*, James Griffioen, Michigan, 2007–10

Figure 3.4. From *Foreclosures: Florida*, Bruce Gilden, Florida, 2008

Figure 3.5. From *Foreclosures: Florida*, Bruce Gilden, Florida, 2008

a reconsideration of private property rights: figured as empty, Detroit appears not as disaster but as "a lucrative frontier for development."[18]

Whereas depictions of Detroit as an empty frontier (not-yet-civilized and awaiting inhabitants) were deployed to buttress privatization schemes, depictions of Detroit and other post-crisis communities as feral (uncivilized and inhabited by savages) underwrite more violent forms of dispossession carried out in the name of property values, public safety, civic responsibility, and the rule of law. The representation of an unruly nature capable of decomposing culture participates in an imperialist ideology that imagines racialized subjects as recalcitrant to the ordering principles of modernity, culture, and civilization. As Rachel Hughes notes, "The trope of fecund, tropical nature as endangering civilized cultures . . . cast[s] racial different as natural threat."[19] Thus the feral, with its implied danger and lawlessness, appears to necessitate an especially forceful response on the part of the state: not simply exploitation but enclosure, not simply privatization but population control. Griffioen's coinage of "feral houses" thus resonates more than incidentally with the idea of "feral cities," a concept developed by Naval War College scholar Richard Norton, author of an influential paper on the emerging threat to US economic and security interests represented by places like Johannesburg, Mogadishu, and Mexico City—all of which risk, Norton insists, "going feral." Describing these "lawless" cities as having "descended into savagery," Norton presents an understanding of ferality that clearly provides an alibi for neocolonial military intervention and forced structural adjustment.[20] In his framing of the feral houses series, Griffioen similarly emphasizes the temporality of degeneration, describing the houses as "reverting to a wild state, as from domestication" and underscoring the irony of the *domus* becoming wild.[21] His emphasis on reversion thus marks another distinction between these images and the optimistic frontier discourse that Safransky identifies. The latter is future oriented, yoking national or civic identity to not-yet-cultivated land (thus the evocation of the modern urban "pioneer" or the reference to the homesteader in projects like the Michigan Homesteaders Act). In contrast, the idea of feral decomposition implies a backward movement—the descent of once-civilized spaces into racially marked natural decay—and evokes the melancholy of lost imperial power, here clearly linked to the ravages of deindustrialization not only on cities like Detroit but also on the US working class and economy as a whole.

Whereas Griffioen's use of the "feral" metaphor registers the process of decivilizing as (racial) reversion, Gilden frames it as (moral) tragedy. Gilden turned to Detroit after finishing his Florida series, and he uses the difference between the two regions to frame degeneration in terms of class rather than race. Comparing the spaces he photographed in Florida to those he shot in Detroit, he laments, "What was really sad for me in Detroit was that many of the destroyed houses were well made and beautiful houses at one time, they were like Grande Dames.... This makes the destruction even sadder, it's not like a dilapidated trailer in ruins. There was an elegance here—the houses were beautiful— it's so sad.... When these houses were built there was pride in craftsmanship and you saw it in the houses. It's sad."[22] Contrasting the "dilapidated trailers" of rural Florida to the lost beauty of the Detroit "Grande Dames," Gilden makes his nostalgia for a lost past clear but also flips the commonplace racialization of Detroit as a failed black city. Instead, he uses Detroit to construct a narrative of class otherness: whereas the ruined homes of Detroit once stood for wealth and beauty, the rusted trailers and modest houses of Fort Myers seem to be always already decomposing, easily lost because they were never invested with meaning or care. The "pride in craftsmanship" he sees in the formerly upper-class neighborhoods of Detroit—but not in the working-class towns of rural Florida—transforms a narrative of economic decline into a tale of declining morality, diminishing work ethic, and deteriorating social values.

These photographs of natural degeneration echo common depictions of the housing crisis as a symptom of moral degeneration—the "erosion of our common values," in President Obama's phrasing.[23] As legal scholar Brent White has documented, media invective against defaulting homeowners has represented debtors as "unseemly, offensive, unethical" and "a blight on society," and these characterizations have been cultivated and encouraged by the financial services industry as a form of social control.[24] We see the traces of this sentiment reflected in the photos by Gilden and Griffioen, which literalize the metaphor of "blight" by figuring it as a kind of organic disorder, a natural prodigality whose wanton lushness quickly slides into dissolution and ruin. If credit is to continue to be associated with civilization and sociability, then failure to repay can be represented only by the horrifying encroachment of nature. The fantasy of (moral) dissolution shows up not only in images of houses but also in Gilden's portraits of the inhabitants themselves, portraits that present the apparently neglected bodies—often half naked or with wild, unkempt hair—of the former homeowners as an extension of their empty, untended houses (Figures 3.6 and 3.7). These portraits draw our attention to the apparent "otherness" of their

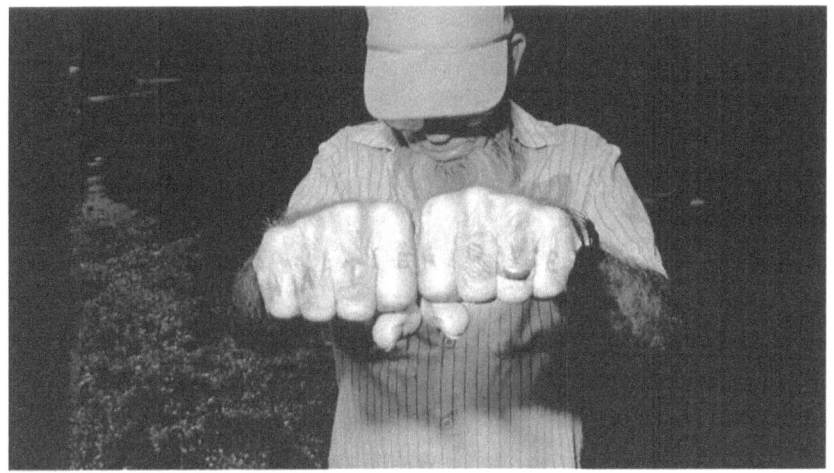

Figure 3.6. From *Foreclosures: Florida*, Bruce Gilden, Florida, 2008

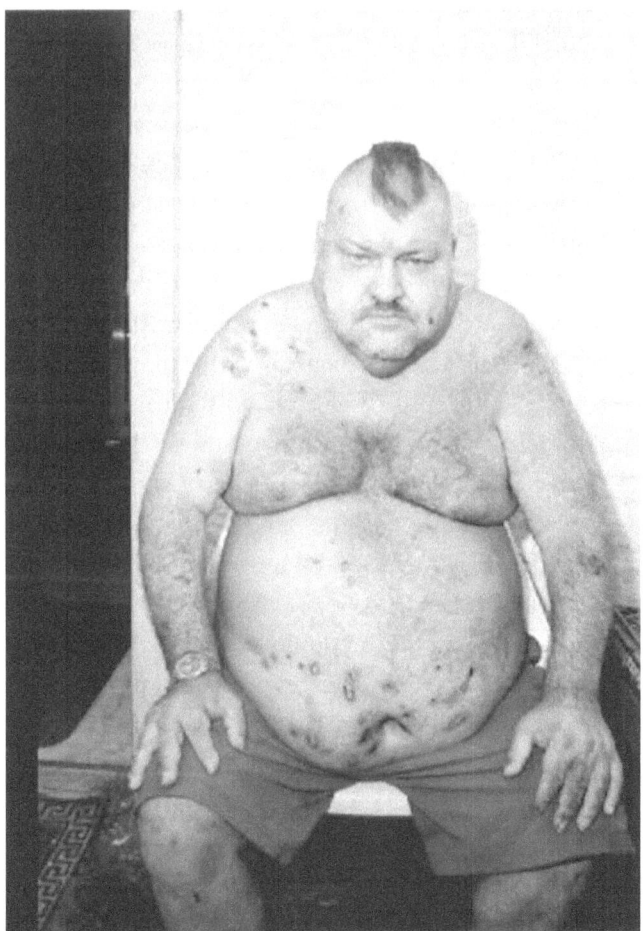

Figure 3.7. From *Foreclosures: Florida*, Bruce Gilden, Florida, 2008

subjects, transforming human figures into abject spectacles marked by hardship; often the marks of damage are literal, whether the aggressive handmade tattoos shown in Figure 3.6 or the scars and burns shown in Figure 3.7. Gilden's portraits particularly emphasize their subjects' bodily size: among the many portraits in Gilden's Florida and Detroit foreclosure series, nearly half are topic-tagged with the marker "overweight," including images that show only a woman's upper arm or a pair of legs and feet. Gilden's focus on the debtor's body—which might be viewed as the counterpoint of "The Three Score Guys" ad discussed in Chapter 2, with its association between physical and fiscal fitness—suggests that it is no coincidence that fear of an "obesity epidemic" rose alongside anxiety about the indebtedness of US families, since both obesity and debt are often portrayed as failures of personal will. Journalist Michael Lewis, for instance, describes the rise in consumer debt as symptomatic of an American "cultural disease" analogous to obesity. Lewis begins by offering an intentionally provocative, but scientifically inaccurate, comparison between the disease of indebtedness and the so-called reptilian brain that "cannot think [in terms of the future] when faced with chocolate cake" and that finds itself unable to limit its consumption in an "environment of extreme abundance." Lewis then shifts from analogy to correlation, writing, "A color-coded map of American personal indebtedness could be laid on top of the Centers for Disease Control's color-coded map that illustrates the fantastic rise in rates of obesity across the United State since 1985 without disturbing the general pattern."[25]

In their tendency to turn their subjects into aestheticized spectacles for a presumed middle-class viewership; in their treatment of the neglected body as a sign (or even a cause) of economic hardship; and in their attempt to represent these subjects and these bodies as unfamiliar others, Gilden's portraits also recall WPA-era works by Margaret Bourke-White.[26] Like Bourke-White's photographs of impoverished Dust Bowl farmers, Gilden's portraits efface the real lives of those affected by the foreclosure crisis by transforming them into symbols.[27] Also like Bourke-White's images of regional poverty, both Gilden's and Griffioen's photographs of degeneration (degeneration of either the evicted home or of the evicted body) present the foreclosed neighborhoods of Florida and Detroit as radically, terrifyingly Other, the spectacular sites of exotic catastrophe.

However, these photographs also suggest a more historically particular response to the problem of representing indebtedness in the wake of the contemporary credit crisis. The bourgeois viewer of Bourke-White's photographs could satisfy a kind of vicarious curiosity about the experience of economic precarity by seeing it as a condition suffered by people radically different from himself. According to Fredric Jameson, by imagining the underworld of the underclass as "irredeemably other," such representations provide the bourgeoisie with "the double bonus of sympathy . . . on the one hand and of class reconfirmation and the satisfactions of the bourgeois order on the other."[28] The housing and debt crisis of 2008, however, had devastating consequences for this once-protected middle class. As economist Edward Woolf has reported, "Between 2007 and 2010, the median net worth of U.S. households fell by 47 percent, reaching its lowest level in more than 40 years. . . . In other words, middle class wealth virtually evaporated in this country." By 2007, Woolf's data suggest, the average US middle-class household owed sixty-one cents for every dollar of wealth, up from forty-one cents a mere six years earlier.[29] Read in the context of these data—read in recognition of the fact that there were very few people not damaged by the housing crisis—Gilden's attempt to imagine the economic hardship as happening only to Other people and only in Other places appears less a self-satisfied form of middle-class sympathy and more a pathological disavowal of material reality.

Dienst describes the invisibility of debt as paradoxical, since "we should be able to find its traces everywhere." Yet as Gilden's portraits suggest, the "everywhere-ness" of debt also makes it difficult—even terrifying—to render debt visible. Platt's widely circulated AP image of a blank house takes debt's *everywhere* and transforms it into a kind of *anywhere*, while Gilden and Griffioen represent indebtedness as an abject *elsewhere*, a wild space that we might visit but can always leave. Yet the data on middle- and working-class debt suggest that this fantasy of removal or distance is impossible to fulfill. Rather, the very attempt to disavow the near universality of indebtedness cannot help simultaneously registering an anxiety about the precarity of US middle-class housing. Even as they try to represent the feral houses of the crisis as the signs of racial or economic Otherness, these photographs ultimately reveal that indebtedness is a condition more widely shared than ever before, a condition that can no longer be banished to the margins of either national space or of collective consciousness.

Eviction, Photography, and the Police

More narrative, more populated, and more classically documentary than the images just discussed, photographs of forced eviction have similarly become frequent emblems of the human consequences of the financial crisis. Eviction turns the house inside out and displays its contents for public view, and images of eviction necessarily exploit this newly commonplace spectacle of public exposure. The two documentary series I address in this section—documents of eviction taken by photojournalists Anthony Suau (*Time*) and John Moore (Getty Images)—were awarded highly prestigious World Press Photography Awards in 2009 and 2012, respectively. Moore and Suau reflexively explore the way in which the photographer's presence on the scene is underwritten by the capacity of both the state and the bank to violate individual privacy. Moore and Suau's photo series explore the anxious visibility of eviction by depicting the police's "home invasion" and the photographer's voyeuristic entry as mutually supporting forms of violent exposure.

Photography has long had to negotiate the problem of domestic privacy. As a new technology, the camera was alluring precisely because it made it possible to enter the lives of strangers, and also to enter their homes. Photographers often represented themselves—as James Agee characterizes himself and Walker Evans in *Let Us Now Praise Famous Men*—as "spies," or "bodiless eye[s]," invisible presences in the homes and lives of others. Indeed, many of Evans's interior photographs appear to have been taken while peering out from behind a wall or around a corner.[30] Susan Sontag similarly avers, "We want the photographer to be a spy in the house of love and death, and those being photographed to be unaware of the camera."[31] The photographer-spy's claim to invisibility produces, even as it reverses, the medium's imperative of visibility: the subject can be transparently herself ("unaware") because the photographer has hidden himself. Not only does this serve to naturalize the power dynamic between those who produce the image and those who are produced as the image; it also renders the impropriety of photography's domestic voyeurism unthreatening to the sanctified privacy of family life. In a manner similar to the process Jameson describes, wherein an image of poverty enables both sympathy and complacency, a relatively secure middle-class consumer of photos like those by Evans could enjoy the pleasure of voyeurism by contrasting the indiscriminate living conditions of the rural poor—in whose homes there is seemingly never any privacy—to her own.[32] Put simply, one's own home can be imagined as inviolable to the exact extent that the homes of others are porous.[33]

Far from being deemed a threatening invasion, then, domestic photography has tended to shore up attitudes about domestic property and propriety. Thus, the paradox of the "invisible spy" returns with the voyeuristic fascination with domestic interiors common during the twenty-first-century housing bubble. Television critic Shawn Shimpach argues that even as they allow the home "to be visualized, made accessible, imaginable, and desirable," such narratives sustain "the ideology of domesticity" and the fantasy of total privacy.[34] In fact, pre-housing-crisis television shows like *House Hunters* revise Sontag: what we really want is to be a spy in the house of love and *money*.[35] The opportunity to glimpse the private lives of the rich, like the chance to peer into the homes of the poor, thus does not threaten the sanctity of domestic space. This paradox is perfectly reflected in the opening credits of the *Real Housewives of Orange County*, a show representative of housing-boom culture not only because it was fascinated with conspicuous real estate consumption but also because many of the "housewives" were either professionals in industries connected to the mortgage boom or were the beneficiaries of the cheap credit offered during it. After an aerial shot of Orange County, we approach that ultimate signal of domestic privacy, the entrance to a "gated community." The gate opens to allow us inside, at which point we are introduced to each of the show's housewife characters, but the final shot is of the gate closing, seen as before from the outside. Although we seem to enter these communities as gate-crashing voyeurs, in the end the gate also shuts us out.

Like Evans's Depression-era photographs, housing-bubble narratives like *Real Housewives* defend the sanctity of domestic space precisely by violating it.[36] But this salutary link between the aesthetics of eavesdropping and the ideology of domestic privacy fails in the context of the contemporary housing crisis and the subsequent wave of foreclosures and evictions. There are few US communities in which the image of families forced out of their homes is not crushingly common. The consequence of this ubiquity is that the relationship between the invasion of privacy and the very act of representing domestic space becomes both more visible and more troubled. Once a symbol of financial security (a kind of "*real* estate" set against the abstraction and fluidity of the market), domestic property is transformed into an emblem of speculative risk. As a material environment, likewise, the home no longer represents certainty but a looming precarity: the possibility of a violent unhousing.

This anxiety around domestic insecurity is captured in *Newsweek* photographer John Moore's award-winning images of eviction in and around the Denver, Colorado, metro area. Part of a series documenting one family's experience of foreclosure, Moore's photographs show us the aftermath of forced eviction. In one particularly powerful image (Figure 3.8), the central figure, evicted renter Tracy Munch, is buffeted by the wind and enveloped by a darkening sky. The photograph's depiction of her vulnerability to the natural elements reminds us that eviction constitutes an act of both visual and material exposure. The family's domestic belongings appear transformed from objects of value (both sentimental and material) into mere debris, a transubstantiation whose drama is heightened by the way the family's stuff is haphazardly piled into jumbled trash bags. Moore's photo emphasizes the impropriety of turning the home inside out and the improper treatment of property once removed from its "proper" place. Whereas the real estate porn of the housing bubble allowed us access to the domestic interiors of real estate boomtowns without threatening the sanctity of domestic property and personal privacy, here the blurred line between private and public produces anxiety rather than security. No longer protected from material exigencies or economic rationality, this home is the site of a forced entry.

From one perspective, such images of eviction and hardship explicitly endorse the sympathetic voyeurism also found in Depression-era photographs of domestic poverty. Yet in these contemporary photos, the photographer does not conceal his presence as an invisible spy (pace Evans and Agee). No longer is private life rendered visible to public view by an act of mediation that is itself invisible. Rather, Moore's image of the Munch family eviction troubles the relationship between private domesticity and public consumption by marking Moore's own presence in the house and contrasting it to the family's absence. In another photograph (Figure 3.9) Moore shows the literal screen that interrupts the relationship between the camera and its subjects: as the photographer looks out from within the protected and private interior of the house, the home's material contents and human residents are exposed both to the elements and to the camera's gaze. This photograph imagines foreclosure as a kind of world inside out: the home's inhabitants and all the furniture are out-of-doors while the photographer—the stranger, the spy—stands inside the door. Another image in the series views the former inhabitants—again situated outside the home—from a recently emptied upstairs room. Here the camera has not just hovered at the home's threshold but fully entered it, moving into the more private spaces of the Munch family's second floor. Moore's series indexes the withdrawal of the material preconditions for privacy: the photographer doesn't simply slip

Figure 3.8. From *Newsweek* coverage of foreclosure crisis, John Moore, Colorado, 2009

Figure 3.9. From *Newsweek* coverage of foreclosure crisis, John Moore, Colorado, 2009

inside the family's house as a secret guest; rather, he occupies the home while the family is forced outside. The photographer's presence is thus uncomfortably affiliated with the very forces of state power that enable the family's eviction. The evicted residents themselves stand uneasily in the background or on the outer edges of the image, as if they have already been rendered irrelevant to the home's future life as a commodity.

The camera has long colluded with the state to invade the bourgeois interiors (psychic as well as domestic) that both sought to naturalize. The camera not only contributes to an ideology of visibility; it also makes certain forms of visibility materially possible. As Sekula convincingly argues, from criminal photography to surveillance, aerial landscapes to mug shots, the photograph "introduce[d] the panoptic principle into daily life." Photography, he continues, yoked a model of the self rooted in property rights to "its lurking, objectifying inverse in the files of the police."[37] In photographs documenting eviction, the relationship between the private self, private property, the photographer, and the police becomes part of the photograph's content. The results are complex and ambiguous: these images condemn eviction as an act of violent exposure while participating in that violence; they recoil from the power of the state while borrowing some of that power for themselves. Those contradictions appear most powerfully in Anthony Suau's award-winning photographs of the housing crisis in Cleveland. Taken in 2008 for *Time*, the series shows us a Cleveland police detective entering a foreclosed home to make sure that the residents have left. Like Moore's photographs, Suau's series asks us to reckon with the complicity between the photographer and the state. Not concealing his own dependence on the support of the cops, Suau enters the home not with the quiet cunning of the eavesdropper but with the brutality of the forced entry. In shot after shot he draws a visual parallel between the twinned and mutually dependent intrusions of the law and photographic capture. In one image, the policeman peering down the barrel of his gun echoes the photographer looking through his lens (Figure 3.10); in another, the glare of the policeman's flashlight is mistakable for a lens flare. Suau's images insist on the interdependence of property, the police, and photojournalism. In Figure 3.11, the blurry head and shoulders of one of the cops blocks Suau's shot; included in the series rather than discarded as an accident, this photograph reveals that Suau's work depends on the presence of the police. By acknowledging the ways in which documentary photography relies on the power of the state, these images transform

Figure 3.10. From *Time* magazine coverage of foreclosure crisis, Anthony Suau, Ohio, 2008

Figure 3.11. From *Time* magazine coverage of foreclosure crisis, Anthony Suau, Ohio, 2008

domestic transparency from an act of seemingly benign voyeurism to one of material violence.

They also momentarily redirect our attention from the frequently invoked opacity and virtuality of MBSs to the visual transparency and material vulnerability of the household under police power, the police who help transfer private property from the defaulting homeowners to the bank. In these episodes of complicity between capital and the cops, the bank is the only participant in the transaction that is allowed any privacy. In the forced entries that Suau documents, the bank's right to invisibility is secured by its police representatives, who appear as unseemly interlopers in the aftermath of domestic tragedy. In this sense, post-crisis photographs of eviction illuminate a specifically contemporary set of historical conditions: they are not simply an example of the property panopticon described by Sekula; they are also evidence of a new legal framework around bankruptcy, foreclosure, and punishment for debt. In 2005, as some banks and lenders were beginning to realize that the rising levels of consumer debt presaged an eventual crash, Congress introduced the Bankruptcy Abuse Prevention and Consumer Protection Act (BAPCPA), referred to by some as "no creditor left behind."[38] This legislation significantly strengthened the power of creditors over debtors and was supported not only by banks but also by the highly profitable debt-collection industry, which first emerged amid the inflationary crises of the 1980s. As a result of BAPCPA and other legal changes lobbied for by the debt-collection industry, a growing number of states now allow nonjudicial foreclosure, a process of foreclosure "preauthorization" that is cheaper and faster for the lender because it requires no court appearances. Banks and debt collectors have also been granted additional legal leeway to use harassment and intimidation to force tenants to vacate foreclosed homes, including tactics like "threatening to change the tenants' locks or removing their property . . . threatening to damage the tenants' credit . . . [and] shutting off the tenants' water or electricity."[39] As more tenants and homeowners attempt to forestall foreclosure through post-housing-crisis federal programs, more and more of them are still occupying their residence on the day of eviction. The result is that processing foreclosures has required ever-more-intensified use of police and sheriff's departments.[40] Such evictions often take place in the middle of the night and involve a significant use of force. In Georgia, for instance, the Frazer family were thrown out of their home at three in the morning by dozens of armed police officers; in North Carolina, a family attempting to return to their repossessed home to retrieve some personal belongings were met by a large SWAT team equipped with submachine guns.[41] Elsewhere, banks have chosen not to bother with the legal procedures required to get a city or county police force to perform an eviction and instead have used "rent-a-cops"—private police officers hired directly by the bank—to do the work of removing individuals from their homes.[42]

A way for banks to "expropriate assets and future earnings through coercive means," as scholar Adrienne Roberts puts it, contemporary practices of forced eviction represent the instrumentalization of state violence as the means for the maintenance of private property relationships.[43] Eviction thus becomes not only a way to police individuals but a means to govern an entire "subprime" population through violence and dispossession. In many cities, the flood of evictions served as the alibi for intensified policing. Much as the land enclosures of the eighteenth century created a population of vagrants and vagabonds who could then become new objects of police power, twenty-first-century forced evictions have created a new population marked by housing precarity and thus vulnerable to intensified scrutiny and violence by the state.[44] Suau's and Moore's photographs insist on the terrifying everydayness of these spectacles of violent foreclosure. Their images convey the realization, consequent to the housing crisis itself, that the threat of physical force—enacted or authorized by the state—underwrites the "promise" of credit. The fantasy that credit bonds us to our neighbors or that its promissory form constitutes a kind of social intimacy is here undone by the violence of foreclosure. The photographic image of forced eviction substitutes the ostensible mutuality of the contract with a scene of dispossession, fear, and domestic precarity. Moreover, such images make plain the argument articulated in Chapter 2: the trust on which credit claims to depend is secured not through the alienation of the debtor's morality but by the material power of the state to act violently on the debtor's body and belongings.

Haunted Houses and the Uncanny of Debt

The photographs in John Francis Peters's *Foreclosed: 2008–2010* do more than bust through the front door: they gaze into bathrooms and pry into children's bedrooms. The photographer enters the basement of the home, opens cabinets, and crouches on the floor as if checking for a lost object under the couch. Peters's photos accentuate the small items that are left after the home has been cleaned out: in Figure 3.12, an opened closet door reveals the clothes apparently

Figure 3.12. From *Foreclosed: 2008–2010*, John Francis Peters, New York

Figure 3.13. From *Foreclosed: 2008–2010*, John Francis Peters, New York

not worth taking, while a chest of drawers, haphazardly pushed against the wall, is covered with toys and detritus; the background of the image, showing open doors and their empty frames, emphasizes the acts of departure that preceded this leaving-behind. These photographs also attend to the traces of items that have been removed: plugs and cables connected to nothing, shadows on the wall where pictures were hung, impressions on the carpet (Figure 3.13). These are the ghosts of the lost material of daily life. They point toward lacunae in the spaces once given over to commodity value, capturing in that absence what Ann Carson, in *Economy of the Unlost*, describes as "an uncanny protasis of things invisible, although no less real."[45]

Carson also reminds us that we have a name for the feeling of domestic non-belonging, dis-ease, and uncertainty produced by photographs like Peters's: Freud's *Unheimlich*, or unhomely, uncanny. Freud opens his 1919 essay with a thorough etymology of the word *Unheimlich*. The term is typically glossed, he says, as "uncomfortable, uneasy, haunted." But in order to properly understand *Unheimlich*, Freud observes, we must first understand its apparent opposite, *Heimlich*. To be *Heimlich* is to be secure and of the home: the word is associated with comfort, with familiarity, with what "arous[es] a sense of agreeable restfulness and security as [is felt] by one within the four walls of his house."[46] The *Unheimlich*, however, is frightening, unknown, dangerous—to be *Unheimlich* is to reveal what should be kept private. In this section, I explore photographs of abandoned, "haunted" homes like those in Peters's *Foreclosed*. By taking up the various ways the idea of the "uncanny" has been yoked to a critique of private property, I argue that these uncanny domestic still lifes index an anxiety about private domestic property as an alienated and alienating form.

Like Peters's *Foreclosed*, Todd Hido's series *Foreclosed Homes* suggests that the interiors of abandoned houses are both haunting and haunted. In images like Figure 3.14, Peters plays with eerie tones of light and shadow, but by using only available ambient light, he resists the aestheticization of these interiors that would be produced by a starker chiaroscuro. Using a more gradual, natural contrast between light and dark, Hido emphasizes the fact that these houses are closed up. Images like Figure 3.15 are almost reminiscent of Mark Rothko's color field paintings, attuned to the rectangular planes of empty walls and floors, surfaces that appear simultaneously flat and deep, at once luminous and muted. And like Rothko's paintings, they also evoke tombs, such that these houses no longer feel like homes at all but like uncanny ruins long since deserted.

Figure 3.14. From *Foreclosed Homes*, Todd Hido, California, 1996

Figure 3.15. From *Foreclosed Homes*, Todd Hido, California, 1996

In *The Architectural Uncanny*, Anthony Vidler suggests that the uncanny is a "quintessentially bourgeois kind of fear: one carefully bounded by the limits of real material security."[47] It is certainly possible to read in Hido's and Peters's photographs a nostalgia for the rights of privacy and private property the US middle classes lost under a regime of housing debt. Yet the uncanny aesthetic of these photographs seems more to unsettle than to secure the privileges accorded to property ownership. In these photographs, as in Freud's essay, ownership itself is the source of fear and loathing. As Freud writes, "Whoever possesses something that is at once valuable and fragile is afraid," suggesting the anxiety that attends the inevitable insecurity of possession.[48] Peters's and Hido's photographs imply that all commodity objects are marked by this fragility and thus that insecurity haunts all property ownership. Their photographs represent not only the forced entry of the economic into the domestic but also the absolute devaluation of domestic commodities, their terrifying failure to signify any value at all. The imprints on the carpet and the shadows on the wall where pictures once hung disclose traces of absent value, and these depictions of eradicated commodities make it apparent that, as Melinda Cooper and Angela Mitropoulos put it, "the value form can come undone, fail to reproduce, or produce otherwise." The so-called reality of real estate becomes what Cooper and Mitropoulos term "a social liquefaction escaping even the most liquid of securities markets": not the grounded stability of real estate and the foundational security of bourgeois domesticity but a more unstable, uncanny liquidity.[49]

These photographs also reveal an undercurrent in Freud's account of the unhomely home: the way in which (contra Vidler) the uncanny disturbs the very idea of property itself. Freud implies that the uncanny is not simply the experience of feeling alienated from our property but a realization that alienation is reflected in our property. Indeed, it turns out that a range of critics have used the language of uncanniness to describe our relationship specifically to domestic property. In *Minima Moralia*, for instance, Adorno first clarifies that Nietzsche's critique of ontological homeliness is linked to a more literal critique of home ownership and then offers his own account of the uncanny of private property:

> "It is part of my good fortune not to be a house-owner," Nietzsche already wrote in *The Gay Science*. Today we should have to add: it is part of morality not to be at home in one's home. This gives some indication of the difficult relationship in which the individual now stands to his property, as long as he still possesses

anything at all. The trick is to keep in view, and to express, the fact that private property belongs to no one.[50]

For Adorno, the uncanny experience of feeling not at home even in one's own home defines our relationship to private property. Marx, of course, had long before suggested that all commodities are uncanny, a characterization most apparent in his description of the dancing table in *Capital*.[51] However, the more interesting depiction of a specifically domestic property as uncanny appears in Marx's earlier writing, when he describes what it means to live in a mortgaged or rented house, a description that clearly traffics in the conventions of the ghost story. "The cellar dwelling of the poor man is a hostile element," Marx tells us. He goes on, sounding rather like Edgar Allan Poe, to describe this "hostile space" as

> a dwelling which remains an alien power and only gives itself up to him insofar as he gives up to it his own blood and sweat—a dwelling which he cannot regard as his own hearth—where he might at last exclaim "Here I am at home"—but instead he finds himself in *someone else's* house, in the house of a *stranger* who always watches him and throws him out if he does not pay.[52]

Marx suggests that the constitutive alienation of private property becomes most visible when one obtains consciousness of debt: when one realizes that neither the pleasures of ownership nor the protections of domestic privacy are given (as it might appear with a commodity one purchases outright) but that they depend instead on the ability to continue to pay over and over and over again. Moreover, Marx's description of the feeling that "everything is itself something different from itself" implies the uncanny nature of debt, what Dienst describes as the world of debt in which "nothing really belongs to itself."[53] In Freud and Nietzsche, Marx and Adorno, the uncanny results from an alienation constitutive of domestic property, especially of borrowed, rented, or mortgaged domestic property: even before we are evicted or foreclosed upon, debt has already unsettled our relationship to domestic property. Housing debt, in other words, is the uncanny's own hidden history.[54]

As the Introduction to this book already suggested, the idea that there is something particularly uncanny about living in a mortgaged property goes back to the very etymology of the word "mortgage," or dead pledge. As collateral for a loan, property could be either "dead" to the lender, if the loan was paid, or "dead" to the borrower, if he defaulted. What this etymology suggests is that the house has a kind of liminal status while the loan is still owed; neither living nor dead, the mortgaged home has a strange ontology. The dead pledge of the mortgage defamiliarizes domestic space, which instead of being a place of comfort and security becomes a space of unease and alienation. (In fact, the exploration of post-crisis domestic invasion thrillers in Chapter 4 suggests that insecurity and unease so permeate the sites of debt and eviction that even when the house is repossessed by new owners, it retains the haunted traces of violent dispossession.)

If Hido's and Peters's images associate the absence of commodity objects with a kind of alienated melancholy, T. J. Proechel's photographs of abandoned foreclosed homes in Minneapolis represent the uncanny of property not simply as loss or unease but as a more frightening form of hostility, one registered by the objects that remain rather than by those that are missing. Proechel's photos fully embrace Marx's sense that under the conditions of capital, all commodities are alien beings. The objects Proechel captures are very familiar items left behind by the evicted family, grouped by Proechel into strange still lifes, as in Figure 3.16, which depicts a stuffed hedgehog resting surreally on a tanning bed. They were all photographed in the room in which they were found, which invests them with an uncanny feeling: we know what these objects are, but we do not know why they are there. Proechel's photos recall Freud's reading of the spatial dimension of coincidence: uncanny coincidences create a dreamlike disorientation akin to "wander[ing] about in a strange dark room, looking for the door or the electric switch, and collid[ing] time after time with the same piece of furniture."[55] The objects in Proechel's still lifes are likewise endowed with a kind of uncanny agency: in Figure 3.17, a bare-bottomed doll, facedown beneath a cot and next to a listing plastic Christmas tree, seems, like Hoffman's automata, to have stilled its uncanny motion just as the camera turned its gaze in its direction. The property captured in these images resembles what Evan Calder Williams describes—in an echo of Marx's "hostile element" in the previous passage—as "hostile objects," objects that are neither waste nor value, neither useful nor exchangeable, but "uncertain, unstable, loathing or loathsome, dangerous, and weirdly incommensurable with the purpose for which they were designed."[56]

As these singularly discomfiting photographs suggest, moreover, the alienation produced by ownership is not merely subjective and individual but also social or, more particularly, antisocial. For Freud, the fear of losing our valuable

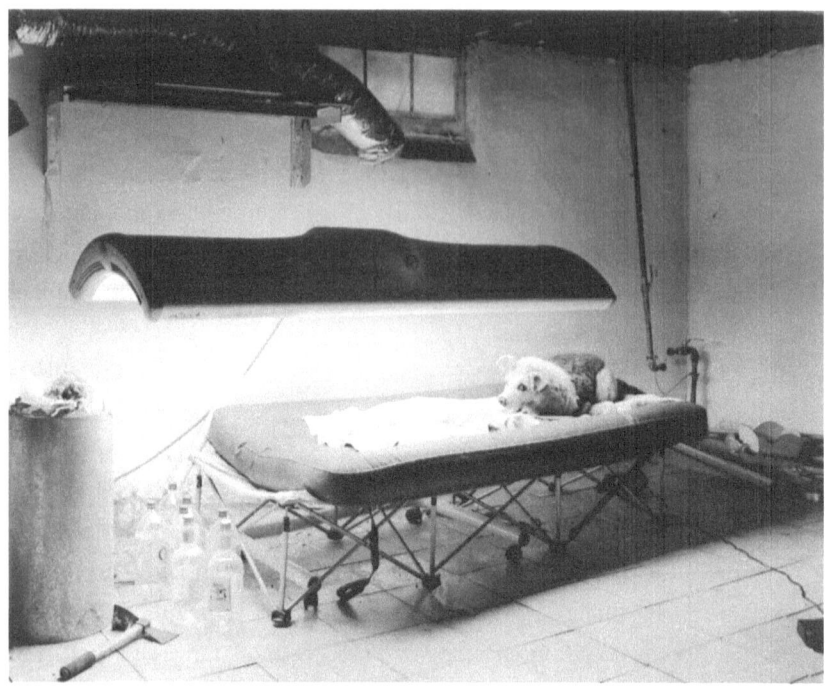

Figure 3.16. From *Dream House*, T. J. Proechel, Minnesota, 2009

Figure 3.17. From *Dream House*, T. J. Proechel, Minnesota, 2009

objects—a fear that defines the very fact of owning in the first place—manifests first as an anxiety that these objects have "an uncanny and secret intention of doing [us] harm" and then as a hostile envy of others, who we jealously imagine are secure in their capacity to possess.[57] That is, we first grant a specifically malignant agency to (commodity) objects and then attribute that hostility to the human subjects around us. In Freud's reading, then, not only does the commodity obscure or reify social relations, but ownership as such entails a kind of hostility. The hostility of the arranged objects in Proechel's photographs thus discloses the uncanny double of the hospitality the home ostensibly invites: they do not suggest the exposure or opening up of the once reassuringly private abode but the terrifying, tomblike form of enclosure the home has always represented, here fully realized as the house finally rids itself of all human presence.

Both debt and the uncanny exhibit a singular capacity to alienate us from private property while revealing property's underlying antisociality, the antisociality that inheres both in our relationship to commodities and equally in our relationship to the world mediated by them. Fred Moten and Stefano Harney's manifesto "Debt and Study" describes this hostility as debt's essential "fugitivity." They regard debt as the place at which it becomes apparent that "something is wrong," as the site of radical devaluation.[58] In the *unheimlich* houses photographed by Hido, Peters, and Proechel, the devaluation of the home is reflected in the uncomfortable wrongness of an uncanny aesthetics. These photos index debt's uncanny trafficking in epistemological and ontological uncertainty, whether Moten and Harvey's "fugitivity" or Cooper and Mitropoulos's "liquefaction." In the photographs considered in the next two sections, however, this relationship between the uncertain and the fugitive, between the not-quite-right and the radically devalued, appears as the ambient atmosphere of the contemporary credit crisis itself. In them, the uncanny is not simply the alienated, hostile strangeness of property but the anticipatory temporality of a total, systemic crisis in the making.

Haunted Factories and the Postindustrial Uncanny

The widely circulated series *The Ruins of Detroit*, by French photographers Yves Marchand and Romain Meffre, emphasizes the ruined, abandoned spaces of Detroit, focusing particularly on derelict infrastructure (train depots, libraries, police stations, schools) and deserted industrial buildings (especially shuttered car factories). Taken between 2005 and 2009 and released as part of an art book in 2011, these photos, like other similar images of Detroit, have frequently been interpreted as representations of the 2008 financial crisis—and just as often criticized for that representation, labeled as "ruin porn," real estate porn's uncanny double.[59] Like the images of abandoned domestic interiors by Hido and Peters, Meffre's and Marchand's photographs depict buildings emptied of use, meaning, and value: factories without equipment, salesrooms without commodities. A photograph of the Fischer Body Plant, once home to equipment that made the Buick and Cadillac bodies praised under the marquee "Body by Fischer" and housed in a light-filled building designed by Albert Kahn, the "architect of Detroit," thus captures the building—decommissioned as a car production facility in the early 1980s—in ruined disrepair (Figure 3.18).[60] In Marchand and Meffre's photograph, the Fischer Body Plant's concrete walls are peeling and dramatically discolored, and its wooden floor blocks, protected by their coating of creosote, are in disarray. As if to emphasize the way the factory has become a kind of cave or crypt, the image reveals the tiny stalactites that form on the ceiling in the winter months as ice and snow make their way into the building.

Figure 3.18. *Fischer Body Plant* from *The Ruins of Detroit*, Yves Marchand and Romain Meffre, Ohio, 2009

John Patrick Leary argues that by using Detroit as an "uncanny spectacle" for the larger economic crisis, Marchand and Meffre (and others like them) inaccurately present the city as "ground zero of the collapse of the finance and real estate economy in America."[61] Leary is persuasively critical of such "Detroitism," but I suggest that reading these images in terms of the uncanny actually affords something more interesting than Leary allows. Marchand and Meffre's ruined industrial landscapes present Detroit not merely as a backdrop but as a metonym for the financial crisis, a metonymic representation that indicates both the spatial proximity and figurative intimacy of factory closure with home foreclosure. Leary is right, of course, to note that Detroit's economic ruination preceded the collapse of the markets in 2008 by many decades, spurred on by deindustrialization, the globalization of manufacturing labor, and persistent structural racism. Well before 2008, after all, Detroit was facing high unemployment and an overabundance of empty housing stock and was unable to provide basic services to its citizenry. For Leary, the fact of this much longer crisis makes Detroit an inadequate and inaccurate symbol for the financial crisis of 2008 and makes photographs like Marchand and Meffre's a particularly pernicious form of bad historicism. "Though they trade on the peculiarity of Detroit as living ruin," Leary argues, "these are pictures of historical oblivion. The decontextualized aesthetics of ruin make them pictures of nothing and no place in particular."[62] According to Leary, Marchand and Meffre fail at both causality and chronology: their suggestion that Detroit's collapse was the result of the market crash of 2008 precludes viewing those spaces in the proper context of an earlier history of deindustrialization.

Yet if we ask instead *why* these photographs emerged as (un)cannily improper figures of the economic crisis of 2008, we might find that their metonymic historicism actually links the events of 2008 to the collapse of US industry in the 1970s in important ways.[63] As the Introduction outlined, the stagnation of the industrial economy in the 1970s both prefigured and is the prehistory of the twenty-first-century credit crisis. As Robert Brenner has persistently and persuasively argued, "The long term weakening of capital accumulation and of aggregate demand" that began in the mid-1970s has, in the ensuing decades, forced economic authorities to "stav[e] off ... crises ... by resorting to ever greater borrowing."[64] Gopal Balakrishnan similarly claims that as income from production declined, capital became "increasingly dependent on turning savings into interest-bearing debt, which under the right conditions can grow out of all proportion to the streams of income that ultimately support it."[65] When labor is expelled—when its profitability ceases to satisfy and it is sent abroad, as happened in the automobile industry metonymically represented by the city of Detroit—credit and finance come in to work their uncanny magic. But when credit itself is thrown into a state of crisis—as in the current moment, when loans cannot be paid, when value cannot be extracted even through the most extreme threat of retribution—the edifice of credit crumbles and exposes the crisis of productivity. As metonyms of the twenty-first-century credit crisis, photographs of abandoned industrial and civic spaces in Detroit reveal the relationship between these two historical moments and these two forms of crisis: the crisis of deindustrialization and the crisis of finance that came in to repair it. These photos disclose the prior lacunae of value that credit and finance once attempted to cover over, limning the relationship between the decimation of profitable labor and the rise of financialization. The unnerving sense of discovery that subtends these images—the eerie feeling of entering spaces that have remained empty for a long time, for instance—is not simply an "archaeological fantasy," as Leary maintains; it also indicates the power of crisis to reveal what capital attempts to hide.[66] Thus, while Balakrishnan (following Fredric Jameson) emphasizes the difficulty of "mapping an opaque ... world of financial markets," photographs like Marchand and Meffre's show that in moments of crisis, such mapping may become easier.[67] When Marchand and Meffre capture the relationship between a stock market crisis and a crisis of productive labor, they reveal the mutual imbrication of these two seemingly independent spheres of value production.[68] By metonymically folding together these two histories—the long and structural history of a crisis in production and the more punctual, immediate, spectacular history of the seizing up of credit markets in 2008—these photographs of an abandoned city refuse the ahistoricism associated with moments of crisis and insistently return our gaze to the prehistory of the present.[69]

This return to the past, in turn, mirrors the temporality of debt, inasmuch as debt concerns the continued presence of the past, its frightening inescapability. In its anxious, backward gaze, debt, like the uncanny, doubles, reverses, and returns.[70] This feeling of being haunted explains what might feel uncanny about being in personal debt: it is the experience of being followed by something we left behind, of carrying our past with us like a dead weight. Yet I am suggesting that by understanding this backward glance as a mode of historicism, we can understand what is uncanny about debt in broader, more systemic terms as well. Put simply, the uncanny of debt is as collective as it is individual. Freud tells us that the origin of the uncanny lies in the return of a "long familiar" cultural belief from the past: "The primitive fear of the dead is still so strong within us and always ready to come to the surface at any opportunity."[71] We imagine ghosts and zombies, Freud insists, because the premodern fear of corpses is itself a return of the historical past—from a collective prehistory—that we thought we had left behind.

For Marx the financial economy similarly depends on the return of a repressed past: credit at once requires and conceals the past dead labor that underwrites it. Thus, in Marx's writing the seemingly dematerialized magic of credit (its power to create value "as with the stroke of an enchanter's wand") ultimately gives way to a more unnatural and uncanny movement: by volume 3 of *Capital*, credit seems to give money the power to walk around of its own accord, to be "possessed," or to have "an inherent secret quality, as a pure automaton."[72] Of course, this automaton—like Hoffman's in Freud's essay—is an illusion, and credit's real magic depends on exploitation. Beneath credit's dark alchemy, Marx explains, lies something altogether more mundane and familiar: the rule of capital and dead labor over the living, the presence of a "hidden abode of production" that comes to resemble a kind of zombie workshop. In both Marx and Freud, then, the object becomes most uncanny when its animation allows us to see again some past source of value and meaning: Freud's insistence that the source of the uncanny is its weird "primitive" familiarity echoes Marx's account of the uncanny of credit and debt, whose "magic" conceals its more familiar origins in labor and the primitive dispossession of exploitation. When credit works, it lives only in the future, transfixing in its seemingly magical power to move itself ever forward. But when it fails, credit is pulled back into its own uncanny past, back into the reality of labor and production that it so desperately attempted to disavow, confronted with the material limits it thought it had overcome.

It is thus no coincidence that Marchand and Meffre's photographs of Detroit's decaying industrial architecture—much of it abandoned decades ago—prove such mesmerizing spectacles in a moment of credit crisis. In Figure 3.19, for instance, we see the Packard Plant, unused since the early 1960s. The Packard Plant was also a Kahn-designed edifice but far more massive than the Fischer Plant: it takes up thirty-five acres of land and comprises millions of square feet of industrial space; although long abandoned, fully ransacked, and

Figure 3.19. *Packard Plant* from *The Ruins of Detroit*, Yves Marchand and Romain Meffre, Ohio, 2009

empty, its ruins are nonetheless massively, inescapably present.[73] As Figure 3.19 emphasizes with its image of a long road leading nowhere and its attention to crumbling buildings denuded of value but nonetheless taking up an immense amount of space, the plant is a kind of Potemkin village in reverse, its uselessness and anachronism belied by its intractable materiality and substance. Images like this make it clear that the industrial economy that Detroit represents is the uncanny double of the shiny glass towers emblematic of transnational financial institutions, of the gleaming sexiness of techno-innovation and the amped-up volatility of stock market value. Detroit's deserted factories are not merely historical ruins but an uncanny zombie architecture: they are the past of industrial labor that is jerkily, incompletely reanimated in a moment of crisis, when the destruction of that past becomes visible through the utter breakdown of the forces of financialization thought to have "surmounted" it. If these images are, as Leary argues, mere fragments that "provide the details of a familiar story whose major plot points we can't piece together," the reason for this fragmentation is not the images' ahistoricality but rather that they capture a totality itself in pieces.[74]

Haunted Landscapes and the Uncanny of Crisis

The ever-growing power of debt and dead labor over surplus value and living labor produces more than elegiac images of loss; it also portends economic futures. Thus in a moment of debt default, the sudden failure of credit to work its magic foreshadows the coming failure of capital to realize its own anticipated value. I conclude by exploring this sense of an eerily anticipated crisis in satellite images of the "ghost cities of China." The ghost cities are massive Chinese real estate and commercial developments that are almost entirely empty; according to most estimates, there are currently at least sixty-four million empty houses built in massive complexes that also include empty theaters, government buildings, sports arenas, and malls. Scholar Michael Alexander Ulfstjerne describes the ghost cities as an exemplary consequence of "an overproduction of real estate developments financed through an unregulated economy of private high-interest lending."[75] It is no coincidence that this description could just as easily apply to similar, if smaller-scale, spaces in the United States, such as abandoned exurban construction projects in Arizona, California, and Florida. Despite this familiarity, however, the ghost cities have proved fascinating to US observers. Perhaps the most photographed and discussed ghost city is Ordos, in Inner Mongolia, which Ulfstjerne calls "a place where boom and bust co-exist and where creativity takes elusive forms. Nothing is what it seems."[76] Ordos, situated about forty miles from the "old city" of Dongshen, was intended to be a "shadow city" to house employees of the mining companies that moved to the area to take advantage of the region's recently discovered coal deposits, the largest in China. The city was also intended to be home to the proposed "Ordos 100" project, headed by Ai Weiwei, for which one hundred international architects would create fantasy housing as China sought to make the city a gleaming paean to economic and cultural globalization. Although "Ordos 100" attracted the attention of architects and designers across the globe when it was announced, currently only one of the projects has actually been completed, and the site remains full of massive empty shells, filling up with blowing sand. The rest of Ordos is similarly isolated and largely empty, a vast swath of concrete, glass, and steel, home to towering high-rises and gleaming malls but relatively few residents or commercial tenants.

Although Ordos is the most well known of the ghost towns, financial journalist Anne Stevenson Yang claims that "the ghost city issue in China, far from being about a few extreme cases like that of Ordos, is absolutely ubiquitous," adding that she has "not seen a single city, town, or hamlet without massive empty housing stock. . . . The ghost developments stretch along Beijing's southern Fourth Ring and through Shanghai's Pudong and Xuhui. The East District Zengzhou looks like a post-apocalyptic landscape."[77] As Yang's depiction of the region as "post-apocalyptic" and Ulfstjerne's portrayal of the "elusive" enigma of the cities both suggest, the discourse around the Chinese ghost city is markedly ideological. Some of this Orientalist rhetoric is familiar—the *Economist*'s description of China's real estate market as "adolescent" recalls nineteenth-century developmentalist accounts of the lagging "Asiatic mode of production," while a *Forbes* report on "Chinese Late Stage Growth Obesity" rather strangely echoes the aforementioned association between consumer debt and obesity as instances of arrested development and antiwill.[78] The idea that China is, on the one hand, backward, adolescent, and effete and, on the other, proleptically, threateningly post-apocalyptic reminds us of the overdetermined ways in which the Asian body has often signified both the precivilized past and the posthuman future.[79] Further, the association of China and the Chinese economy with apocalyptic catastrophe reinscribes what Colleen Lye identifies as the long-standing representation of "the Asiatic as a dark figure of futurity." As Lye suggests, "the Asiatic" has been a particularly significant figure for portentous economic anxiety, from early twentieth-century fear about Asian immigrants, to the worry over Japanese dominance in the auto industry in the 1980s, to the "China threat" of the twenty-first century.[80] If the figure of the Asiatic worker, as Rachel Lee maintains, tends to "render intelligible the contradictory disequilibriums of post-Fordist, transnational capital and its flexible modes of production," then we might say that the Chinese ghost city renders intelligible the contradictions inherent to deindustrialized speculative capitalism and its increased dependence on asset bubbles fueled by national, corporate, and consumer debt.[81]

What then are those contradictions, and what becomes intelligible about them when we confront images of these ghost cities? The answers to these questions become more apparent when we consider the ways the ghost cities entered the Western social imaginary through aerial photographs. The first widely circulated images of the ghost towns were satellite pictures discovered (using economic reports from market analysts for Forensic Asia Unlimited) through Google Earth and published in 2010 by *Business Insider* (Figures 3.20 and 3.21).[82] These images focus on the sprawling size of the developments, which appear as regimented grids dividing up an otherwise empty landscape: even though many of the ghost cities are actually fairly close to older existing cities, since they were built to house anticipated workers in and beneficiaries of China's once booming extractive industry, the published version of the aerial photographs often crop this context from the frame. By thus emphasizing the cities' geographic isolation, these images depict the empty cities as an uncanny reverse image of the frontier: fully territorialized and enclosed before being inhabited. They are also the reverse image of the eviction photographs discussed earlier: their glimpse of something hidden is made possible not by a slip into the back door of an imagined home but by the machines that give us visual access to the eerie vastness of an interconnected global economic system—the satellite, the surveillance camera, and the digital platform through which such images are accessed, collected, and displayed.

The photographs of ghost cities thus reframe the tropes of abandonment, depopulation, and ruin that have appeared throughout this chapter. Rather than depict spaces that have been forcefully deinhabited—areas where the population has packed up and left or been violently evicted—these images capture places that have never been inhabited. This lack of human habitation is most compelling in on-the-ground photographs of Ordos by Michael Christopher Brown for *Time*. Unlike the photos of Detroit, which capture the slow devastation of built space—its steady disintegration back into nature and its transformation from use into ruin—images like Figure 3.22 show us gleaming perfection, clean streets, and the absence of both population and nature. The low-rise housing developments pictured in Figure 3.23, in turn, resemble a newly built American subdivision, full of "dream homes" that never leave their moment of perfect potential, that are never sullied by actual

Figure 3.20. Satellite image from "Ghost Cities of China," *Business Insider*, 2011

Figure 3.21. Satellite image from "Ghost Cities of China," *Business Insider*, 2011

Figure 3.22. From "Ordos, China: A Modern Ghost Town," *Time* magazine, Michael Christopher Brown, 2010

Figure 3.23. From "Ordos, China: A Modern Ghost Town," *Time* magazine, Michael Christopher Brown, 2010

use. If Marchand and Meffre find a kind of uncanny beauty in the ravages of economic history and organic time, Brown's images find an equally uncanny sublimity in the beauty of no history whatsoever. What these photographs represent is not the substitution of civilization for nature, as in Gilden's abandoned landscapes, but a much more disconcerting emptiness, as if the ghost cities were made neither by nor for humans at all. These cities are assets whose value has never been realized—they are commodities that have never completed what Marx calls the *salto mortale*, or fatal leap, into value; they are the dancing table frozen in the middle of its movement.[83] This feeling of being frozen also manifests in the strangely static quality of the images. Without even the implicit temporality of natural decay, and without the presence of human beings or of any sign of human life, they register the anxiety of an end of history, what Balakrishnan describes in his essay on terminal crisis as a period of devastating economic stagnation, in whose absence of moving and movable capital "a new kind of 'worldlessness' and drift begins."[84]

Despite the frequent evocation of their post-apocalyptic quality, the temporality of the "post" does not quite get at the particularly strange temporality these images register. They are haunting because they also suggest a more uncanny mode of futurity, one built into the function of credit itself. As suggested earlier, whereas the temporality of debt—the continued presence of something from the past—makes a backward glance, credit is a form of anticipation. Credit makes it possible to postpone the realization of value, to defer actual profitability into the future while collecting on it now, to borrow on the basis of an anticipated future. But it cannot do this forever. In this way, credit's temporality is not just the futurity of deferred losses and anticipated profits but equally the foreshadowing of a vast and destructive crisis. Thus, when Marx argues that credit capital depends on "past or dead labor" commanding "living surplus labor," there is another crucial clause: mediated by credit, this domination "lasts only *as long as* the capital relation." When Marx observes that the power of dead labor over living labor—of the past over the present and the future—is historically contingent and functions "only as long as" capitalism itself, he invokes the specter of a terminal crisis. Credit's duality is thus obvious in the way credit's spokesmen have "the nicely mixed character of swindler and prophet."[85] As a swindle, credit attempts to forestall crisis by anticipating the as-yet-unrealized profits of future living labor and future production. As a prophecy, the expansion and intensification of credit offer an uncanny glimpse into a future in which this anxious and hyperactive effort at crisis management has utterly and catastrophically failed.

It is here that the uncanny finds its final temporal articulation in Marx's account of credit and debt, and here that we see the relationship between this proleptic uncanny and the images of the ghost cities. Credit is uncanny because despite its seemingly infinite temporality of deferral and anticipation, the future it glimpses is that of terminal crisis, the future that cannot be deferred forever. Uncannily prophesying the collapse and destruction of the very system they propel, credit and debt thus resemble Freud's description of an uncanny feeling that one has glimpsed a future that has not yet arrived. We fear doubles, Freud says, because they are "an uncanny harbinger of death."[86] The gleaming, flawless emptiness of the ghost cities thus registers what Marx describes as credit's ability to "raise the material foundations of the new mode of production to a certain degree of perfection."[87] They are figures of this magic perfection, of credit's seeming capacity to create something out of nothing, and in them we see the calm before the catastrophe, the bubble in the shimmering, glossy moment before it pops. Yet in their strangely frozen stasis, they also anticipate the moment at which credit stutters and stalls out and the future, rather than being a perpetually deferred site of anticipated value, comes crashing into the present. These images are powerful because they concatenate all that is both thrilling and terrifying in what Marx describes as a "violent eruption" or the "violent disintegration of the old mode of production." In the context of the present, credit's uncanny prophecy is both the promise and the threat of a vast devaluation in the world system of capital, a crisis that feels at once familiar and strange, at once anticipated and entirely unimaginable.

As suggested earlier, all the photographs of abandoned houses and empty cities here are attempts at realizing Benjamin's ideal of a "dialectic at a standstill." Describing Benjamin's interest in the "still life," Theodor Adorno observed that Benjamin "was drawn to the petrified, frozen or obsolete elements of civilization, to everything in it devoid of domestic vitality."[88] The absence of specifically "domestic" life is precisely what these images so strikingly capture and also what explains why they draw on the aesthetics of Freud's similarly nondomestic *Unheimlich*. Post-crisis photographs of foreclosure and eviction, ruin and abandonment, make it possible for us to think in terms of the economic structure precisely by stilling it. The photographs of Detroit and China are in a sense the final realization of this dialectics at a standstill, making stillness the logic not simply of artistic mediation but indeed of the historical moment itself. In these images the aesthetic of stillness figures, or prefigures, the total cessation of movement and growth. To revise the famous Althusserian axiom, they suggest the possibility that crisis is a process without subjects. What remains is the stagnant stillness of capital in crisis, a worldless or posthistorical landscape that shows us an "after" just before it has become an "after." Taking this prospective glance, the ghost cities of China allow us not only to "recognize the monuments of the bourgeoisie as ruins even before they have crumbled," as Benjamin puts it, but also to see these unused, empty buildings as ruins even before they have become "of" any historical subject in the first place, before their value has been realized but after it can never be realized.[89] The imminent contradictions they invoke—the disequilibriums they reveal by stilling them—are thus not simply the temporary contradictions of global, financialized, late capital but the terminal contradictions of capitalism as such.

4 Houses of Horror

From the depiction of derivatives as "Frankenstein's monsters" to the evocation of the dark arts of "shadow banking," uncanny specters of the gothic haunt the post-crisis moment.[1] Although finance capital's uncanny abstraction and specterlike virtuality have long been associated with the ghostly and the occult, more everyday forms of credit and debt are also now being described in the language of horror and haunting. The home mortgage has become a particular locus for these terrors, whether they are private nightmares (as in the so-called zombie mortgages that result from sloppy bank record keeping) or public fears (such as an *Economist* article about the global housing market titled "House of Horrors").[2] This chapter seeks to understand the prevalence of this discourse, arguing that it does not merely reflect the fear associated with market volatility but also is an attempt to register historical transformations in the economy itself: the financialization of risky credit that preceded the crisis and the material experience of housing risk that followed in its wake.

I turn to a set of horror films that bring together fear, foreclosure, and financialized credit: *Drag Me to Hell* (dir. Sam Raimi, 2009), *Dream Home* (*Wai dor lei ah yut ho*, dir. Pang Ho-cheung, 2010), *Mother's Day* (dir. Darren Lynn Bousman, 2010), and *Crawlspace* (dir. Josh Stolberg, 2013).[3] All four films explicitly link the formal trappings of horror to the context of real estate lending, mortgage speculation, and foreclosure risk. *Mother's Day* and *Crawlspace* are home-invasion thrillers in which the former inhabitants of a foreclosed home seek vengeance on the new owners, who are framed as savvy investors taking advantage of a distressed market. *Dream Home* and *Drag Me to Hell* are explicitly concerned with the financialization of the mortgage market. Pang's ultraviolent slasher flick, set in Hong Kong in 2007, explores the consequences of the post-handover Hong Kong housing bubble. Its female protagonist goes on a gory killing spree after struggling to purchase an apartment in a city where real estate prices often increase by the day. Raimi's campy *Drag Me to Hell* tells the story of Christine, a young, ambitious bank employee who is cursed by an old woman after refusing to give her an extension on her overdue mortgage.

Taken together, these films register the transformation of economic uncertainty into speculative risk and refigure this risk as precarity, dispossession, and fear. Bringing together the "gothic economy" of high finance and the "dead pledge" of the mortgage contract, these post-crisis films suggest that contemporary debt works less by securing our moral obligation to repay than by making us fear the material consequences of default. In them, debt is frightening not because it produces shame and guilt but because it opens up the possibility of economic precarity and vulnerability. *Drag Me to Hell*, *Dream Home*, *Crawlspace*, and *Mother's Day* use the horror genre to capture the spectacular nature of both the bubble and the bust and to expose the seismic shifts in conceptions of property ownership that have followed as a result of real estate speculation and the foreclosure crisis. Engaging with changing accounts of property rights, these horror films dramatize noncontractual understandings of ownership grounded in ideas of sentiment and utility rather than market exchange and legal formalism. Moving from individual experience to structural critique, they figure liquid credit as a dangerous toxicity, which allows them to represent a credit economy in which unpayable debt leads to social violence, and they depict the violence of dispossession and resettlement consequent to the globalization of financial risk. Finally, their shared recourse to the revenge plot reveals that the imperative to repay our debts produces not the balance and closure of justice but the ceaseless excess of retribution: from paying back to payback.

Risk and Real Estate

The previous chapters considered the various ways the relationship between risk and credit has been transformed in the late twentieth and early twenty-first centuries, from new explanations for market volatility, to the development of risk-quantifying credit-rating systems, to the dangers of global debt imagined through images of empty suburbs and decommissioned factories. In this chapter, I turn to the ways in which the securitization of credit introduced new forms of risky speculation. These new forms of securitized risk, I suggest, were the origin of much of the irrational market volatility that the novels of Chapter 1 misattribute to individual actors; they were the mechanism through which the uncertainty involved in what Chapter 2 described as "control by risk" could appear quantifiable and controllable; and they made it possible for the houses shown in photographs in Chapter 3 to become liquid, global, speculative commodities.

In the frantic search for profitability after the industrial crises of the 1970s, productive capital was driven into ever-more uncertain territory. Financial risk had formerly been a danger to be mitigated, minimized, or hedged against, but by the 1990s, financial profit depended on finding "rewarded risk." After the repeal of the 1933 Glass-Steagall Act in 1999 (which had separated risk-seeking speculators from risk-averse commercial banks), even once-conservative banks sought out riskier investments promising ever-higher rates of return.[4] The growing acceptance of risk was perhaps most significant for the manner in which it transformed credit markets. In the early 1990s and through most of the 2000s, federal interest rates were cut to historic lows. Because banks had to pay almost nothing for their own debt, they lent more and more readily.[5] As Chapter 2 explains, technical developments in the capacity of banks to collect and analyze consumer data had made it possible for lenders to price risk more precisely. Yet as they penetrated ever deeper into the market of previously undiscovered potential borrowers, lenders eventually began to ignore their own formulas, since they had to relax requirements for background and credit checks to keep up with the demand for lucrative high-risk debt.[6] As a result, the once fundamental idea that institutional creditors should lend only to credible borrowers was abandoned. Between 1999 and 2006, the so-called subprime market—the market in the riskiest debt—increased from 5 percent to 30 percent of all lending.[7]

Securitization made all this risky lending possible. Simply put, securitization "makes a debt a saleable commodity," as nineteenth-century economist Henry Dunning Macleod put it.[8] Securitization creates a secondary market in traded debt to fund further lending. Securitization techniques were applied to many forms of lending, including car loans and credit cards.[9] But the primary site of securitization was in the mortgage market. The first MBS was created by the FHA as a means to improve the liquidity of the mortgage lending market after the Great Depression, and most MBSs were financed and sold by the government-sponsored enterprise known as Fannie Mae. For decades, Fannie Mae could purchase only FHA-approved home loans, but in the 1970s Fannie Mae's charter was altered so that it could purchase non–FHA mortgages as well, opening up new terrain for the securities market. In the early 1980s, Congress deregulated the savings and loan industry as well, giving more investors access to increasingly complex securities like MBSs. It also repealed ceilings on mortgage interest rates, making the adjustable-rate mortgage (and ultimately the subprime loan) commonplace and providing a new source of demand for the debt that backed financial instruments like the MBS.[10] By the mid-1980s, aided by these institutional changes and encouraged by the demand for high-risk debt, investment banks had created a new and powerful innovation in the securitization of credit, the structured financing device known as a collateralized mortgage obligation (CMO). Whereas MBSs pay all investors in the same way, CMOs create a range of different investments, both long and short term and high and low risk.[11] CMOs repackage individual securities into bundles and then divide the bundled debt into various "tranches" offering different degrees of risk—and of potential profit.[12] In 2007, Federal Reserve Chairman Ben Bernanke described this shift from reliance on specialized mortgage lenders to a greater use of capital markets as "a great sea change in mortgage finance."[13]

Securitization was supposed to create a virtuous cycle: banks could grant loans to previously unqualified buyers while diluting the risk by reselling those loans as securities to speculative investors around the world. However, by transferring credit risk to very minimally regulated intermediaries, securitization also created opportunities for high-risk activities like arbitrage (the practice of taking advantage of small price differences) and leverage (the practice of borrowing to fund investments) and radically altered the use of structured finance techniques by consumer banks.[14] Banks and investment houses often held on to most of the mortgage-backed instruments they issued rather than spread the risk by selling them to other investors. As the bubble got even bigger, banks created "squared" or even "cubed" CMOs—instruments whose revenue stream came not from the original mortgages but from another CMO or from a CMO of a CMO. Commercial banks took on massive amounts of debt to buy financial instruments based on the risky loans made by other lenders. Consequently, the banks were linked such that a single default could trigger a chain reaction that would spread swiftly and virally throughout the economy.[15] When housing prices fell and the mortgage-default rate climbed, many investment banks found themselves deprived of income, without credit, and leveraged to the hilt. Effectively, the banks themselves were bankrupt.

And of course, as the previous images of eviction have already made starkly apparent, the damage wrought by the introduction of speculative risk into the housing industry extended beyond the crash of stock markets. The result, indeed, was another kind of risk: what Karen McCormack and Iyar Mazar term "radical risk," a form of lived risk that is distributed unevenly across classes, races, genders, and categories of citizenship and that extends the other forms of uncertainty and instability that characterize contemporary economic life for these populations.[16] The nearly eleven million high-risk subprime borrowers who were given credit during the bubble suffered a particularly high rate of foreclosure during the bust. From 2006 to 2008, the frequency of default on non-fixed-rate (that is, both subprime and adjustable-rate) mortgages jumped from 10 percent to 40 percent.[17] In 2008 the child advocacy group First Focus predicted that nearly two million children would be directly affected by the housing crisis, largely because of the increase in homelessness caused by both homeowner and renter evictions.[18] The crisis devastated borrowers of color in particular: 39 percent of the mortgages given to single African American women during the bubble were subprime, and African Americans were the population hardest hit by the wealth-destroying effects of the financial crisis.[19] In short, the forms of speculative risk created in and exploited by the securitized credit market were transferred as material precarity to working- and middle-class borrowers and renters, particularly those of color.

Meanwhile, some speculators have profited almost as much from the housing bust as from the housing boom. Private-equity firms like Lewis Ranieri (described as "the inventor of the mortgage bond") are currently investing tens of billions in the market for foreclosed homes. Blackstone, a large hedge fund, has spent a billion dollars purchasing homes in the Tampa Bay area alone and has made a multi-billion-dollar investment in the foreclosure-to-rental industry as a whole.[20] An Urban Strategies Council study on foreclosure in Oakland, California, showed that nearly half of foreclosed homes purchased there after 2007 went to equity and hedge fund investors. According to a story in the *New Republic*, these hedge fund owners "make life really miserable for renters, especially in areas without strong tenant protections" like the typically underregulated suburban communities where a large proportion of post-crisis foreclosures took place.[21] One of the ways these new landlords create misery is by subjecting renters to the same kind of credit scrutiny that home buyers might face. For example, one of Blackstone's partners, Riverstone Residential, has partnered with credit-reporting-bureau Experian to compile a national database of tenant payment histories, which means, as an article in the *New*

Republic puts it—in figurative language apt for this chapter—that "one late rent payment could haunt a renter throughout his or her financial life."[22] Moreover, these rental revenues are being aggressively securitized in the same way mortgage revenue was securitized in the 1990s, with investors chasing high-risk assets and then attempting to render them more liquid through various techniques of financialization.[23]

When investors voraciously pursue high-risk/high-reward debt securities, they encourage mortgage brokers to seek out high-risk borrowers and charge those borrowers dangerously excessive interest rates as the price of credit; when those risky debtors default, property investors are able to speculate in the houses they leave behind and to fund those speculations by creating further risk-tranched securities on the basis of the rental income. Thus from the housing boom to the housing bust, the relationship between mortgage debt and housing property is now routed almost exclusively through risk-seeking forms of speculation. One consequence of this shift has been the remapping of both the national landscape of and the global market in US housing. The ubiquity of "reverse redlining"—a kind of discrimination by inclusion that produces a high-risk subprime population subjected to unpayable debt and inflated housing prices—has meant that the spatial grid of dispossession no longer looks quite as simple as it did in the days of white flight. In the later discussion of *Mother's Day*, for instance, I describe the reshaping of certain suburban and exurban peripheries from white, middle-class enclaves into impoverished subprime communities with high rates of unemployment, eviction, and default. Globally, as my account of *Dream Home* makes clear, the emphasis on market liquidity transformed US real estate into a form of global capital by turning concrete, rooted assets like homes into financial commodities.[24]

As a result of these changes in the US real estate market, dominant ideologies of property ownership have become incoherent, even contradictory. The rhetoric of owner responsibility is belied by the growth of large-scale, impersonal, speculative proprietorship, and the fantasy of the owner's sacrosanct right to resist trespassers is contravened by the increased likelihood that she will be evicted from her own property by door-busting cops. The fiscal stability purportedly made possible by property ownership is negated by the reality of subprime mortgages, while the supposedly sacred right of deed is destabilized by the chaos that results when mortgages are bundled and their titles change hands over and over again. Finally, the sentimental and nationalist logic of ownership is contradicted by the conversion of houses into liquid assets and investment opportunities.

The films addressed in this chapter take up the ways in which all these changes have transformed our cultural and affective relationship to the home. Drawing on the long association between the gothic genre and real estate, they expose the fears produced by contemporary housing insecurity, offering a subtle critique of the forms of population control that such insecurity produces and exploits. They refuse to see increased real estate market liquidity—the ability to treat houses and homes as purely speculative assets, transferable with a single keystroke—as an economically rational or socially salutary transformation. Moreover, they suggest that the collapse of conventional understandings of property rights might lead to more than just greater fear and disorder: such a crisis might also provide an opportunity to rethink the priority given to property as a social form.

House of Horrors

The relationship between real estate and horror film has deep roots.[25] From *The Uninvited* (1944) to *Pet Sematary* (1989), American horror films have long been interested in the uncanny transaction of purchasing a home. They have also long done so in historically specific ways: for instance, the particular popularity of the haunted-house film in the late 1970s and early 1980s—classics such as *The Amityville Horror* (1979, *The Shining* (1980), *The Hearse* (1980), *Poltergeist* (1982)—can clearly be attributed to the specific economic anxieties of a period of low growth and high inflation. Writing on *The Amityville Horror*, for instance, Stephen King details the film's "subtext of economic unease" and notes that "in terms of the times—18 percent inflation, mortgage rates out of sight, gasoline selling at a cool dollar forty a gallon—*The Amityville Horror* . . . could not have come along at a more opportune moment."[26]

Whereas *The Amityville Horror* spun out the anxieties of stagflation, the films discussed here dramatize the financialization of real estate markets and its consequences for the security of property ownership in a period of credit crisis. Produced in the midst of the post-crisis period—in a long aftermath in which foreclosures and other forms of dispossession appeared as the flip side of financial speculation—these films repurpose the standard tropes of the horror genre to explore the dangers of economic risk. While the formal mechanisms of suspense serve as an index of the somatic tolls of risk taking, the visual excesses of gore provide signs of financial contagion and toxicity. Locating gothic horror not in property itself but in the uncanny transactions that render ownership terrifyingly precarious, these films represent the shift from the commodification to the collateralization of property. They rewrite the demonic possession of the body and the home as the equally terrifying "repossession" of property. In them, the contractual form of the mortgage—a promise that binds the borrower more than the lender and that is immune to pleas for clemency based in sentiment or justice—becomes the dead pledge of debt under capital.

King's reading of *Amityville* tellingly invokes the facts and numbers specific to the economy of 1979: the rate of inflation, the cost of a mortgage, the price of fuel. Yet as King acknowledges, the film itself does not invoke these details; rather, they are its latent "subtext." It is only "*beneath* its ghost-story exterior" that *Amityville* unconsciously gives figurative expression to the economic anxieties of the period.[27] Like most critics on the genre, King suggests that horror film engages economic concerns symbolically or allegorically rather than mimetically. Indeed, horror's ideological effectivity is generally seen to depend on the way it renders historical processes only latently. In his seminal essay "Dialectic of Fear," Franco Moretti argues that Bram Stoker's *Dracula* and Mary Shelley's *Frankenstein* depict workers and capitalists "in disguise," through metaphor and allegory. Manifest ideology "does not show through" but is instead "filtered." Such figurativity—the fact that texts like *Frankenstein* do not explicitly address the relationship between labor and capital—allows horror narrative to "express an unconscious content and at the same time hide it."[28] Yet this tendency to hide historical or political content is also why horror is typically understood to be somewhat conservative. Thus, we find scholars of horror describing the genre's effort to "restore the rational, normative order" or to "bring things back to a more stable and constructive state."[29] Even in horror's treatment of historical and economic transformation, critics find an "orient[ation] towards the restoration of order" and a desire to "alleviate political-economic anxieties" and "domesticate . . . manage and sublimate" economic fear.[30] Although its indirection allows horror to express fears that might not otherwise be named, critics agree that the genre does so in the interests of catharsis and comfort rather than change and critique.[31] For Moretti, for instance, *Dracula* and *Frankenstein* express the fear of a radically divided society, but they also convey a desire to preserve rather than transform that society. Fear, in these novels, "is a means to obtain consent to . . . ideological values."[32]

The films I survey neither contain economic anxiety nor imagine a restored calculus for accountability. Nor do they filter or hide their economic content. Rather, they include strikingly specific expositions of economic changes and processes. The high price of particular commodities and the volatility of the market are not merely the ambient atmosphere or political unconscious of these films. They are the films' explicit content. *Mother's Day* and *Crawlspace*, for instance, speak explicitly to the relationship between speculation, gentrification, and the "opportunities" presented to investors by foreclosure. *Mother's Day* includes both a realtor and a mortgage broker, and *Crawlspace*'s patriarch is the head of lending at the foreclosing bank. *Drag Me to Hell* and *Dream Home* are even more wonkish: the latter tells us the specific prices of Hong Kong apartments, while the former advises us about the rate of interest on a US mortgage loan, and both films use phrases like "long-term debt restructuring," "trapped equity," "loan tenure," and "disclosure fraud." In short, these four films are not figurative responses to the housing boom and credit bust; they are explicit representations of it. Their almost obsessive inclusion of the figures and terminology of the speculative economy in real estate dramatizes the processes that also define that economy: the introduction of calculation, risk, and finance into all aspects of everyday life. The narrative they tell has all the power of reportage; it is a systemic account rendered with all the explicit, mimetic detail one would expect of a realist novel. At the same time, they draw on the particular, uncanny capacity of the horror genre to defamiliarize, to turn ideological comfort into embodied fear. Rather than simply perform what Fredric Jameson famously describes as "imaginary solutions . . . to social contradictions," they oscillate between the imagined and the real or between, as the opening credits of *Dream Home* put it, "true stories" and "crazy" nightmare.[33] As a result, the contradictions they explore appear at the level of both form and content—they are both representational and material—and, as with the ongoing credit crisis itself, there seems to be no resolution to them.

Caveat Emptor

There is nothing new about the home-invasion thriller, a subgenre of horror that dates to the 1950s and 1960s. Home-invasion narratives, not surprisingly, are typically understood to express anxieties concerning the ever-thinner line between public and private space, as well as fears of the world outside the safety of domestic space.[34] Despite its persistent popularity, however, the home-invasion thriller has had two peaks in terms of both sheer quantity and innovation: the 1970s and the mid-2000s.[35] These two apogees happen to map quite precisely onto record highs in the cost of housing: the mid- to late 1970s marked the first real estate boom in the postwar era, and the mid-2000s marked a historically unprecedented upsurge in home values. Like the haunted-house film, the home-invasion thriller quite clearly dramatizes fears and fantasies about the economics of real estate. I argue here that post-housing-crisis home-invasion films *Crawlspace* and *Mother's Day* indicate the shifting understandings of property and ownership consequent to the foreclosure crisis, a crisis in which one's investment of either sentiment or "sweat equity" in a property—or one's belief in the meaningfulness of the "ownership society"—is not enough to save one's home from foreclosure. These two films also convey the belief that the forced transfer of such property has socially catastrophic consequences. Figuring foreclosed homes as what real estate law calls "stigmatized property," property that a buyer might wish to avoid for reasons unrelated to its physical condition, *Crawlspace* and *Mother's Day* literalize the doctrine of caveat emptor in horrifying ways.

Crawlspace, released in 2013, opens with the tagline "Based on real life events." Although one should accept "based on" rather loosely, director Josh Stolberg has claimed that the film was inspired by an incident in Japan in which a man discovered an elderly homeless woman living in his closet and eating food from his refrigerator.[36] The plot of *Crawlspace* concerns the Gateses, a family of five, who have recently purchased their dream home. As the Gateses move their belongings into the house, they find that the previous owners, the Webbers, left behind boxes filled with children's toys and photographs. Watching the new owners cavalierly tosses these items into the trash, we cannot help recalling the more melancholic representation of the detritus of foreclosure represented by the photographs discussed in the previous chapter. When the Gates children ask their father about the items left behind, they learn that the two Webber children drowned in the family swimming pool and that soon after this tragedy the Webber family lost the house to foreclosure. The viewer, meanwhile, learns that the former owner, Aldon Webber, did not in fact move out of the house after the foreclosure sale and is living in the attic, determined to repossess the house and take the Gates children as substitutes for his own lost daughter and son.

A remarkably similar set of circumstances appears in *Mother's Day*, a remake of the infamous 1980 film of the same name directed by Charles Kaufman.[37]

The original *Mother's Day* is at once a B movie and a parody of B movies: in it, three women go on a camping trip and are captured by Ike and Addley Koffin, brothers in a criminal family run by their disturbed mother, who goads the boys into acts of increasing sexual violence. After two of the three women escape, they arm themselves and return to seek revenge against the brothers and their mother. Both a rape-revenge narrative and a "hillbilly horror" film, the original is a perfect example of what Carol Clover identifies as the "urbanoia" horror narrative, wherein "it is not just that the city men [or women, in this case] have more money than the country people; it is that their city comforts are costing country people their ancestral home."[38] Bousman's *Mother's Day* remake dramatically revises the plot of the original and dispenses with its parodic tone, though it too has its moments of self-consciousness (the casting of Rebecca de Mornay, famous for her turn as the evil nanny in *The Hand That Rocks the Cradle*, as the sinister Mother Koffin, for instance). The 2010 remake is a home-invasion thriller wherein the brothers Koffin (there are now three: Ike, Addley, and Johnny) have just committed an unsuccessful bank robbery. Seeking safe haven, they flee to their mother's house only to discover that Mother Koffin lost the house to foreclosure and that it is now occupied by new owners, Beth and Daniel Sohapi. The Sohapis are having a housewarming party with a group of friends, whom the Koffins quickly lock in the newly refinished basement. When Mother Koffin shows up, things take a more vicious turn as the Koffin family tortures and sexually menaces the Sohapis and their friends. Only two of the women—including Beth Sohapi—survive, and they go on to kill two of the brothers, in the process burning down the house. Much as *Crawlspace* revised a "true story" to create a narrative about ownership in the context of the post-crisis moment, Bousman's *Mother's Day* rewrites the original 1980 film, transforming its narrative from a story of rape and revenge into a meditation on what it means to live in a house lost to foreclosure.

Taken together, *Crawlspace* and *Mother's Day* indicate a fundamental tension in ideas of property consequent to the housing bubble and bust. These tensions can be located first in the rhetoric of the "ownership society," a discourse frequently invoked by President George W. Bush as justification for the vigorous pursuit of new home borrowers (through the deregulation of mortgage lending and the lowering of federal interest rates) in the wake of the economic crises of the early 2000s. "Owning a home is part of the American dream, it just is," Bush averred, "so somebody can say, this is my home, welcome to my home."³⁹ Bush's rhetoric makes property ownership identical not only with economic independence but also with sentimental attachment, moral legitimacy, and freedom. In a 2004 position paper in support of Bush's policy proposals, the Cato Institute likewise claims that "a system of property requires people to treat others with respect," an opinion for which they cite Locke and Aquinas as philosophical grounding.⁴⁰

Bush's emphasis on home ownership provided a ready metaphor for national exceptionalism in the insecurity of a post-9/11 world. It framed US citizenship through the logic of consumption, and the policies attached to this discourse boosted the consumer economy in the absence of real wage gains. But it also provided ideological cover for a set of institutional and economic transformations that actually made home ownership increasingly insecure and then turned that insecurity into a securitizable asset. When Alan Greenspan reflects in his memoirs that he "believed then, as now, that the benefits of home ownership are worth the risk," he frames the risks involved in deregulating mortgage credit as the price to be paid for the ideological benefits of property.⁴¹ In fact, however, the ideological utility of home ownership was itself merely a fringe benefit of Bush's and Greenspan's policies. The real point of these policies was to increase opportunities for restless speculative finance to take advantage of—and thereby increase—risk. Moreover, in the resulting foreclosure crisis, the sentimental rights that once appeared to naturally accrue to home ownership were superseded by the legal right of the mortgage holder to seize the home as collateral. The long-standing and distinctly American legal tradition of residential protectionism became the practice of preauthorized, nonjudicial foreclosure, through which banks can foreclose on owners without even bothering to go to court. Most of the new homeowners produced by Bush's and Greenspan's policies were able to purchase their property only because they had been offered mortgages in impossibly high amounts or with impossibly draconian terms. When those owners proved unable to repay their loans, banks were more than willing to unceremoniously deprive them of both their property and the "rights and respect" they had ostensibly earned. Thus, we note the cynicism in the suggestion by the Cato Institute that home ownership secures "respect" by creating the right of exclusion: "Owners have the right to exclude others from the use of what belongs to them."⁴² Read alongside the images of evictions that appear in the previous chapter, there is nothing self-evident about the association between inhabitation and the right to exclude if the entity you want to exclude is the bank that loaned you money to buy the house. Underlying the ideology of the ownership society is thus a deep contradiction between the ideology of ownership as stability, self-sufficiency, and social commitment, on the one hand, and the material reality of credit arrangements and foreclosure law on the other.

Crawlspace's subtle revision of the home-invasion genre captures this ideological torsion, pushing the violence of foreclosure to its horrifying extreme. The home-invasion film typically narrates the terrifying penetration of the inside by the outside—manifesting what Paula Cohen describes as "an increased fear of the erosion of distinctions between private and public space . . . a sense that the outside world is more dangerous and unpredictable than ever before."[43] But as *Crawlspace* opens, the killer is already—or, put better, still—inside the house. The home is thus occupied by two tenants simultaneously, an idea that is realized visually when Aldon, taking advantage of the Gates family's temporary absence, moves downstairs from the attic and places his own "Welcome" mat outside the front door. Indeed, *Crawlspace* is surprisingly unwilling to identify one of these two competing property owners as the "rightful" one. On the one hand, the film clearly seeks to secure our identification with the Gates family, who are Aldon's unwitting and seemingly innocent victims—the family's very name conveys the desire for the right of exclusion invoked by the Cato Institute, though ironically the Gateses' obsession with security systems and automatic doors also ensures that the menace remains inside. Yet the film also presents Aldon as a highly sympathetic claimant, both because of the horrifying fact of his children's deaths and because we eventually discover that Mr. Gates, who works for the bank that owned the Webbers' mortgage, took advantage of Aldon's financial distress to obtain the house for his own family.

The film treats this double occupancy as a problem without a clear solution by anxiously invoking competing philosophies of ownership. The family first realizes that something is wrong in the house when they discover that someone not in the family is taking out the garbage and closing the garage door. The work is being done, we soon discover, by Aldon, who keeps a to-do list posted in his attic hideaway. Aldon not only does small chores but also performs regular household maintenance like fixing the garbage disposal and the air conditioning, subtly implying that the performance of this labor expresses his legitimate claim to ownership of the house. We recall that the Lockean theory of property invoked by the Cato Institute holds that "no man but he [who mixes his labor with property] can have a right to what that [labor] is once joined to."[44] Aldon thus represents the idea of what is now called "sweat equity," a phrase that suggests the still-resonant, if now anachronistic, sense that there is a relationship between labor and the economic right to property. The film goes on to invoke not only the use-based imperatives of Lockean property theory but also what legal theorist Margaret Jane Radin influentially termed the "personhood" theory of property, which links property to the sanctity of the self and gives ownership sentimental justification.[45] When we see the new owners encountering the wall on which Aldon and his wife tracked their children's growth, we are made to understand that these marks constitute a morally, if perhaps not legally, legitimate form of territoriality: that through its sentimental association with the nuclear family, domestic property is an extension of the private self and that insofar as the house is a container for personal memories, it cannot simply be transferred intact to a new owner.

Although *Mother's Day* hews more closely to the conventions of the horror genre by consistently villainizing the Koffins, it contains an almost identical evocation of sentimental ownership, as Mother Koffin explores the house and comes across a room in the process of being renovated but in which a still-unpainted door frame shows the spot where she marked her children's growth on the wall. The film engages with the discourse of ownership and value throughout, most explicitly during a scene in which the Koffin boys are taking everything of value (jewelry, cell phones, wallets) from their captives. One of the women objects to turning over her ring by saying, "It belonged to my grandmother." Intervening, Mother Koffin allows her to keep the ring. "Oh wait," she tells her sons, "family heirloom. It's irreplaceable." Mother's defense of this small piece of personal property as nonfungible and particular, and her emphasis on the grounding of ownership claims in sentiment, is the logical extension of her belief that the Sohapis' house is likewise still rightly hers because it is where she raised her family. *Mother's Day* further explores the meaning of ownership by flipping the conventions of hospitality: on entering the house, Mother immediately begins to act as if she is the owner by treating the current occupants as her guests. Entering the basement, where the captives are lying on the floor, she announces (addressing first her sons and then the captives), "Sometimes you boys are just savages. I don't want you lying there on the floor. Please, make yourselves comfortable. Let's just talk. Please, sit down." Hospitality, as Derrida famously reminds us, is based not on pure generosity but on the principle of ownership, which is what allows one not only to exclude the stranger (according to the Cato Institute) but also to invite him in.[46] If property is the site of personal and familial memory, irreplaceable in its particularity (one can't transfer the wall on which one marked the height of one's children any more than one can replace a grandmother's ring), and if the responsibility that attends ownership is expressed through the requirement to welcome guests, then the Koffins are indeed the rightful owners of the house in which the Sohapis live, making the Sohapis the invaders.

Mother's Day adds one final noncontractual understanding of property, supplementing its account of property as sentimental attachment or as hospitality right with an older, even more antimarket theory of ownership. Replying to Addley's melancholic admission, "It's not our house anymore," for instance, Ike responds coolly and pragmatically, "It is now." Addley invokes the durational temporality of past ownership ("anymore"). But Ike, advocating the "now" of temporary expedience, insists on a view of property as a matter of pure utility: the house is their house for the moment because they need it right now, because they are using it right now, because they are in it right now. Ike's theory of property breaks from the liberalism of sentimental or social theories of property, offering instead an understanding of ownership as nonpermanent, noncontractual, and not oriented toward exchange—an understanding that the right to use something is based on that thing's concrete, and also potentially temporary, use value.

Aldon Webber's understanding of property as labor and as sentimental attachment, Mother's understanding of property as nontransferable value and the site of hospitality, Addley's understanding of property as temporal and personal, and Ike's view of property as primarily a matter of contingent need contradict one another. And yet what these contradictory understandings of property have in common is that they are all incompatible with the contemporary treatment of the house as fungible property and liquid investment. One result of a market glutted with cheap foreclosed homes has been that foreclosed properties have been bought not by owners intending to take up residence but by firms who operate as absentee landlords, acquiring thousands of homes and either kicking out the current renters or forcing them to pay higher rent.[47] Because these homes are owned in such large quantities, often by a hedge fund located across the country, they are possessed in a manner that doesn't guarantee upkeep, sentimental investment, or even use (many end up vacant and crumbling into disrepair). *Crawlspace* implies a critique of these kinds of equity owners—investors who exploit other families' hardships and who might not even care about the home they are buying—by making Mr. Gates a stand-in for the bank he works for and by emphasizing his inability to properly care for the property. Likewise, in *Mother's Day* we learn that the Sohapis were able to purchase the house because Beth is a realtor who "snapped it up before it went on auction." When Beth, fearing for her life, promises that she can "get the title back" to the Koffins, Mother Koffin replies, "Would that it were that easy, my dear." Mother Koffin is right for entirely literal reasons: it's unlikely that Beth actually can hand over the title, since it is probably held by her own bank or by the financial institution to which her bank sold her mortgage. Indeed, problems of title holding were incredibly common during the foreclosure crisis, as in cases of "zombie titles" in which owners were assessed fines or taxes on homes that had long before been repossessed by the bank. Given that the legal regulation of domestic property rights through deeds and contracts has failed in the post-crisis era, it is little wonder that older and more primitive meanings of ownership—from utility to hospitality, sentiment to labor—have come back to life like zombies.

In taking up competing theories of property and in framing these alternative understandings as responses to a failed regulatory regime and to the bankrupting of ownership society ideology in the wake of the crisis, *Mother's Day* and *Crawlspace* also inevitably lay the ground for a discussion of so-called squatters' rights, a legal and political claim that became particularly salient in the wake of the foreclosure crisis. A claim for squatters' rights—more properly termed "adverse possession"—is an attempt by the current user or possessor of a property to establish title without the express consent of the original legal owner. Legal scholarship on adverse possession imagines property as more than merely a fungible commodity mediated by markets and regulated by contract law. The doctrine of adverse possession originated in claims made by frontier homesteaders, but defense of the principle often involves other understandings of ownership rights as well, including some of those appealed to in *Mother's Day* and *Crawlspace*. Oliver Wendell Holmes's seminal justification of adverse possession laws, for instance, emphasizes the fact that "a thing which you have . . . used as your own, takes root in your being and cannot be torn away."[48] Likewise, another scholar suggests that the goal of adverse possession laws is to "mov[e] land into the hands of parties who value it more highly than do the record owners," implying that such transfers ought to be permitted when they benefit the community as a whole.[49] The conflict between the formal market understanding of property and these other views of property—the homesteader's justification of first possession, the ontological or embodied account of ownership that Holmes defends, the distributionist belief that everyone is better off when property belongs to someone who cares about it—returned in the wake of the housing crisis when former owners started squatting in their own foreclosed homes. These adverse possessors have variously claimed to be the "first possessors" of the property, to have "taken root" in its sentimental value, and to be helping the community by ensuring that the property is cared for.

The discourse around these contemporary cases has, perhaps not surprisingly, been largely negative, representing squatters as a threat to the community and as an illegitimate response to a housing problem. As Hannah Dobbz puts it in her study of property and resistance in the United States, "Horror stories [about adverse possession] cascaded into the news. Each story presented the property owners . . . as virtuous victims in unpredictable times, always blaming the squatters."[50] Yet *Crawlspace* and *Mother's Day* are actual horror stories that present a somewhat more ambivalent response. These films treat the social and ethical utility invoked by squatters—the benefit of making expedient use of abandoned property and the squatter's right to thereby prove an ownership stake in it—as a potentially meaningful social value. The articulation of this fairly radical position depends first on the films' capacity to secure some amount of viewer sympathy with the claimants. In *Crawlspace*, this sympathy emerges when Mr. Gates confesses his own malfeasance to his family. "I'm the one who foreclosed on [Aldon Webber]," he admits. "There were thirty ways I could have helped him get back on his feet and I chose to do nothing." This admission buttresses Aldon's claim to rightful ownership not just morally but also legally, since the doctrine of adverse possession is intended in part to protect owners against a competing claim to title based in fraud: his debt takes on a moral status something like the "odious debt" that in international law describes a national debt incurred by dictators against the will and interests of citizens. Much as Aldon's claim to ownership is validated by the immoral or possibly fraudulent circumstances that led to his foreclosure, real foreclosure squatters have argued that when a bank can no longer prove that it holds the title to a mortgaged property because it passed on the titles to the mortgages it bundled and sold as securities, the bank is no longer the property's rightful owner. Similarly, in *Mother's Day*, it turns out that Beth has been stealing from the Koffins: Ike, Addley, and Johnny were sending Mother Koffin money to help her pay the bills, including the mortgage, and when these envelopes full of cash appeared in her mailbox, Beth chose not to return them to their rightful owner but instead to sock them away as her own form of security. Because Beth has taken property that doesn't belong to her—thus helping ensure the foreclosure she was able to profit from—the Koffins have a legitimate right to protest her theft of their home by taking adverse possession of it.

Mother's Day offers one final meditation on ownership that allows us to understand the particular anxieties expressed by post-crisis horror. The plot hinges on a literal as well as figurative expression of the doctrine of caveat emptor, buyer beware. According to the tradition of caveat emptor, the purchaser of an asset is responsible for determining any potential problems with it, including those that could affect its ability to be resold. In the mid-twentieth century, the doctrine of caveat emptor was largely superseded in real estate law: since then, the law has tended to rule that the owner or realtor of a property is responsible for disclosing potentially adverse information about it.[51] The precedent remains murky, however, around instances of so-called stigmatized property: relevant stigmas include public stigma (the example typically given is the "real" Amityville Horror house, whose notoriety made it hard to sell); criminal stigma; and phenomena stigma, or haunted houses.[52] In fact, it was a 1989 case adjudicating a claim of phenomena stigma that set much of the precedent for distinguishing between the older doctrine of caveat emptor and modern requirements concerning realtor disclosure: given the connection between domestic property and the horror genre described here, it almost comes as no surprise that the language of the decision referenced the movie *Ghostbusters*.[53]

As these references to *Amityville* and *Ghostbusters* suggest, the law around property stigma often refers to horror films; so too, however, do horror films make reference to the problem of stigmatized property. In *Poltergeist*, for instance, an avaricious real estate development company built the house in question on top of sacred Native American land and burial grounds, recasting the film's treatment of the uncanny horrors of domestic real estate as a colonial allegory. The generic relationship between stigmatized property and the haunted-house film appears self-reflexively in *Crawlspace*: when the teenage Gates daughter learns that the two Webber children died on the property, she refutes her father's description of it as a "dream home" by saying it is "essentially built on an Indian burial ground!" *Mother's Day* even more clearly addresses the law around stigma disclosure in a scene in which a policeman, alerted to the escape of the Koffin brothers from the scene of the bank robbery and knowing their old address, knocks on the door of the Sohapis' house to check on them. With Addley Koffin's gun to his back, Daniel Sohapi opens the door to persuade the policeman that everything is fine. "Violent criminals lived in my house?" he says shakily. "You'd think they'd have to disclose something like that." "I'm not sure, sir," replies the cop; "you'd have to check with your realtor." Daniel's realtor is, of course, his own wife, which means (to use the lingo of the horror genre) that the disclosure fraud is coming from inside the house. Beth, putting her faith in the doctrine of caveat emptor and failing to disclose the property's history to her own husband, discovers that the "caveat" of caveat emptor is not just the threat of depreciating value but the threat of death itself. The film's figuration of this danger attests to the fear that property purchased after a foreclosure is similarly stigmatized, haunted both by the fact of its prior ownership—whose ghostly signs remain everywhere—and by the forceful withdrawal of rights from the former owners.

Under the law of disclosure, a final form of property stigma is known as "debt stigma." If the former owners have unpaid debts, collection agents may come aggressively looking for them at their old address and may not take no for an answer. Thus the stigma of the house in *Mother's Day* doubles back on itself: since Beth owes the Koffins the money she was able to get access to via her own change of address, they are not just debtors but also debt collectors. At once justified in their claim to the property and horrifyingly violent in the means through which they realize that claim—both owing and owed; invoking debts simultaneously legal, economic, and moral—the Koffins represent not only the problem of property but also the violent obligations imposed by debt. I return to these obligations in the discussion of payback at the end of this chapter.

Speculation and Liquidity

As these readings suggest, *Mother's Day* and *Crawlspace* are largely concerned with the home as a fixed asset: in the difference between real estate as a commodity and real estate as the site of sentiment and personal attachment, and in the various theories of property that emerge to mediate and complicate these various understandings of home economics. *Drag Me to Hell* and *Dream Home*, in contrast, are more specifically interested in real estate as a speculative asset and in the transformation of uncertainty into risk. These films expose the blurring between economic reason and financial risk, between rational desires and speculative excess, that occurs in a period of "irrational exuberance." They consider the ways risk seeking has been introduced into mortgage markets, opening up new opportunities for arbitrage among investors in capital markets. In particular, they dramatize the emergence of securitization as the defining logic of real estate investment by exploring both the metaphor and meaning of monetary liquidity.

Ben Bernanke described the securitization of mortgage financing as a "sea change" in contemporary markets, and his aquatic metaphor is apt given that the main effect of securitization is to increase asset liquidity: the speed with which assets can be sold with no loss or with which value can be transferred within an economy. For Bernanke, this increased liquidity is an unquestioned good, a belief he shares with a long tradition of classical and neoclassical economic ideology. As political economists Bruce Carruthers and Arthur Stinchcombe put it, "If exchange constitutes the elementary form of market life, liquidity means that exchange occurs easily and frequently."[54] The emphasis on the importance of liquidity shores up both the institutions of free markets and their ideology. Thus, laissez-faire rhetoric describes monetary liquidity as a means of social connection to present markets themselves as socially salutary. In *Wealth of Nations*, for instance, Adam Smith treats the circulation of money as equivalent to the blood pumped by the human heart, warning that blockages to the "blood vessel" of Britain's foreign markets were "very likely to bring on the most dangerous disorders upon the body politic."[55] Drawing on developments in anatomical science like William Harvey's 1628 treatise "On the Motion of the Heart and Blood," classical economists used the metaphor of liquidity to connect circulating money with both individual and collective well-being.[56] Likewise, neoclassical economists like Bernanke understand liquidity as among the greatest virtues of competitive markets, a figure for the benefits of economic flexibility and freedom and for the natural power of markets.[57]

As Bernanke's remarks also make clear, since Smith compared money to blood, all sorts of economic transformations have changed what we mean by liquidity: the creation of paper money, the removal of the dollar from the gold standard, the digitalization of currency. Until the contemporary securitization revolution, however, the one thing that remained fairly constant was the view that real estate was among the most illiquid of all assets. Fixed assets like homes are concrete objects literally rooted to the ground, and their value is highly dependent on their location. As political economist Kevin Fox Gotham puts it, "Real estate is by definition illiquid, spatially fixed and immobile, relatively durable and costly, and defined by local particularities and idiosyncrasies." In this sense, real estate poses a problem for capital, which "seeks to eradicate the local peculiarities and place distinctions that characterize the buying and selling of commodities and thereby eliminate the spatial barriers to the circulation of capital."[58] Mortgage securitization made this eradication of the concrete and the local possible, allowing illiquid assets like homes to be transformed into liquid ones. By making the market more liquid, securitization also made the mortgage market more global, creating a borderless market in the international flow of housing debt. Mortgage securitization, writes historian Louis Hyman, allowed "oil money from the Middle East [to] finance housing developments in the Mid-west." The truly global commodities of this period were thus not only Nike shoes and world music but collateralized credit card debts and mortgage-backed speculative instruments.[59]

Bernanke's enthusiasm about the sea change of securitization notwithstanding, flexible, swift-moving markets tend to cause material insecurity for most of the world's population. According to Pasanek and Polillo, securitization allows money "to acquire a momentum of its own, breaking down existing barriers and boundaries, dissolving traditional, sentimental, and sacred distinctions."[60] Liquidity's destructive power thus caused John Maynard Keynes to famously and controversially insist, "Of the maxims of orthodox finance none, surely, is more anti-social than the fetish of liquidity." Whereas for Smith liquidity was a figure for social connection through economic circulation, for Keynes capital in its most liquid state increases the violent volatility of an economic system in which pure self-interest—the desire "to outwit the crowd, and to pass the bad, or depreciating half-crown to the other fellow"—rather than the long-term good of the social whole rules the social world.[61] It is this non-neoclassical understanding of liquidity as antisociality that *Drag Me to Hell* and *Dream Home* take up. *Drag Me to Hell* does so by exploring liquidity's relationship to mortgage securitization while *Dream Home* considers the globalization of high-risk real estate investing.

Drag Me to Hell is a remarkably complex meditation on the link between risky investment and the insecurity of daily life caused by the conversion of homes into collateral for securitized credit. *Drag Me to Hell*'s protagonist is Christine, an ambitious young woman who works as a loan officer at a Los Angeles bank.

Pressured by her boss to get tough on her customers, Christine denies an elderly Eastern European woman named Sylvia Ganush an extension on her mortgage payment deadline. After a campily horrific fight scene that takes place in the bank parking lot, Mrs. Ganush curses a button she has pulled from Christine's coat. Christine soon learns from a fortune-teller named Ram Jas—whom she has to pay $50 for the information—that as long as she possesses the cursed button, she is doomed to be dragged to hell by a demon known as the lamia. Christine scrapes together enough money to purchase exorcism services, but the exorcism fails and she continues to be tormented by the lamia, who not only leads Christine to kill her cat and makes blood spew from her mouth but also causes her to lose out on a promotion at the bank. At the end of the film, Christine digs up the grave of the now-deceased Mrs. Ganush and shoves the button, sealed in an envelope, into the coffin, hoping that by passing the cursed object back to its original owner, she has prevented her fate. The plot as a whole thus is intimately concerned with mortgage financing, money, and the link between debt and payback.

Drag Me to Hell also has much to say about the relationship between liquidity and the mechanics of monetary circulation. Although it is primarily engaged with liquidity as the defining logic of contemporary mortgage financing, it underscores this interest with a very noncontemporary figure of liquid circulation: a rare coin. Early in the film, Christine gives Clay, her professor boyfriend, a coin she came across at the bank; Clay, an amateur numismatist, recognizes its value immediately: "It's a 1929 standing Liberty, and it's almost fully struck," he says in nerdy wonderment. "You found this in regular circulation at the bank?" This coin—which ends up changing hands a number of times over the course of the film's narrative, from Christine to Clay and back again—also serves as a figure for historical changes in what we mean by monetary liquidity. Prior to the virtualization of money, cash—especially the coin, which was less dependent on the potentially volatile fortunes of national banks and national economies than paper money—was the perfect expression of circulatory liquidity: even in Keynes's twentieth-century critique of liquidity, the central image is of the half-crown coin. As Deidre Lynch has argued, the circulating coin was once so central to the economic imaginary that in the eighteenth century it even had its own narrative genre, the "talking-coin narrative," a story narrated by a piece of currency. Talking-coin narratives, she suggests, imagined "a community of mutual dependence." Stories of coins' journeys from hand to hand produced a new sense of collective economic life—one forged through trust and interdependence—and thus humanized an economic system otherwise marked by risk, "affording the reader a kind of comfort." The talking-coin narrative was particularly effective in making monetary liquidity look like a social good rather than a form of dangerous risk: it took everything that was potentially frightening and seemingly asocial about liquid value—its impersonality, abstraction, and lack of particularity or context—and turned it into what Lynch describes as "a marker of social agreement."[62] Like Adam Smith's economic treatises, these fictional narratives treated coinage circulating within a country as a sign of economic health and connected this circulation to the forms of social trust and economic well-being ostensibly enabled by modern credit.

The coin in *Drag Me to Hell* both cleverly invokes this tradition and suggests the extent to which we have moved beyond it. The liquidity of cash typically depends on its capacity to be immaterial and impersonal. Clay, on the other hand, is excited by his coin's material specificity and its potential to be a personal asset rather than a medium of exchange. Whereas liquid currency's value depends on its ability to change hands, Clay's coin must be removed from future circulation to remain valuable, so he immediately seals the coin in a small white envelope to protect its value. (In fact, a 1929 standing Liberty coin isn't as valuable as Clay imagines, worth perhaps a few hundred dollars; a 1927 standing Liberty is worth far more, which suggests that Raimi chose the 1929 date intentionally as a nod to the resonance between the 2008 financial crisis and the crash of 1929.) Sealed off and put away, Clay's coin is no longer a meaningful form of circulating currency; instead, a platinum credit card represents his actual liquid wealth, and Clay proudly brandishes this card at psychic Ram Jas when he pays for Christine's fortune-telling session. The electronic money represented by Clay's credit card can be transferred across the globe instantaneously; compared to such perfect liquidity, Clay is right to see coins not as a measure of value but as a kind of historical curiosity. Whereas the talking-coin narrative produced a sense of spatial and social interconnection by treating money as a circulating medium coursing throughout the social body, Clay's credit card represents the dissolution of social space, the apotheosis of capital's drive toward placeless abstraction.

Far from allegorizing this economic content, *Drag Me to Hell* treats it quite explicitly, including a notably detailed account of Mrs. Ganush's transactions with the bank and, later, a parallel narrative in which Christine, who is competing for a promotion, is working out a much larger loan deal with a corporation seeking to expand into new markets. In the first scene following the opening credits, the film deploys the jargon of speculative investment to indicate the violence of real estate financialization. Mrs. Ganush thrusts a stack of papers at Christine and asks her to explain them; Christine replies, "The bank is informing you of their intent to repossess your property today." By describing Mrs. Ganush's house as a property that can be repossessed, Christine represents the home as a commodity whose possession is as precarious as it is alienated. Moved by Mrs. Ganush's plight, however, Christine approaches her boss, Mr. Jacks, and explains that Mrs. Ganush is on a fixed income and has almost paid off her thirty-year mortgage, translating her sympathetic response and moral hesitation into the language of quantification and contractual obligation. In response, Mr. Jacks shifts from Christine's description of the house as a commodity to a newer language of pure, liquid value. "Apparently we've already granted her two extensions," he explains to her, "and you know in this type of foreclosure we seize the trapped equity and the bank makes a sizable amount in fees." As the expression on Mr. Jacks's face slowly changes from irritation to greed, what Mrs. Ganush calls a "home" and Christine calls "property" is transformed into "trapped equity."

Mr. Jacks's use of the term "trapped equity" is significant not only because it is one of many moments in which the film uses highly specific professional language (elsewhere, for instance, we hear of "asset-based lending" and "long-term debt restructuring," terms whose specificity suggests the film's thematic interest in the particularities of the twenty-first-century credit economy). It is also significant because Mr. Jacks's use of the expression is slightly unusual. Typically, trapped equity describes a situation in which the owner of a home wants to access the home's value without having to sell it. Put colloquially, it is the condition of being "house rich and cash poor," of owning a valuable home in which you live but not having the money to pay for other needs or wants. Here, however, the "trap" that keeps the value of the equity from being realized is the physical house itself: Mr. Jacks and the bank want to make Mrs. Ganush's house liquid again, to make it a tradable asset easily exchangeable for other assets.

That this desire to liquidate Mrs. Ganush's home—to turn a concrete habitation into a profitable, fungible investment—is connected to the bank's own role in the financial economy becomes clear later on, as Clay's upper-class mother condescendingly imagines Christine's job as the dreariness of handling actual money: "With all that counting and repetition—it must get so tedious."

Clay's mother imagines that Christine is a mere functionary in the "nonexotic" or "vanilla" economy of cash deposits and personal withdrawals—the kinds of things local banks used to do prior to the Glass-Steagall Act of 1999, after which even small banks could go after the big bucks of speculative investment. But Christine corrects the error and restores her place in contemporary finance: she is not a teller but a loan officer on the verge of a major professional coup. Christine describes the "big loan" she has been working on: "Well, I was reading in the *Wall Street Journal* about this medical supply company who was looking to expand but didn't have the necessary liquidity. So I met with their CFO and presented him with a formula for restructuring some of their long-term debt." What Christine is describing is a company that wants to get bigger but has no money. By helping the company with its "debt restructuring," Christine wants to allow a business that has debt to go into even more debt, which is of course precisely the kind of arrangement that she denied Mrs. Ganush, who likewise had inadequate liquidity to make her mortgage payment. The reason the bank is interested in this kind of debt restructuring but not in the kind that would allow Mrs. Ganush to keep her house is that investing in corporate debt—helping a corporation become more "liquid," to use Christine's euphemism, by bundling the debt into a corporate debt derivative and selling it again—is risky enough that it is also immensely profitable. Debt securitization, Dick Bryan, Michael Rafferty, and Randy Martin point out, "give[s] a liquidity to capital as a social relation of value in movement" by making it possible for "the capital embodied in fixed or illiquid assets"—whether houses or boxes of medical supplies—to be "transformed into a fluid, competitively-driven capital."[63] For Christine's bank, the competitive profitability of helping the medical supply company go into more debt is precisely correlated to its riskiness. As the exorcist Christine and Clay hire puts it, "I must put myself at great risk, and I will not do this for free."

By positing a connection between liquidity and risk, *Drag Me to Hell* allows us to put a finer point on the particular form of economic horror that is the film's manifest content. The image of monetary liquidity as blood has a well-known antecedent in Bram Stoker's *Dracula*. In that novel, as in its later filmic adaptations, blood is the vital fluid whose circulation fuels both the social and the economic body: thus Moretti argues that Count Dracula represents the nineteenth-century fear of corporate monopolies. The relationship between the figure of the vampire and financial crisis also has a more contemporary resonance, reappearing in somewhat weirder form in journalist Matt Taibbi's 2010 description of Goldman Sachs as a "blood-sucking vampire squid."[64] For Taibbi, as for Stoker, such blood suckers steal the circulatory medium and deprive the economic body of its vital lifeblood: thus it appears as if social and economic well-being are endangered not by liquidity itself but by any obstacle to its flow. Taibbi's representation of "blood-sucking" banks hoarding money rather than allowing it to circulate freely ultimately reinforces the idea that the contemporary crisis was the result of the "drying up" of liquidity rather than (as was actually the case) a sign that the banks were insolvent.

Yet *Drag Me to Hell*'s connection between currency and bodies—between financial liquidity and vital liquids—differs from both Stoker's and Taibbi's representation of vampiric threats to circulation and is far less sanguine than the beating hearts and hydraulic engines imagined in the economic accounts of the eighteenth and nineteenth centuries. When Christine goes to Mrs. Ganush's house, hoping to apologize and have the curse revoked, she is admitted into the house by Mrs. Ganush's niece, who takes her downstairs to the basement. To her horror, Christine realizes that she has arrived at Mrs. Ganush's funeral, but as she tries to backs out of the room, she knocks over the coffin, which promptly falls on top of her. In perhaps the film's most infamous moment, Mrs. Ganush's corpse falls onto Christine as a cascade of grotesque liquid is expelled into Christine's mouth (Figure 4.1). Whereas Dracula bites and sucks, Mrs. Ganush gums and spews. Over and over in the film she emits saliva, mucus, embalming chemicals, and other noxious fluids. In an earlier scene, Christine herself becomes a horror image of liquidity, spewing copious blood from her nose. Mr. Jacks, who is standing in front of her, is drenched in blood, having apparently gotten the liquidity he had coming to him: "Did I get any in my mouth?" he asks frantically (Figure 4.2).

Whereas Dracula is frightening because he siphons off the circulatory medium, then, Christine is frightening because she spreads it around. Far from imagining liquidity as economic vitality, Raimi's film depicts liquidity as economic virality. From the perspective of financialization, pure liquidity is to be desired: it is liquidity that Christine's medical supply company lacks and that Mr. Jacks wants to restore to Mrs. Ganush's house. Yet for *Drag Me to Hell*, the liquids involved are not life fluids but death fluids, resembling the "toxic assets" that contaminated the portfolios of even risk-averse investors like pension plans and local governments. The film thus suggests that it is no longer possible to represent the speed and fluidity of value circulation as the lifeblood of the market. Instead, for *Drag Me to Hell* liquidity appears as Keynes described it: capitalism's most "anti-social . . . fetish."[65] Far from reassuring its audience of the stability and naturalness of a social body fueled by the exchange of currency and credit, *Drag Me to Hell* depicts an exchange in which monetary transactions threaten rather than support the social whole, in which the infinite fungibility of liquid value becomes the inevitability of toxic contagion.

Drag Me to Hell imagines the economy of liquid circulating capital through the smaller scales of individual transactions. *Dream Home*, in contrast, takes up the more systemic contradiction between the fixity of real estate and the liquidity enabled by securitization. In the film, this contradiction becomes the site of global economic contagion, a crisis that spreads virally not simply through the contagious effects of economic panic but also through securitization's liq-

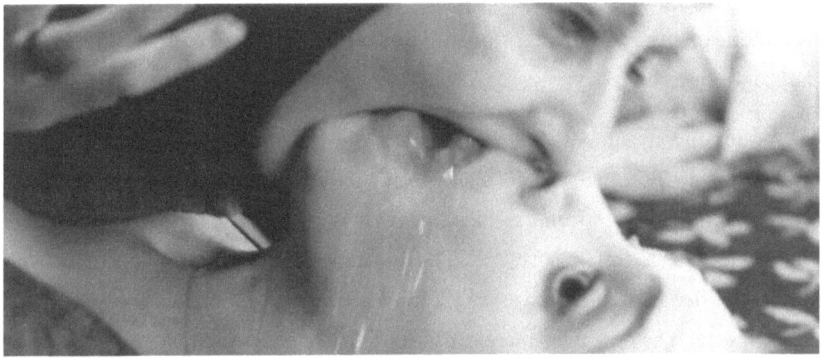

Figure 4.1. Mrs. Ganush attacks Christine, screenshot from *Drag Me to Hell*, dir. Sam Raimi, 2009

Figure 4.2. Mr. Jacks improves his liquidity, screenshot from *Drag Me to Hell*, dir. Sam Raimi, 2009

uid forms of value. *Dream Home*'s central plot concerns the events of October 30, 2007. Over the course of a few nighttime hours on this date, the film's protagonist, a seemingly meek young woman named Cheng Li-Sheung, kills eleven people in one apartment building: a security guard, a pregnant woman and her maid, the pregnant woman's husband, two young party boys, a drug-dealer, two prostitutes, and two cops. The rest of the narrative flashes backward and forward over the course of Sheung's life prior to her killing spree. We are given the story of Sheung's childhood, between 1991 and 2002, as she grows up in one of the city's public housing developments and as her family faces the likelihood of being forced out of their home by property developers. In the sequences set in 2007, we see Sheung as a young woman working two part-time jobs—as a bank telemarketer and a salesgirl at a shop—while she also attempts to purchase a luxury flat in the high-priced high-rise No. 1 Victoria Place, the "dream home" of the film's title.[66]

The film opens with a rather surprising screen text, which foregrounds its treatment of the Hong Kong housing bubble as neither secondary contextual material nor as allegory:

> A 2007 survey shows that the average monthly income of Hong Kong people is HK$10,000. But there are still 24% of people who aren't up to that line yet. Since the handover, HK's income rate has increased by 1%, but in 2007 alone, house prices shot up by 15%. In HK, a flat of 600 sq. ft costs more than HK $7 million. Flats with harbor view can reach HK$30,000 (US$3,200) per square foot. In a crazy city if one is to survive he's got to be more crazy. This is based on a true story.

The detail and specificity of the statistics about the Hong Kong housing market are striking. The numbers here provide an impressively thorough account of the boom in Hong Kong. They aptly link economic changes to "the handover"—the transfer from British to Chinese sovereignty in 1997—and place the increased cost of housing in the context of wage stagnation (the negligible increase in the income rate). In observing that a quarter of the population is effectively living in poverty, the title sequence explicitly draws attention to Hong Kong's growing income gap. Ultimately, the "true story" the film claims to be based on is not a story at all but the economic context itself: as Pang states in an interview, "It's true that many people would like to buy a flat in Hong Kong. But the plot and the killing scenes are fictitious."[67] Although we are all accustomed to postmodern play with the fiction-fact distinction, Pang's claim here remains noteworthy. The familiar invocation of "real-life" events—a commonplace in the post–*Blair Witch* horror film—is separated from the actual events of the plot and applied instead to the horror of the market itself. The economy thus appears not merely as part of the film's allegorical unconscious but as the narrative's central and explicit preoccupation.

The history *Dream Home* narrates also points toward both the ideological parallels and the direct links between financialization and housing speculation in the United States and in Hong Kong. The Hong Kong government derives high premiums through public land auctions and by taxing property trades; by 1997, real estate taxes accounted for 50 percent of annual public revenue in the region.[68] Although public housing was for many decades the main source of housing for residents of Hong Kong, in recent years the government and real estate developers have succeeded in representing home ownership as a traditional element of Chinese culture.[69] As in the United States, in Hong Kong there is now a "pervasive and deeply ingrained set of pro-homeownership values with various newspaper columns and regular television programmes focusing on home purchase."[70] Yet it has become more and more difficult for Hong Kong residents to purchase homes, as inflated prices, slow wage growth, and a 70 percent loan ceiling make it very hard for first-time buyers to enter the market.[71] As a result, the most sought-after buyers of property are "cash-rich Chinese corporate and individual investors purchasing houses outright," a situation that serves only to amplify citizens' sense that buying a house in the city is a speculative investment.[72] Housing scholar Chan Kam Wah observes that because of the soaring values of real estate, "individual households . . . treat buying and selling real estate as a central part of their investment activities (and life worlds)." The cultural impact of the ongoing real estate bubble has thus been felt not merely in the demand for homes but also in the transformation of speculation into a "way of life."[73] As Helen Hau-ling Cheng notes in her analysis of Hong Kong real estate marketing, "Since flats are traded so often, there is no clear-cut boundary between property as home and as investment, or between buying property as home-making and as making a fortune," and "the belief in the upward movement of property prices seems unshakable."[74]

In an essay about the relationship between economic and political change in Asia and Hong Kong martial arts cinema, Bhaskar Sarkar has tied the "postmodern excess" of Hong Kong cinema to "the intense pace of [economic] transformation" that followed the so-called Asian miracle. The dizzying speed of

Hong Kong action films, he argues, represents the region's sense of a loss of control, rendering it as a kind of affective and aesthetic "hysteria."[75] There is no doubt that Pang's film indexes the dislocation produced by high-speed political economic transformation, but it also offers a somewhat more specific type of hysteria: Alan Greenspan's idea of "irrational exuberance," influentially cited by Robert Shiller to describe the collective enthusiasm for a particular form of investment, whether tulips or tech stocks, that characterizes—and then fuels—an asset bubble. Yet the film also refuses to turn this irrationality into an individual affect, as behavioralists like Shiller and Greenspan do; rather, irrational exuberance is tied to the volatile, risk-seeking hysteria of the market itself and, formally, to the filmmaker's frenetic attempt to incorporate the meaningful systemic details of the economy as a whole. Although the film as a whole is noticeably minimal in its use of dialogue, it teems with an excess of numbers and information. For instance, we hear how loans at Sheung's bank are managed, including interest rates, monthly payment amounts, and the kinds of credit reporting used; we are told how much Sheung earns per loan currently and how much she might earn at another bank; we are privy to extensive conversations about the bureaucratic process around insurance and real estate; we learn not just that the Hansheng Index is at a historic high but also what that high is (31,638). The film thus seems to use this excess of numerical detail to suggest that the prices themselves, inflated as a result of the speculative bubble, are illogical and immoderate: its lavishly "inflated" use of detail blurs the distinction between rational and excessive costs inherent in the very concept of irrational exuberance.[76]

Moreover, in an amazing ironic twist, Sheung's violence does not ultimately express the hysterical desire of the naïve consumer. Instead, it is a form of market rationality, since her violence enables a basically rational price correction. After she has killed the last of her victims, the film cuts to the following day, and we see her receiving a call at work from her realtor. The owners of the flat, who earlier attempted to raise the price by 50 percent over the course of a few hours, have now agreed to "cut the price to HK$4.9 million." A smile begins to play across Sheung's face as she informs the agent that she has just read in the paper that eleven people were murdered in the building the night before; it is only then that we realize that she embarked on her killing spree with a single purpose in mind: to lower the price of the apartment by stigmatizing it and dampening demand. Coolly, she offers HK$3.9 million. When the sellers' agent begs her to reconsider a better deal, she replies, "In fact all my friends think even at

3.9 million I must be crazy to accept it." Like a speculative arbitrager, she takes advantage of a fast and momentary drop in the price, acquiring the apartment for less than the estimated value. In *Dream Home*, the apotheosis of financial logic is violence: the irrationality of speculation, the film suggests, produces violence as the consequence of risk seeking yet also renders it a corrective force.

Dream Home addresses the relationship between liquidity and dispossession by connecting both of these economic forces to the haunted atmospherics that attend rapid urbanization. Through the work of financialization and credit securitization, the concrete local specificity of real estate is turned into abstract universal equivalence. Liquidity thus becomes a quality not just of money but of the entire urban landscape under a regime of speculative capital, as the turn toward a more volatile, speculative real estate market enables destruction and dispossession. The effect of this transformation of asset fixity into monetary liquidity on Hong Kong—the effect, that is, of both securitization and frenzied asset speculation—is figured in *Dream Home*'s visual aesthetic. The "dizzying" speed of economic transformation Sarkar describes reappears in the film's sense of vertical spatiality. At one point, for instance, the film's narrative moves backward into 1997 for a silent scene of fewer than thirty seconds in which all we see is the reflection (in a window) of buildings falling. This shot is mirrored a few minutes later, when the transition from 1999 to 2004 is represented with a sped-up image of a row of tenements being slowly shadowed by a rising construction crane. These images capture not only the liquid speed of circulating value but also the spectral shadows of what that value displaces, allegorizing what is euphemistically called "capital flight," the deterritorializing process through which capital first transforms the solidity of production into the air of speculative capital and then flies off, abandoning one region or one form of accumulation for another.

The film also creates a stark visual contrast between the relentless verticality of the Hong Kong skyline and the claustrophobia of the city's interior spaces, a contrast that heightens the sense of the historical contradictions the film indexes. Despite the magnificence of the Hong Kong skyline and despite the city's incredible construction boom, both housing precarity and substandard housing conditions have become a way of life there. Fewer and fewer citizens can afford property in their own city, and as many as one hundred thousand are currently estimated to live in "cage homes": actual cages measuring six feet long and three feet high that are piled on top of one another and for which renters pay the equivalent of around $200 a month.[77] Given this context, in the end it's not so surprising that, as the film's American tagline puts it, "In a cut-throat property market, [one] would kill for a harbor view."

Although the last scene of the film shows Sheung happily moving into her new apartment, in the final shot before the film cuts to black, she stares out the window and listens to the following newscast:

> America's subprime mortgage crisis, triggered last July, has now spread globally. Financial firms on both sides of the Atlantic have been proven vulnerable, resulting in a global stock market crash. In the US, more borrowers can't keep paying their mortgage. Major companies such as UBS, Citibank, Merrill Lynch, Morgan Stanley, and Lehman Brothers have recorded huge losses. The subprime mortgage crisis could trigger a credit crunch, bringing about recession in businesses and property markets not just in the US but the entire world. Investment opportunities in 2008 look very gloomy. Under these circumstances, the market is extremely volatile, but the worst is yet to come.

These lines mark a shift in scale, from the microeconomics of individual home ownership (as represented by Sheung's violence) to the ways in which those economic transactions fuel and are fueled by a global economy whose agency and interests are as unlocatable, unfixed, and diffuse as contemporary currency itself. They suggest that a view of the relationship between liquidity and credit necessitates a global understanding of an economic totality, one that might see credit and debt not only as the means through which capital extends and revives itself but also as the economic form most likely to create and exacerbate crisis. Indeed, the film offers us an impressive "high-rise" view of the global economic system: despite the specificity of its Hong Kong context, *Dream Home* is unique among the four films considered here in attending to the global context of real estate speculation and securitization, which it captures by drawing attention, in these final lines, to the relationship between East Asia and the United States. Although the standard narrative of the 2007–8 financial crisis typically emphasizes the United States as the origin of both the real estate bubble and the techniques of financialization that underwrote it, many of these changes occurred first in Asia.[78] East Asia as a whole was central to and a leader in neoliberal expansion, and its financial markets became the primary site of direct US investment in the mid-1980s; by the time of the handover in 1997, the Hong Kong Stock Exchange was entirely dominated by finance and real estate.[79]

Moreover, because of this interconnection between the two economies, the US financial crisis affected the Hong Kong property bubble in a seemingly paradoxical way, causing the further inflation of housing prices. The US financial rescue packages injected trillions of dollars of cash (largely through "quantitative easing," designed to increase global liquidity and open up credit markets) into the global economy, and much of this capital has flown to Hong Kong via China. In a climate of market volatility, many US investors have felt that Hong Kong real estate—highly liquid, highly profitable—is a good place to keep their cash. The global financial crisis has thus pushed the Hong Kong housing market beyond all possible limit, and most market analysts see it as poised for a devastating crash. The *Economist* estimated that as of 2012, property in Hong Kong was 58 percent above fair value, making it the second most overvalued market in the world.[80] Thus, Sheung's once stigmatized property is, by the end of the film, again accruing value and becoming increasingly liquid. Yet higher interest rates in the United States (Hong Kong currency is pegged to the US dollar) or a crisis in the Chinese economy would cause prices in Hong Kong to crash, with consequences not only for the Hong Kong and Chinese economies but global markets as well. When in December 2015 the Fed raised US interest rates for the first time since 2008, home sales in Hong Kong plummeted, dropping to the lowest levels since researchers began tracking them in 1996. Remarking on the likelihood of a coming bust in Hong Kong, one economic journalist produced a flurry of provocatively mixed metaphors: "If and when this global housing weakness crosses back into the Chinese border, all bets about the Chinese economy will be off . . . as China does everything in its power to keep the house of $30 trillion in cards from toppling and sending a deflationary tsunami around the entire world."[81] If the image of a house of cards is a figure for the instability of real estate built from perilous, vertical risk, the image of the tsunami suggests the fear that the liquidity preference will wash the market away.

From this global perspective, there is no easy resolution to the bad weather or contagion of financial crisis. Appropriately, then, *Dream Home* refuses to provide an easy narrative resolution—instead, it gestures immediately toward its own unresolved future: a future still not yet reached, a future in which "the worst is yet to come." Issuing from an unseen radio or television, these lines are more diegetic than the film's opening text but still disconnected from any locatable body, spoken instead as if from the mouth of a narrative deus ex machina.

In the film's final moments, the economy itself gains structural agency, becoming the film's ultimate villain. The economic system no longer even needs to be personified (à la Stoker's Count Dracula) but rather simply lurches into view in all its monstrosity, the way a conventional horror film might end with a final shot of the slain villain once again rising from the grave. Because this villain cannot easily be vanquished, *Dream Home* refuses to produce the cathartic relief associated with horror, making it impossible for us to "com[e] contentedly to terms with a social body based on irrationality and menace," as Moretti would have it.[82] Without such a symbolic representative whose punishment (or redemption) could allow us to repress again the fear of financial crisis, we are left instead with an unresolved awareness of systemic economic violence.

Paying Back and Getting Even

The connection between the logic of debt and the logic of revenge is long-standing.[83] In the modern credit economy, however, the association between paying back and payback had to be insistently disavowed. As the idea of restorative justice replaced the retributive violence of the blood feud, the development of modern, contractual forms of credit and debt was supposed to supersede debt slavery and other forms of economic violence. The ideological insistence on modern credit as a form of exchange based on trust, confidence, and social cohesion depended on credit's separation from both the language and the logic of vengeance. However, these relationships of trust continued to be secured by excessive and violent forms of social and state coercion, a coercion partially enabled by the turn toward contractualism in law. As Amanda Bailey notes, the introduction of imprisonment as a state-mediated alternative to retaliatory violence did not actually serve to delink the right of revenge and the failure to repay, since "even those who maintained that imprisonment was intended to secure custody of inmates' bodies rather than enact retribution acknowledged that an insolvent debtor was useless to his creditor who could use the objectionable conditions of prison as a means to exact revenge." Debt, in short, was always an obligation secured "in terrorem."[84]

This link between debt and the fear of reprisal profoundly shapes the four films discussed here. The introduction of speculative risk makes it clear that credit is neither balanced obligation nor a form of mutuality. Because debt both underwrites private domestic property and makes ownership relations more precarious—whether the danger of the subprime loan or the threats of dispossession that attend both bust and boom periods—these films also reveal the risk and violence that inhere in a system where the very roof over one's head is subject to the insecurity of private ownership. Yoking the economic act of paying back to violent acts of payback, these films thus reimagine credit as social violence rather than social cohesion. In their various narratives of personal payback and historical reprisal, the films make clear that the social force of credit contracts depends not on the promise of trust but on the threat of revenge.

In *Drag Me to Hell*, debt and revenge are treated as part of the same excessive exchange economy. At first it seems as if the final revenge is Christine's on Mrs. Ganush, since the film's penultimate scene shows Christine digging up Mrs. Ganush's corpse and shoving what she thinks is the button Mrs. Ganush cursed into her mouth. The image of Christine emerging from Mrs. Ganush's grave triumphant and mud splattered clearly and cleverly references the classic horror movie trope that Carol Clover famously terms the "final girl," the heroine with whose suffering we are led to identify both narratively and visually.[85] Yet the film does not end here. Thinking she has defeated her enemy, Christine happily goes to meet Clay for a romantic train voyage. On the train platform, she embraces Clay and tells him (in words that almost directly echo Mr. Gates's confession to his family in *Crawlspace*), "I could have given Mrs. Ganush an extension on her mortgage payment, and I didn't. The choice was mine, and it was wrong." She shows off the new coat she has just impulsively bought for herself and tells him she threw the old one away. "Well that's too bad," he says, "because I found this in the car after you left last night" and takes out the cursed button. Christine immediately realizes that she has not "paid back" Mrs. Ganush the button after all. As she recoils from him in horror, she falls onto the tracks just as a train comes barreling toward her. The ground beneath her opens up, and she is pulled into a fiery pit by the hands of demons. As the film ends with a smash cut to the title screen, it becomes clear that the story has concluded with the punishment that Christine (and the viewer) thought she had avoided. The sudden and irreversible horror of these final shots suggests that Christine is not the film's avenging heroine but its villain, subject to the violent retribution that is the debtor's only recourse. *Drag Me to Hell*'s revenge narrative is not Christine's but Mrs. Ganush's, and the payback of the victimized mortgage holder on the villainous banker who refused to grant her clemency implies that proper payback is not the restitution of the creditor but the payback of the debtor on the creditor.

Whereas *Drag Me to Hell* imagines the link between revenge and *repossession*, *Dream Home* uses the structure of payback to avenge a prior act of *dispossession*. In his writing on land speculation, Jameson remarks that only in Hong Kong has he ever heard of haunted high-rises. The idea of ghosts haunting a building that itself has no past, according to Jameson, suggests a nostalgic "wish to be haunted" and a longing for history.[86] However, *Dream Home*'s representation of a Hong Kong high-rise whose residents are imperiled by an assassin with ghostlike stealth gives a somewhat different answer, connecting the logics of speculative possession that attend contemporary real estate development to the history of territorial displacement. In the film's flashback sequences, we learn that Sheung's family was forced out of their apartment by an alliance between the government and the Triads, a Chinese crime syndicate described by Mike Davis as "the major informal property developers in Hong Kong," whose collaboration with the state made it possible to "fre[e] up the maximum surface area for high-rise offices and expensive market-price apartments."[87] Sheung's grandfather warns, "Hong Kong is going to be hijacked by property developers soon," to which her father replies, "What 'soon'—they've fucking done it already." Over the course of the film we realize that Sheung's fixation on buying an apartment in this particular building, No. 1 Victoria Place, stems from the fact that it was built on precisely the spot where her grandfather, a former sailor, used to look out to the ocean before they lost their home to the developers. Her desire to reclaim this lost past takes the perverse form of a desire for precisely the object that displaced it: a home in the expensive high-rise developments built on the ruins of the harbor tenements in which she grew up. Sheung herself thus functions as what Bishnupriya Ghosh describes, in an essay on real estate horror in South Asian cinema, as the "concrete remainder" that spectral capital seeks to replace with shimmering high-rises and liquid value. In this way, *Dream Home* depicts the consequences of transforming collectively held resources—whether natural, as in the case of the sea and the air, or built, as in the case of the state-subsidized housing destroyed by Hong Kong's land speculation boom—into private assets.[88] In contrast to the Bollywood films of Ghosh's analysis, however, in *Dream Home* Sheung is a threat that cannot be "reasoned away" or "relocated": she may represent the "return of the repressed," but she is not going anywhere, and the property itself is always already stigmatized by this prior violent displacement. Sheung terrorizes the residents of No. 1 Victoria Place, whose very possession of this property indicates their guilt, in order to fulfill her historical obligation to exact revenge on behalf of her family. As in *Drag Me to Hell*, *Dream Home*'s payback model does not suggest that the debtor is a wrongdoer who owes amends to the creditor; rather, here the debtor is an avenger who owes a debt of blood on behalf of others. The revenge that Sheung exacts makes no distinctions and offers no reprieve or respite, forcing not only the property owners but the property market itself to pay the price for her family's dispossession.

Mother's Day uses the home-invasion genre to suggest a related concern over the shifting spatial dynamics of white flight, suburbanization, and gentrification. Carol Clover discusses the original 1980 version of the film as an instance of the "city/country horror," which "takes as its starting point the visit or move of suburban people to the country" and in dramatizing "the revenge of the [city] woman on her [country] rapist" also dramatizes "the revenge of the city on the country."[89] The remade *Mother's Day* both recalls and rewrites the city/country horror film's dramatization of a violent encounter between classes. The Sohapis repeatedly frame their move to the Koffins' house and neighborhood as a move out of a psychically destructive urban space: "I *had* to get out of the city," Beth says repeatedly. That the Sohapis are complicit in the economic destruction of the nonurban, as Clover argues in her account of the urbanoia genre, is true in more than a merely structural way in the 2010 *Mother's Day*, since it is literally Beth's fault that the family has no money because she was the one who took it. Like the films of Clover's account, Bousman's *Mother's Day* also evokes a still older story of real estate plunder: genocide, land expropriation, and other forms of violent primitive accumulation.[90] The first dialogue between the Koffins and the Sohapis is an exchange between Daniel and Addley, where the former asks, "What the hell are you doing in my house?," to which Addley replies, "What the hell are *you* doing in *our* house, pilgrim?" If Daniel Sohapi is a pilgrim, it seems that Ike and Addley and Johnny represent what Clover describes as the twinned "redneck"/"redskin": despite their claim to be literally the "first possessors" of land and home, the Koffins' primitive violence robs them of their right to formal ownership, making it appear as if they, not the Sohapis, are the intruders on another's property.[91]

But why does *Mother's Day* take pains to remind us that the Sohapis are from the city while erasing all the "country" qualities the Koffins had in the original? The Koffins in the remake are not, after all, presented as the "threatening rural other" that Clover identifies in the original. Comparing the images of

Mother Koffin in the two films, we see that the wild-haired "hillbilly" granny of the 1980 film could, in the 2010 version, be any mini-van-driving soccer mom (Figures 4.3 and 4.4). And why does the remake take place not in the isolated rural landscape of the original but in the suburbs? After all, we would hardly describe the suburbs a space where, as Clover puts it, "the rules of civilization do not obtain," nor are the suburbs typically associated with decay, incivility, and poverty, as rural space often is.[92] How can the Koffins represent the racialized Other to the white, urban, moneyed Sohapis, given that the phrase "threatening *suburban* Other" does not seem particularly resonant?

Unless, of course, it is. As Alex Schafran points out in an important essay on media and the suburban housing crisis, in 2008 it became apparent that the financial crisis "was not just about Wall Street or Main Street, but about Elm Street, that quintessential American street found in towns across the metropolis. And it certainly was a nightmare."[93] Schafran's invocation of horror film—which should by now be familiar to us as the exemplary discourse of the housing crisis—suggests that whereas the city/country relationship functioned effectively as a metonym for rich/poor (and for white/nonwhite) in the 1970s and 1980s urbanoia films of Clover's account, this spatial dynamic has been transformed by the contemporary housing crisis. Schafran's description of the effects of the housing crisis on areas neither cosmopolitan nor rural also suggests the extent to which it is now impossible either to consign one's economic and racial Other simply to the country or to assume that the exploited periphery is always a space of underdevelopment. Economic growth and relatively cheap credit made suburban home ownership possible for black, Latino, and working-class families once excluded from these spaces, although often under subprime terms that made repayment difficult if not impossible. After the crash of the housing market, homes in these exurban communities plummeted in value, losing all of the value they had gained in the housing boom and increasing the wealth gap between an affluent urban core and a suburban periphery that had in many cases already been the site of sustained disinvestment over the last two decades.

Read across the two versions of the film, the Koffin family's journey from rural space to the suburbs to homelessness thus allegorizes the history of what has been called "reverse redlining," or discrimination by inclusion. Moving from rural poverty to the relative stability of a twenty-first-century middle-class suburb, the Koffins became not an excluded but an included Other. Once

Figure 4.3. Mother Koffin as hillbilly, screenshot from *Mother's Day*, dir. Charles Kaufman, 1980

Figure 4.4. Mother Koffin as suburban housewife, screenshot from *Mother's Day*, dir. Darren Lynn Bousman, 2010

they were unable to continue to pay the mortgage on this home, however, they were deprived of any claim to land or property, and they end the film as the mobile homeless, living in their van. From this perspective, the relationship between the Koffins' displacement and the Sohapis' profit exposes a link between finance and territorial land grabs, between possession and dispossession. In its departure from the original 1980 original, *Mother's Day* dramatizes the racialized and class-specific anxiety produced by the entrance of nonwhite and working-class families into spaces from which they were once excluded. It also attests to the fact that as redlining becomes a logic of inclusion, the affluent white homeowner is ever more likely to have to confront the consequences of the gentrification or dispossession in which she is complicit. Under these conditions, it is little wonder that the ultimate revenge of the film is the Koffins' on the Sohapis. Like Christine in *Drag Me to Hell*, Beth Sohapi is no triumphant "final girl." Rather, the film ends with the remaining Koffins reunited, plotting their revenge on Beth. Like *Dream Home*, *Mother's Day* uses the revenge drama to think about revenge not simply as personal reprisal but as a kind of historical redress. The revenge of the debtor's own payback is as cumulative as financial risk and as mobile as liquid money; it has neither end nor outside but is the logic of dispossession turned back on itself. The "red line" this payback draws across the landscape of expropriation does not mark the exclusions and inclusions mapped by bankers and brokers, politicians and planners, but is a demarcation of blood and fire.

In their explorations of the social relations mediated by twenty-first-century forms of credit and debt, these economically informed horror films argue that the credit economy itself depends not on formal equality and "balance" but on the unrelenting excess of retribution. They emphasize the gap between a narrative economy of resolution and a credit economy of retribution by refusing the notion that horror films and revenge narratives must end in the restoration of order and balance. *Dream Home*, *Drag Me to Hell*, *Mother's Day*, and *Crawlspace* give us powerful insight into why twenty-first-century economic discourse seems so haunted by a language of horror: only through such terrifying imagery can we adequately represent a credit economy in which risk and fear are a source of profit. They suggest that it is now less and less possible to see debt as anything other than a socially destructive force. Under a regime of securitization and exploitable risk, of expropriation and eviction, credit no longer appears as balanced obligation or mutuality.

By delineating contemporary transformations in the economics, demographics, and ideology of private property—one visible only with the collapse of property values and the crisis in credit that caused that collapse—these postcrisis films also reveal a longer, more continuous fact about the relationship between property, political economy, and violence. The Cato Institute's favorite philosopher of ownership, John Locke, famously argued that private property both defines and defends itself against "fears and continual dangers."[94] In these films such fears and dangers are part of the very constitution of property, and there is no defense against them. The righteous revenge exacted by the films' debtors is not simply vengeance against their particular creditors. It is also an attempt to get payback on the entire economy of private property underwritten by credit and debt, an act that refuses both calculation and closure. Understanding that the debt economy of the present exploits a fear of reprisal rather than a sense of social obligation, it seizes on debt's dead pledges and makes them its own.

Coda
The Living Indebted (on Students and Sabotage)

Contemporary debt, this book has argued, no longer appears as a form of exchange that reinforces social cohesion.[1] In an age of securitization, speculative risk, and default, credit cannot function as a form of balanced obligation or mutuality. To be in debt today—to owe one's livelihood to the willingness of a bank to extend credit, to owe the roof over one's head to a lender who can take one late payment as cause for eviction—is to be caught in an endless cycle of discredit and dispossession. Thus, in the twenty-first century, credit and debt are no longer two reversible perspectives on the same circular exchange (money passing from lender to borrower and back again); rather, they represent two fundamentally antagonistic subject and class positions. Today, most of us number among the ever-growing hordes of the living indebted. While the previous chapters have sought to show the different ways this widespread condition of indebtedness has taken cultural form, they have also tried to remind us that debt itself is not cultural or representational, that it is not merely made of words or a matter of perspective. Though we think through debt at the level of culture, we nevertheless live it—and can only hope to contest it—on a more strictly material plane. With that in mind, I conclude by moving from the realm of cultural representation to the realm of political action to highlight the practical and tactical actions and affiliations that remain available to those of us for whom a life of debt is not the only life we wish to know.

Consider, for instance, just one way that the aesthetics of uncanniness and horror (as discussed in Chapters 3 and 4) uncannily prefigure a more material genre of housing violence. Soon after the foreclosure crisis began to wreak havoc on homeowners and renters alike, reports emerged about the willful destruction of homes being foreclosed. Sometimes these incidents were merely the collateral damage inflicted when dispossessed owners attempted to remove objects of possible salable value from the home: appliances, electrical fixtures, copper piping, exterior landscaping. In other cases, however, the acts of vandalism were pure revenge. Homeowners poured cement down the drains. They punched holes in the walls. They left dead fish to rot in basements. They broke pipes to flood their houses with water or sewage—cleverly turning the problem of their home's asset illiquidity on its head. One California man planted fake pipe bombs all over his foreclosed property.[2] What do these acts accomplish? Of course, they do not help foreclosed homeowners reclaim their homes. Yet they do powerfully produce an utterly different way of relating to the commodity that is one's house. As if to subvert the strange transfer of agency that defines every instance of commodity fetishism, these acts of sabotage reassert the resistant agency of the vandal. And the vandal's agency is not single-minded but systemic. Her act of destruction does not merely ruin a single house for a single person; it effectively removes the commodified object from circulation altogether. Against the perverse attempt to defend the sanctity and rights of commodities, property destruction thus seeks to upend—one flooded home at a time—the entire system of exploitation and profit that subtends capitalist exchange.

This is the politics of sabotage. Sabotage is one of several crucial political frameworks that allows us to understand the shifting dynamics of organization and resistance under contemporary conditions of indebtedness. Removing commodities from circulation or blocking the paths by which they (and money) might circulate, sabotage addresses itself not so much to what Marx famously described as "the hidden abode of production" but to what Jasper Bernes powerfully terms "the sites of social reproduction." For Bernes, social reproduction encompasses "industries involved in the circulation or realization of commodities (transportation and retail), industries designed to manage the reproduction of capital (finance) or labor (education, health care); and finally industries concerned with the administration of flows of goods and bodies . . . spheres that accelerate and direct flows of capital and labor from site to site, quickening their turnover and reproduction." This shift from production to reproduction, or from productive capital to circulating capital, means that our basic relation to capitalism is no longer governed primarily by the workplace. Instead, as Bernes urgently points out, "the working class confront[s] capital as circulation or reproduction, as storefront and trade union office, prison and university, as riot cop and shopping mall"—or, as this book has added, as subprime mortgage broker and sheriff's department, as foreclosure summons and payday loan bill.[3] The result is a mode of accumulation characterized by precarious, short-term, typically nonunionized service work supplemented by debt and driven by a form of financial capital so mobile and liquid that it can outmaneuver any form of organization designed to resist it. Under these circumstances, traditional forms of radical organization meet an impasse.

Attempts to slow or block circulation have thus become the tactical correlative of an economy driven by consumer debt. From property destruction to building occupation, port blockades to freeway shutdowns, anti-foreclosure barricades to student debt strikes, clashes with the mode of reproduction and in the zones of circulation reveal a situation in which economic subjects confront their exploitation not in the wage but in the eviction notice. These tactics, which I suggest we can group together under the category of sabotage, are the ones most adequate to a moment in which capital itself has been accruing an ever-larger share of its own profits from underpaid workers' need for credit. Where credit seeks to ensure the smooth transfer of money and commodities while deferring payment to the future, sabotage destroys the commodity, blocks exchange, voids payment.[4] As Morgan Adamson puts it, writing on the Chilean activist Francisco Tapia, who burned student loan promissory notes valued at $500 million and displayed their ashes as art, sabotage "intervene[s] in the material practices of accounting and accountability that undergird forms of exploitation" under crisis capitalism. Acts of sabotage, Adamson persuasively claims, "use property destruction to incapacitate complex networks of capital accumulation."[5] In this way, we might consider sabotage the political equivalent of crisis itself, since circulation—the liquid flow of capital and goods, more important to the contemporary economy than ever before—was already stalled or "frozen" by the credit crisis, which, by destroying market credibility and confidence in the market's own systems of risk management, made it that much harder for capital to outrun its own stagnation.

A form of resistance to the logics of private property and ownership, sabotage thus represents a particularly canny response to the uncanniness of housing speculation and foreclosure. Moreover, to see sabotage as a mode of collective solidarity is to see it as something more than simply destructive. The solidarity of sabotage has been on display, for instance, in community campaigns against eviction that draw on tactics of direct action to disrupt or prevent foreclosures. In Boston's Roxbury neighborhood, a community group called City Life/Vida Urbana has fought on behalf of both homeowners and renters to prevent evictions and foreclosures, often by occupying homes and blocking the entrance of the police.⁶ Barricading the door against the cops, City Life refuses the police power that protects and underwrites private property. The Oakland-based Foreclosure Defense Group has done similar work in the Bay Area. As one participant described it, rather than "acting on the behalf of property ownership, and exclusion, and capital, and individualization, atomization," organizers realized that in the working-class and black communities of Oakland, "these homes were essentially a bulwark against the ravages of the greater system. . . . It was [a way] to get out from underneath a landlord. It was a bulwark against the greater structure."⁷ Here again we see how the fight against eviction works not as a defense of private property but as a refusal of it. The saboteurs of the anti-foreclosure movement seek to devalue property as a commodity in circulation—seizable, salable, liquid—and to value it in entirely different terms: the terms not of debt-driven reproduction but of shared use value. As a tactical response to foreclosure, sabotage transforms the home from the expression of individual identity into the basis of social solidarity.

Sabotage, then, is one politically canny response to foreclosure and seizure. But what happens when the object in default can't be seized either by the debtor or the creditor? That is the increasingly common problem posed by student debt, which has in many ways become the exemplary form of indebtedness in the twenty-first century. More than 65 percent of students take out loans, and more than forty million Americans currently hold at least one student loan. Student loan debt is now the second-largest category of consumer debt (after housing), topping out at $1.3 trillion. It's also the fastest growing: whereas most other categories of consumer debt have declined somewhat in the post-crisis period, student loan debt is on the rise, having increased by more than 160 percent over the last decade. (The US Treasury currently estimates that, by the end of the next decade, total student debt will increase nearly threefold, to more than $3 trillion.) Today the average graduate of a four-year college concludes her education saddled with $29,000 in debt, a figure that has risen twice as fast as the rate of inflation over the last decade.⁸

If the contemporary university has become increasingly inextricable from the financial economy, one reason is that the market in student loan debt has been immensely profitable. Of the total outstanding student debt, $150 billion is from private lenders and banks rather than the government, and that figure is poised to grow even faster than federal student lending.⁹ Private loans often have interest rates as high as 20 percent, allow no subsidization of interest, and have a much stricter set of rules on repayment after graduation. Yet private lenders have marketed these loans so aggressively that many student borrowers take out private loans even when they are still eligible for lower-interest federal loans. Approximately 45 percent of those taking out private bank loans have not used up their full federal loan eligibility, a figure almost exactly the same as the number of prime-qualified mortgage borrowers who unnecessarily ended up with subprime home loans. Students of color have been the most exploited in this market: the percentage of African American students who take out private loans has quadrupled in ten years, making this subprime market uncannily like the subprime mortgage market, in which people of color were disproportionately targeted for high-interest loans even when they were eligible for a better deal.[10]

Even federal student loans, once seen as a potentially wasteful form of state welfare, have become hugely profitable. In 2014, the Congressional Budget Office estimated that the US Department of Education will generate $127 billion in profit over the next decade.[11] Public loans are also being securitized, refinanced, and bundled together into Student Loan Asset Backed Securities (SLABS), which are then tranched and sold to institutional investors, including many pension funds: this means that it's possible for a professor at a university to be indirectly invested in the debt of her own students.[12] Student loans were once considered too risky for private investors because there is no collateral; unlike a mortgage, there is no material asset underwriting the dead pledge of the student loan. But as of 1998 (for federal loans) and 2005 (for private loans), student debt is also the only form of consumer debt that is not dischargeable by bankruptcy. Predictably, this has made student-debt-backed securities extremely attractive to investors. Creditors have also been reassured by state-based efforts to treat professional certification itself as a form of seizable collateral. Much as new practices in eviction processing have made it possible for banks to exert more pressure on mortgage holders, so too have new strategies shaped the student loan collection industry, as graduates working in any job from law to teaching might have their wages garnished and their very right to employment in that field revoked as punishment for failure to repay their debt.[13]

The connection between the university and the credit economy runs in both directions. Not only are banks now invested in education; universities are becoming more like banks. Sometimes, as in the case of private loans, the implication of the university in the profitability of student debt is obvious.

A 2006–7 investigation found that many universities, including prestigious not-for-profit private schools like New York University and public universities like University of Texas at Austin, were colluding with the financing institutions that were offering private loans to their students. These schools received a cut of the fees private lenders charged students, administrators were rewarded for high loan volume with fancy vacations, and in some instances, private lenders even demanded that a bank representative be on university staff.[14] The penetration of financial capitalism into the contemporary university has also happened in less visible ways, as we see when we consider how fast the rate and volume of student lending have increased over the last two decades. Between 1993 and 2015, the average yearly debt load for borrowers increased nearly fourfold.[15] The cause of this ballooning debt was, of course, rapidly increasing tuition: between 1975 and 1990, the cost (adjusted for inflation) of attending a four-year public university increased 50 percent; between 1990 and 2015 it increased 300 percent.[16] The most commonly cited reason for the rapid increase in the price of a degree is the decline in state support. This decline is itself a product not simply of political ideology but also of the pressures on growth of gross domestic product (GDP)—and thus on federal budgets—caused by the productive crisis described in the Introduction. Since 2000, real growth in US GDP has averaged a listless 2 percent, compared with a 3 percent average in the 1970s–90s, and higher rates still in the booming postwar period; in this context, the state surpluses that once funded higher education have dried up. But there is another, less noticed, and perhaps more significant reason for the ongoing tuition bubble. The growth of student debt is not simply the effect of higher tuition; higher tuition is also caused by the increasing availability of student loans (much as easy mortgage credit caused housing prices to rise). As Robert Meister has argued in an important article detailing the relationship between university budgets and student debt, after 1992, when the borrowing limit on the federal PLUS loan program (loans for students signed by their parents) was lifted, universities were left with a completely transformed relationship to tuition. Because the supply of loans was now practically infinite, potential increases in tuition became similarly limitless. University leaders, Meister suggests, were thus active participants in the tuition bubble, since they recognized tuition as "an opportunity for aggressive revenue growth they could not afford to miss."[17] By the start of the twenty-first century, the university had simply become another name for the financial economy.

This fact has not been lost on indebted students themselves. Consider a small but revealing act of defacement that took place amid larger campus protests against tuition increases at the University of California, Berkeley, in 2010. Lining the campus walkways at the time were promotional posters from the university advertising department emblazoned with "Thanks to Berkeley..." and filled in with a variety of motivational and enthusiastic student testimonials. One such poster, though, carried a different message. "Thanks to Berkeley," one protester scribbled onto the sign, "I'm in debt forever." Then even the word "Berkeley" was crossed out and replaced with "capitalism," providing an even more insightful account of the contemporary credit economy: "Thanks to capitalism ... I'm in debt forever."

One might choose to read this clever bit of graffiti as a kind of individual complaint or solitary confession. Yet in the context of the broader campus activism that was its occasion, it stands as one of several examples of a collective movement aimed at putting university life at the center of economic resistance. In the manifestos, reports, and communiqués written by and circulated among student activists, the condition of being in debt has opened up a much-needed perspective from which to view the connection between the university and the economy, as well as between students and workers. One student manifesto, titled "We Are the Crisis," argues that "the massive personal debt required to keep the university and its building projects churning along indicate[s] the unsustainability of current class relations over the long-term."[18] Here, student debt is what connects the "crisis of the university" to economic crisis. More specifically, the crisis of student debt intersects in several crucial ways—in terms of both its history and its resistant politics—with the crisis of housing debt. Joshua Clover has observed the startling overlap between the locations of student militancy in 2009 and 2010 and those places most devastated by home foreclosures. "We can now say," writes Clover, "that higher education militancy proceeds in absolute solidarity with mortgage failure, bankruptcy, and foreclosure."[19] Behind both subprime mortgage borrowers and subprime student borrowers, we find a shared situation in which the conditions of subsistence and reproduction are no longer supported by the wage alone and can thus be sustained only through ever-greater burdens of debt. Similarly, in both cases, the process of securitization has transformed these particular kinds of debt into income streams for speculative investors. In the context of this blurring of public good and private interest, it is not surprising that the most successful and engaged anti-student-debt movement happening today is the debt strike organized by the students of for-profit Corinthian Colleges. Once the "Corinthian 15," the group of strikers has now grown to more than two hundred students who are refusing to make payments on the massive loans they owe to the now-defunct and unaccredited private colleges run by the Corinthian group. The Corinthian students are largely first-generation college attendees, students of color, and nontraditional students, the very same population most devastated by the housing crisis. And of course, these indebted students are also the ones caught up in the most brazenly exploitative education racket, the for-profit college market. Yet even here, the aims of debt strike are not particular or individual but collective, articulated in terms of the shared condition of debt itself: as a manifesto from the Debt Collective—a group comprising the Corinthian students as well as hundreds of other student debtors—states, "Alone, our debts are a burden; together, they make us powerful."[20]

Approached through the framework of debt, the connection between students and workers, like the connection between the university and capital, is not simply analogical. Nearly 75 percent of college students work while in school. Despite the common recommendation of colleges that students work no more than ten hours per week while in school, one in five students works full-time, and of those who are ostensibly part-time workers, greater than half work more than twenty hours per week.[21] And students—above all indebted students—are not just present workers but also future ones, working now to pay for an education whose meager (and increasingly false) promise is to put them in a position to get slightly higher-paying work later.

The fact that students have pledged their lives and livelihoods to the repayment of their debt has often been read as an expression of a certain optimism: as Adamson puts it, student debt is perceived as "the manifestation of the student's entrepreneurial subjectivity, as education is seen as an investment in his or her own human capital intended to yield a future return on that investment."[22] Asserting over and over again that student debt is "good" debt, university representatives and bankers alike have told students that committing their future wages to their present education will be a profitable investment in their own future, encouraging students to view higher education as a means to an economic end. Humanist academics of all stripes have resisted this discourse of higher education as professional investment or technical job training.[23] Depending on the political affiliation of the critic, this resistance has tended to be rooted in one of two complaints: either about the ruinous instrumentalization of liberal human values such changes portend or about the corporate university's capitulation to capitalist imperatives they mark.

The limit of both these objections, however, is that they fail to recognize that the problem with describing higher education as an investment in one's economic and professional future is not merely a moral or political one. The bigger problem with such a description is that it is historically inaccurate. The assumption that going into debt to pay for a college degree will always pay dividends in terms of future employability and income is now less certain than ever before. The theory of education as an investment in valuable human capital—frequently used to support the rhetoric of student debt as a way to speculate on one's professional future, as Adamson suggests—is often seen as a particularly contemporary phenomenon. But in fact it is a rhetoric that was better suited to the boom economy that produced it: human capital theory first emerged to justify state-financed higher education, especially the GI Bill, between the 1940s and 1960s.[24] This midcentury period was an era of rising US hegemony and unprecedented US economic strength, not only in the economy as a whole but also in the portion of economic growth going to workers in the form of wages. In this context, the human capital theory of the 1950s and 1960s both contributed and responded to the historically specific rise of a middle-class technocracy. That rise meant that capital needed more educated workers than it ever had before. The education premium—the increase in lifetime earnings that accrues to those with a college degree—predictably rose to its highest level in this period (as it did again in the 1980s, as the economy changed to accommodate the microelectronic revolution).[25] Yet today, for the first time in US history, the education premium is falling. Between 2001 and 2013, the average wage for workers with a bachelor's degree declined 10 percent. The current unemployment rate among recent college graduates is nearly identical to the national average rate of unemployment. Of those fortunate enough to have a job, half of university graduates have jobs that do not require a college degree. Because this is happening at the same time that college costs have increased many times faster than the rate of inflation, and given the costs of paying off student debt, 25 percent of US universities, by one estimate, now offer students a negative return on their "investment." Put simply, for many students today, the cost of an education is greater than the lifetime income gains it enables, making human capital a rather dire form of speculation indeed.[26]

From this perspective, that melancholic line from the Berkeley graffiti—"I'm in debt forever"—turns out to be startlingly accurate. Largely because of high un- and underemployment, the current rate of student loan default is remarkably high: student loans have the highest delinquency rate of any form of consumer debt, having surpassed credit card debt in 2012. According to the Federal Reserve, half of total student loan balances are not even in repayment. Some are in deferment (typically because the borrowers are in graduate school and thus continuing to accrue debt), while others are in forbearance (a temporary stay of execution possible if a student loses her job or has a health crisis). Of those ostensibly in repayment, 17 percent are officially delinquent. The overall delinquency rate, the Fed thus suggests, is more than 27 percent, or nearly a third of all outstanding loans. Among students who left college in 2010, five years later $71 billion of their $78 billion in debt remains outstanding.[27] For these and many other students, student loan debt—or the consequences of defaulting on it—may well be with them forever.

Of course, these numbers are facts whether the graffiti implies them or not. What really interests me about the graffiti writer's knowing prognosis is how it suggests that students themselves are now fully aware of their dire predicament. Today's student debtors are hardly trapped in some state of false consciousness or foolish optimism. Yet that assumption lingers. Certainly, these students have been told that education debt is good because it will inevitably lead to higher incomes and a better life—much as their parents were told that housing values would rise forever. Belief in these kinds of future fulfillments has been most influentially described by Lauren Berlant as a "cruel optimism": "an optimistic attachment . . . that ignites a sense of possibility"; a belief in the kinds of "conventional good-life fantasies" that we cling too even when they betray us; a persistent faith in "idealizing theories and tableaux about how [we] and the world 'add up to something.'" Berlant's formulation describes an attachment to injurious ways of being (for instance, when we think we have a moral obligation to our creditor) and to forms of optimistic feeling that ultimately default on their promises (for instance, when we go into debt to ensure a future income we will likely never earn).[28]

My own experience discussing debt with my students at University of Wisconsin–Milwaukee (UWM), however, has suggested anything but optimism, cruel or otherwise. UWM is an open-admission institution in Wisconsin's urban center. The city of Milwaukee (along with the state as a whole) has struggled to survive amid the depredations of deindustrialization and post-industrial transformations of the farming economy. My students come variously from urban Milwaukee, rural northern and central Wisconsin, and some of the highest-poverty suburban communities in the state. They come from working- and middle-class families, and many have seen, through their parents, the dire consequences of the real estate boom, adjustable-rate mortgages, "easy" credit, and foreclosure. In addition to their parents' housing debts, these students are burdened with their own student loan and credit card debt. Many are first-generation college students, and their retention and graduation rates are relatively low, while their average time to degree is unusually long. They work, many of them full-time while enrolled. Some work multiple jobs; many are supporting both themselves and their families. They work in a range of jobs exemplary of a deindustrialized circulation and reproduction economy: truck drivers, baristas, line cooks, pizza deliverers, bartenders, retail salespeople, IT help-line staffers, daycare workers, warehouse stockers. They are working hard for their degrees, even as those degrees are delayed by so much work.

All of this—so much work and so many years for an increasingly devalued degree—may well sound cruelly optimistic. But that is not in fact what these students are. These students turn out to have a very different, far darker view of all those cruel reassurances about debt—of the claim that it is an investment in the future or that it is a measure of moral obligation. Today's student debtors are not in the least optimistic. Rather, they possess a demystified, canny, and radical kind of knowledge. They do not believe in a future "good life" of financial security and middle-class mobility. They do not believe that they will own homes like their parents do. They do not believe they will move up the ladder of social mobility. They do not have faith that they will find meaningful, much less stable, work; indeed, many of them assume they will be working the same jobs after they graduate that they're working right now. They do not see their degree as an investment in their future (nor, they report to me, do many of their parents). And they believe they will never be out of debt.

In all of these ways, I see a much different—more radical, less optimistic, more knowing—post-crisis political subject than Berlant does. In turning here to the question of what kind of subjectivity emerges in a time of crisis, I am not at all suggesting that we ought to prioritize the individual, the experiential, or the affective over collectivity, totality, and history. The way we feel about our debt does not change how much debt we are in. Nor does debt itself work primarily by making us feel certain things. If and when we pay our debt, we do not do so because of ideology or affect; we do so because we are literally at risk when we don't. Because of debt's material consequences and real risks, it cannot be enough to change merely the ways we think about our debt. But that is not to say that such thoughts and feelings must immediately be disqualified as irrelevant mystifications or political withdrawals. The abstract and the universal do not lie apart from the concrete and the particular. Rather, the bankrupt unemployed worker, the subprime mortgage holder, the indebted student all are able to glimpse the mechanisms, motions, and limits of the capitalist totality that subsumes them. They are at once the products of that totality and the subjects most capable of reckoning with it. Their political power may find expression as collective agency (for instance, when students join together to resist their debts); or it may find expression as sheer exigency (for instance, when students default on their loans). In either case, we see how political subjectivity—what we think, what we feel, what we believe—is inextricable from political action. No one has put this point more finely and inspiringly than Chris Nealon: "The volatility born of the contradictions in capital might better point to a different, earlier understanding of theory: not the pursuit of a transcendental vantage point or the critique of that pursuit but the relentless surveying of possible grounds for solidarity among those for whom the regime of capital only spells suffering."[29] In our contemporary capitalist landscape, where suffering is most often synonymous with debt, a survey of the grounds for solidarity shows us the shared interests of defaulted students and evicted families, of student workers and union workers. For these solidarities to come into view, we need to know that there is less difference between the debt to a university and the debt to the landlord than we might assume. We need to know that what unites us today is not the "good-life fantasy" of upward mobility we once clung to but the universal knowledge of that fantasy's historical end. We need to know that debt is not an investment in the future but a confrontation with economic coercion and exploitation in the present. To know these things is to have the kind of knowledge I am calling "crisis subjectivity." This is a knowledge that comes from seeing your parents struggle to maintain their class position; from seeing members of your family evicted or foreclosed on; from seeing your neighbors lose their jobs due to deindustrialization and outsourcing; from seeing your fellow students take on a debt load as crushing as your own. New historical conditions produce new modes of historical consciousness. Crisis subjectivity is simply what it means to grapple with history as it happens, to acquire a politics as it slowly emerges out of history's mist.

"I'm in debt forever." Read as the rallying cry of an emergent crisis subjectivity based not in the uncanniness or illegibility of debt but in a canny, clear-eyed reckoning with the poverty of credit's promises about the future, this line becomes not a sad complaint but an empowering threat. After all, an economy founded on credit depends on deferring payment into the future, but it depends even more on the premise that those payments will not be deferred forever. To be in debt forever is thus to refuse to be in debt at all. This affirmation of debt's unpayability robs debt of its calculability, of its quantifiable claim on the future earnings of worker. To be in debt forever is to refuse to balance the books, to resist paying your debt to society, and thus to throw a wrench into the very machinery of social reproduction. Think of it as a kind of irrational exuberance from below: a way of transforming default and devaluation into the very condition of possibility for radical collective politics. "I'm in debt forever" is the radical voice of both the collective debt striker and the solitary debt defaulter, of the saboteur and the bankrupt. Shouted against the false obligations of credit's dead pledges, it is a new kind of promise: one made by a living indebted who cannot and will not pay their debts.

Notes

Introduction

1. Meta Brown, Andrew Haughwout, Donghoon Lee, and Wilbert van der Klaauw, "The Financial Crisis at the Kitchen Table: Trends in Household Debt and Credit," *Current Issues in Economics and Finance* 19.2 (2013), https://www.newyorkfed.org/medialibrary/media/research/current_issues/ci19-2.pdf, 9.

2. Pam Bennett, "The Aftermath of the Great Recession: Financially Fragile Families and How Professionals Can Help," *Forum for Family and Consumer Issues* 17.1 (Spring/Summer 2012), http://ncsu.edu/ffci/publications/2012/v17-n1-2012-spring/bennett.php.

3. David Graeber, *Debt: The First 5000 Years* (Brooklyn: Melville House, 2011); Mauricio Lazzarato, *The Making of the Indebted Man: An Essay on the Neoliberal Condition*, trans. Joshua David Jordan (Cambridge, MA: MIT Press/Semiotext(e), 2012); Richard Dienst, *The Bonds of Debt: Borrowing against the Common Good* (London: Verso, 2011); Angela Mitropoulos, *Contract and Contagion: From Biopolitics to Oikonomia* (Wivenhoe, NY: Minor Compositions, 2012); Fred Moten and Stefano Harney, *The Undercommons: Fugitive Planning and Black Study* (Wivenhoe, NY: Minor Compositions, 2013); Miranda Joseph, *Debt to Society: Accounting for Life under Capitalism* (Minneapolis: University of Minnesota Press, 2014); Andrew Ross, *Creditocracy and the Case for Debt Refusal* (New York: OR Books, 2014).

4. Graeber, *Debt*, 14.

5. Marc Shell, *Money, Language, and Thought: Literary and Philosophical Economies from the Medieval to the Modern Era* (Baltimore: Johns Hopkins University Press, 1993), 7.

6. Mary Poovey, *Genres of the Credit Economy: Mediating Value in Eighteenth and Nineteenth-Century Britain* (Chicago: University of Chicago Press, 2008), 2, 113.

7. Deidre Lynch, *The Economy of Character: Novels, Market Culture, and the Business of Inner Meaning* (Chicago: University of Chicago Press, 1998); Margot Finn, *The Character of Credit: Personal Debt in English Culture, 1740–1914* (Cambridge: Cambridge University Press, 2003); Ian Baucom, *Specters of the Atlantic: Finance Capital, Slavery, and the Philosophy of History* (Durham, NC: Duke University Press, 2005). Quotation from Lynch, *The Economy of Character*, 13.

8. Jennifer Baker, *Securing the Commonwealth: Debt, Speculation, and Writing in the Making of Early America* (Baltimore: Johns Hopkins University Press, 2007), 4.

9. See Otaviano Canuto, "Food Prices, Financial Crisis and Droughts," *Growth and Crisis Blog*, World Bank, November 23, 2011, http://blogs.worldbank.org/growth/food-prices-financial-crisis-and-droughts; Melanie Haiken, "More Than 10,000 Suicides Tied to Economic Crisis, Study Says," *Forbes*, June 12, 2014, http://www.forbes.com/sites/melaniehaiken/2014/06/12/more-than-10000-suicides-tied-to-economic-crisis-study-says/#5adf7e3a1cbb. Sources for the other claims here about unemployment, eviction, bankruptcy, and homelessness appear throughout this Introduction where they are discussed in more detail.

10. For an excellent account of these changes, see Louis Hyman, *Borrow: The American Way of Debt* (New York: Vintage, 2012), and *Debtor Nation: The History of America in Red Ink* (Princeton, NJ: Princeton University Press, 2011); Lendol Calder, *Financing the American Dream: A Cultural History of Consumer Credit* (Princeton, NJ: Princeton University Press, 1999).

11. See Martha Poon, "From New Deal Institutions to Capital Markets: Commercial Consumer Risk Scores and the Making of Subprime Mortgage Finance," *Accounting, Organizations, and Society* 34 (2009): 654–74.

12. See Maya Gonzalez, "Notes on the New Housing Question: Homeownership, Credit, and Reproduction in the Post-war US Economy," *Endnotes* 2 (April 2010), http://endnotes.org.uk/en/endnotes-notes-on-the-new-housing-question; Robin Blackburn, "The Subprime Crisis," *New Left Review* 50 (March–April 2008): 63–106.

13. See Souphala Chomsisengphet and Anthony Pennington-Cross, "The Evolution of the Subprime Mortgage Market," *Federal Reserve Bank of St. Louis Review* 88.1 (January–February 2006): 31–56; Dan Immergluck, *Foreclosed: High Risk Lending, Deregulation, and the Undermining of America's Mortgage Market* (Ithaca, NY: Cornell University Press, 2009).

14. See Alyssa Katz, *Our Lot: How Real Estate Came to Own Us* (New York: Bloomsbury, 2010).

15. Ben Bernanke, "Housing, Housing Finance, and Monetary Policy," Federal Reserve Board speech, August 31, 2007, Jackson Hole, WY, http://www.federalreserve.gov/newsevents/speech/bernanke20070831a.htm.

16. Hyman, *Borrow*, 213. See also Aaron Unterman, "Exporting Risk: Global Implications of the Securitization of US Housing Debt," *Hastings Business Law Journal* 4.1 (Winter 2008): 77–134.

17. See Vincenzo Bavoso, "Financial Innovation, Structured Finance, and Off Balance Sheet Financing: The Case of Securitization," Social Science Research Network, January 1, 2010, http://papers.ssrn.com/sol3/papers.cfm?abstract_id=1746109.

18. John Bellamy Foster and Fred Magdoff, *The Great Financial Crisis: Causes and Consequences* (New York: New York University Press, 2009), 29.

19. New York Federal Reserve Bank, "Household Debt and Credit Report (Q3 2015)," November 2015, https://www.newyorkfed.org/medialibrary/interactives/householdcredit/data/pdf/HHDC_2015Q3.pdf, 3.

20. See Hyman, *Debtor Nation*; Immergluck, *Foreclosed*; and Alyosha Goldstein, "Finance and Foreclosure in the Colonial Present," *Radical History Review* 118 (Winter 2014): 42–63.

21. See Gary Rivlin, *Broke USA: From Pawnshops to Poverty Inc., How the Working Poor Became Big Business* (New York: Harper Business, 2011).

22. See Federal Reserve Bank of New York, "Household Debt Continues Upward Climb While Student Loan Delinquencies Worsen," February 17, 2015, https://www.newyorkfed.org/newsevents/news/research/2015/rp150217.html; Juan Sánchez and Lijun Zhu, "Student Loan Delinquency: A Big Problem Getting Worse?," *Economic Synopses* 7 (April 10, 2015), https://research.stlouisfed.org/publications/economic-synopses/2015/04/10/student-loan-delinquency-a-big-problem-getting-worse/; Meta Brown, Andrew Haughwout, Donghoon Lee, Joelle Scally, and Wilbert van der Klaauw, "Looking at Student Loan Defaults through a Larger Window," Federal Reserve Bank of New York *Liberty Street Economics* (blog), February 19, 2015, http://libertystreeteconomics.newyork fed.org/2015/02/looking_at_student_loan_defaults_through_a_larger_window.html#.Vx5Qa3qgqNM.

23. College Board, Trends in Student Aid, 2008, http://trends.collegeboard.org/sites/default/files/SA_2008.pdf, 6.

24. American Association of State Colleges and Universities, "The Public Realities of Private Student Loans: A Higher Education Policy Brief," April 2008, http://www.aascu.org/policy/publications/policymatters/2008/privatestudentloans.pdf, 2; The Institute for College Access & Success, "Private Loans: Facts and Trends in 2008," May 2014, http://ticas.org/sites/default/files/legacy/files/pub/private_loan_facts_trends_08.pdf.

25. Jeffrey P. Cohen, Cletus C. Coughlin, and David A. Lopez, "The Boom and Bust of U.S. Housing Prices from Various Geographic Perspectives," *Federal Reserve Bank of St. Louis Review* 94.5 (September/October 2012): 350.

26. Saskia Scholtes and Francesco Guerrera, "Banks Rush to Rescue of Credit Card Trusts," *Financial Times*, June 24, 2009, http://www.ft.com/intl/cms/s/0/a600eed0-60f9-11de-aa12-00144feabdc0.html#axzz497dixmLR. Some economic commentators have noted approvingly the decline in indebtedness between 2009 and 2012, suggesting that it was due to consumers paying off debt and saving more, but in fact most of the decrease can be ascribed instead to an increase in the "charge-off" rate: the amount of very delinquent debt being written off by the lenders as uncollectable. Erin El Issa, "American Household Credit and Debt Statistics: 2015," May 2015, http://www.nerdwallet.com/blog/credit-card-data/average-credit-card-debt-household/.

27. Michael Hurd and Susann Rohwedder, "Effects of the Financial Crisis and Great Recession on American Households," National Bureau of Economic Research Working Paper 16407, September 2010, http://www.nber.org/papers/w16407.pdf, 10–13.

28. Thomas A. Garrett, "100 Years of Bankruptcy: Why More Americans Than Ever Are Filing," Federal Reserve Bank of St. Louis, Spring 2006, https://www.stlouisfed.org/publications/bridges/spring-2006/100-years-of-bankruptcy-why-more-americans-than-ever-are-filing.

29. New York Federal Reserve, "Quarterly Report on Household Debt and Credit," February 2011, https://www.newyorkfed.org/medialibrary/media/newsevents/events/regional_outreach/2011/DistrictReport_Q4_2010.pdf, 9.

30. Bennett, "Aftermath of the Great Recession."

31. Jacqueline Ayers, Suzanne Bergeron, Garrick T. Davis, Valerie R. Wilson, and Madura Wijewardena, eds., *2012 State of Black America Report* (New York: National Urban Renewal League, 2012), http://soba.iamempowered.com/sites/soba.iamempowered.com/files/SOBA2012_SinglePgs/index.html.

32. National Coalition for the Homeless, National Health Care for the Homeless Council, National Alliance to End Homelessness, National Association for the Education of Homeless Children and Youth, National Law Center on Homelessness & Poverty, National Low Income Housing Coalition, and the National Policy and Advocacy Council on Homelessness, "Foreclosure to Homelessness 2009: The Forgotten Victims of the Subprime Crisis," 2009, http://www.nationalhomeless.org/advocacy/ForeclosuretoHomelessness0609.pdf, 5.

33. Hyman, *Debtor Nation*, 219.

34. See S&P Case-Shiller Home Price Indices, accessed May 23, 2016, http://us.spindices.com/index-family/real-estate/sp-case-shiller.

35. Henry J. Kaiser Family Foundation, "Health Care Spending in the United States and Selected OECD Countries," April 12, 2011, http://kff.org/health-costs/issue-brief/snapshots-health-care-spending-in-the-united-states-selected-oecd-countries/.

36. Ruth Mantell, "The Numbers on Child Care's Skyrocketing Costs," MarketWatch, April 8, 2013, http://www.marketwatch.com/story/the-numbers-on-child-cares-skyrocketing-costs-2013-04-08.

37. Malcolm Harris, "Bad Education," *n+1* (April 2011), https://nplusonemag.com/online-only/online-only/bad-education/.

38. See statistics from Census Bureau and Consumer Price Index compared by Trent Hamm, "A Dose of Financial Reality," Simple Dollar, August 1, 2014, http://www.thesimpledollar.com/a-dose-of-financial-reality/.

39. Lawrence Mishel, Elise Gould, and Josh Bivens, "Wage Stagnation in Nine Charts," Economic Policy Institute, January 6, 2015, http://www.epi.org/publication/charting-wage-stagnation/.

40. Hilary Wething, Natalie Sabadish, and Heidi Shierholz, "The Class of 2012," Economic Policy Institute, May 3, 2012, http://www.epi.org/publication/bp340-labor-market-young-graduates/.

41. Annalyn Kurtz, "Employment Is Still Near a 30-Year Low," CNN Money, June 6, 2013, http://money.cnn.com/2013/06/06/news/economy/employment-rate/.

42. See Hyman, *Borrow*; Elizabeth Warren, Teresa Sullivan, and Jay Westbrook, *As We Forgive Our Debtors: Bankruptcy and Consumer Credit in America* (Oxford: Oxford University Press, 1989), and *The Fragile Middle Class: Americans in Debt* (New Haven, CT: Yale University Press, 2001).

43. Karl Marx, *Capital, Volume 3*, trans. D. Fernbach (New York: Penguin Classics, 1991), 573.

44. See Robert Brenner, *The Boom and the Bubble: The US in the World Economy* (London: Verso, 2002); Blackburn, "The Subprime Crisis"; Joshua Clover, "Value, Theory, Crisis," *PMLA* 127.1 (January 2012): 107–14; David Harvey, *Seventeen Contradictions and the End of Capitalism* (Oxford: Oxford University Press, 2014); Robert Kurz, "On the Current Economic Crisis," *Mediations* 27.1–2 (Fall/Spring 2013–14), http://www.mediationsjournal.org/articles/current-global-economic-crisis.

45. Neil Larsen, Mathias Nilges, Josh Robinson, and Nicholas Brown, "Editors' Note," *Mediations* 27. 1–2 (Fall/Spring 2013–14), http://www.mediationsjournal.org/articles/editors-note-vol-27-no-1.

46. Norbert Trenkle, "Tremors on the World Market," trans. Josh Robinson, *Krisis* (May 2008), http://www.krisis.org/2009/tremors-on-the-global-market/print/.

47. See David McNally, "From Financial Crisis to World Slump: Accumulation, Financialisation, and the Global Slowdown," *Historical Materialism* 17 (2009): 35–83.

48. Peter Gowan, *The Global Gamble* (New York: Verso, 1999), 8–13.

49. Gopal Balakrishnan, "Speculations on a Stationary State," *New Left Review* 59 (September–October 2009): 11.

50. Giovanni Arrighi, *The Long Twentieth Century* (London: Verso, 1994), 8–14.

51. Balakrishnan, "Speculations," 25.

52. Claus Peter Ortlieb, "A Contradiction between Matter and Form," in *Marxism and the Critique of Value*, ed. Neil Larsen, Mathias Nilges, Josh Robinson, and Nicholas Brown (Chicago: MCM Publishing, 2014), 45.

53. Nor is this position entirely limited to Marxists. Three new books have likewise questioned the possibility of continued growth—books with diagnoses and prognoses startlingly similar to Balakrishnan's despite being written from very different political perspectives. See Mohamed El-Erian, *The Only Game in Town: Central Banks, Instability, and Avoiding the Next Collapse* (New York: Random House, 2016); Satyajit Das, *The Age of Stagnation: Why Perpetual Growth Is Unattainable and the Global Economy Is in Peril* (New York: Prometheus Books, 2016); Robert Gordon, *The Rise and Fall of American Growth: The US Standard of Living since the Civil War* (Princeton, NJ: Princeton University Press, 2016).

54. For a particularly powerful account of the autumnal condition of crisis, see Marija Cetinic, "House and Field: The Aesthetics of Saturation," *Mediations* 28.1 (Fall 2014): 35–44.

55. Claude Levi-Strauss, "The Structural Study of Myth," *Journal of American Folklore* 68.270 (1955): 428–44.

Chapter 1

1. For excellent mainstream accounts of the events of 2007–9, on which I have drawn, see especially Charles Kindelberger and Robert Aliber, *Manias, Panics, and Crashes: A History of Financial Crises*, 6th ed. (London: Palgrave Macmillan, 2011);

Bethany Maclean and Joe Nocera, *All the Devils Are Here: The Hidden History of the Financial Crisis* (New York: Penguin, 2011); Michael Lewis, *The Big Short: Inside the Doomsday Machine* (New York: W. W. Norton, 2010).

2. "25 People to Blame for the Financial Crisis," *Time*, February 2009, http://content.time.com/time/specials/packages/article/0,28804,1877351_1878509_1878508,00.html.

3. For an excellent account of the relationship between the discourse of complexity and the language of individual accountability, see Leigh Claire la Berge's brilliant *Scandals and Abstraction: Financial Fiction of the Long 1980s* (Oxford: Oxford University Press, 2014). La Berge's analysis of "abstraction" as a central "epistemology of finance" emphasizes market complexity, while her chapters on scandal take up the more "narrativized and conclusive" ways in which narratives of scandal deploy ideas about individual greed (15).

4. Here and throughout this chapter, I refer to behavioral economists as "behavioralists" to clarify the distinction between this economic discipline and psychological behaviorism, to which I also occasionally refer. George Akerlof and Robert Shiller, *Animal Spirits: How Human Psychology Drives the Economy and Why It Matters for Global Capitalism* (Princeton, NJ: Princeton University Press, 2009), 5, 4.

5. Sam Lypsyte, *The Ask* (New York: Farrar, Straus and Giroux, 2010); Jonathan Dee, *The Privileges* (New York: Random House, 2010); Adam Haslett, *Union Atlantic* (New York: Nan A. Talese, 2010); Jess Walters, *The Financial Lives of the Poets* (New York: Harper, 2010); Eric Puchner, *Model Home* (New York: Scribner, 2010); Martha McPhee, *Dear Money* (New York: Houghton Mifflin, 2010).

6. For an excellent account of adultery in *Financial Lives*, see Andrew Hoberek, "Adultery, Crisis, Contract," in *Reading Capitalist Realism*, ed. Allison Shonkwiler and Leigh Clare la Berge (Iowa City: University of Iowa Press, 2014), 41–63.

7. Walters, *Financial Lives of the Poets*, 212.

8. "Remarks by Secretary Henry Paulson, Jr. U.S. Housing and Market Update," US Department of the Treasury, March 3, 2008, https://www.treasury.gov/press-center/press-releases/Pages/hp856.aspx.

9. Regina Gagnier, *The Insatiability of Human Wants: Economics and Aesthetics in Market Society* (Chicago: University of Chicago Press, 2000), 20.

10. Daniel Rodgers, *Age of Fracture* (Boston: Belknap, 2012), 63.

11. See Ben Fine, "Economics Confronts the Social Sciences," in *The Rise of the Market: Essays on the Political Economy of Neoliberalism*, ed. Malcolm Sawyer (London: Edward Elgar, 2004), 76–106.

12. Philip Mirowski, *Never Let a Serious Crisis Go to Waste: How Neoliberalism Survived the Financial Meltdown* (London: Verso, 2014), 256–57.

13. See Daniel Kahneman, Paul Slovic, and Amos Tversky, eds., *Judgment under Uncertainty: Heuristics and Biases* (Cambridge: Cambridge University Press, 1982).

14. Richard Thaler, "Toward a Positive Theory of Consumer Choice," *Journal of Economic Behavior and Organization* 1 (1980): 39.

15. Dan Ariely, *Predictably Irrational: The Hidden Forces That Shape Our Decisions* (New York: HarperCollins, 2008).

16. Robert Shiller, "From Efficient Markets Theory to Behavioral Finance," *Journal of Economic Perspectives* 17.1 (Winter 2003): 94.

17. Akerlof and Shiller, *Animal Spirits*, 4.

18. Mirowski, *Serious Crisis*, 259.

19. Qtd. in Paul Slovic, *The Feeling of Risk: New Perspectives on Risk Perception* (London: Routledge, 2013), 87.

20. Of course, this argument about the role of emotions in financial crises is not entirely new: As David Zimmerman argues, early twentieth-century economists were profoundly worried that "prices were, at bottom, only expressions of investors' opinions and moods" and thus turned to crowd psychology to explain the tendency of investors to emulate one another. Shiller himself acknowledges that the "feedback loop" theory proposed by contemporary behavioralists resembles these earlier theories about crowd behavior. However, Shiller explains, theorists of panics like Charles Mackay claimed that individuals are basically rational while crowds are definitively incapable of collective rationality. The contemporary behaviorists, in contrast, argue that individual psychology and group psychology are basically the same: individuals and collectives are equally capable of both rationality and irrationality. David Zimmerman, *Panic! Markets, Crises, and Crowds in American Fiction* (Chapel Hill, NC: University of North Carolina Press, 2006), 96; Shiller, "From Efficient Markets Theory," 91–92.

21. Those commentators who refused behavioralist explanations tended to turn precisely toward complexity itself as an explanation, for instance, in the "black swan" argument popularized by commentators like Nassem Taleb, for whom the crisis was too strange, too particular, and too unprecedented to be analyzed. Nassem Taleb, *The Black Swan: The Impact of the Highly Improbable* (New York: Random House, 2010).

22. John Cassidy, *How Markets Fail: The Logic of Economic Calamities* (New York: Macmillan, 2009); Justin Fox, *The Myth of the Rational Market: A History of Risk, Reward, and Delusion on Wall Street* (New York: HarperCollins, 2009).

23. Robert Shiller, *Subprime Solution: How Today's Global Financial Crisis Happened and What to Do about It* (Princeton, NJ: Princeton University Press, 2008), 3 (emphasis mine).

24. Qtd. in Mirowski, *Serious Crisis*, 211.

25. See Richard Thaler, with Cass Sunstein, *Nudge: Improving Decisions about Wealth, Health, and Happiness* (New Haven, CT: Yale University Press, 2008).

26. J. G. A. Pocock, *Virtue, Commerce, and History, Chiefly in the Eighteenth Century* (London: Cambridge University Press, 1985), 98.

27. See Marieke de Goede, "Mastering 'Lady Credit,'" *International Feminist Journal of Politics* 2.1 (2000): 58–81.

28. Shiller, *Subprime Solution*, 149–50.

29. Ibid., 24.

30. According to political economist Duncan Foley, microeconomics "admits no social category that transcends individual action, or the simple combination of individual action." Duncan Foley, *Adam's Fallacy: A Guide to Economic Theology* (Cambridge, MA: Harvard University Press, 2009), 156.

31. Liesl Schillinger, "Pride and Avarice," *New York Times Book Review*, February 12, 2010, http://www.nytimes.com/2010/02/14/books/review/Schillinger-t.html.

32. John Lanchester, "Show Me the Money," *Financial Times*, March 2, 2012, http://www.ft.com/cms/s/2/2852f9f0-621e-11e1-820b-00144feabdc0.html.

33. Arne De Boever, "It's Not All Rotten Apples on Wall Street: Christina Alger's *The Darlings*," *Los Angeles Review of Books*, November 13, 2013, http://lareviewofbooks.org/review/its-not-all-rotten-apples-on-wall-street.

34. Joseph Peschel, "Social Commentary, and a Seduction of Sorts," Boston.com, June 5 2010, http://www.boston.com/ae/books/articles/2010/06/05/dear_money_presents_social_commentary_and_a_seduction_of_sorts/.

35. Marco Roth, "The Credit Crisis and the Novel," *Dissent* (Fall 2010), http://www.dissentmagazine.org/article/the-credit-crisis-and-the-novel.

36. Christian Lorentzen, "Fictitious Values," *Bookforum* (June/July/August 2012), http://www.bookforum.com/inprint/019_02/9453.

37. Alexandra Alter, "Through the Eyes of the Ultra Rich," *Wall Street Journal*, January 5, 2010, http://www.wsj.com/articles/SB1000142405274870343650457640192701293478.

38. Much as behavioralism wants to insist that individuals caused the crisis but should not be blamed for it, these novels ultimately, and intentionally, produce sympathy for rather than antipathy toward their protagonists. Indeed, this arguably distinguishes these realist novels from the "financial thriller" genre that also boomed in the wake of the crash: thrillers are perfectly willing to render bankers as "evildoers."

39. For a very thorough treatment and critique of contemporary realism's infatuation with individual affect, see Rachel Greenwald Smith, *Affect and American Literature in the Age of Neoliberalism* (Cambridge: Cambridge University Press, 2015). Much of this chapter might be read in conversation with Smith's work, particularly with her powerful distinction between "works of literature that appear to represent human experience realistically" by emphasizing "personal feelings" and works of literature more self-reflexively attuned to "impersonal feelings": to feelings that "do not . . . conform to a market model . . . do not allow for emotional connections to be made between readers and characters; and emphasize the unpredictability of affective connections" (2). Whereas Smith relies on a somewhat generalized account of neoliberalism's production of subjectivity, I emphasize the specific economic methodologies that transform emotions into economic indicators (methods that have a long history, traceable back to the marginalist microeconomics of the late nineteenth century), and attempt to historicize their new dominance as a response to the particular quandaries of a post-crisis economy. Only by doing so, I suggest, can one understand such methods (and their

attendant policies) as lacking the kind of coherence and unity sometimes attributed to regnant "modes of discourse," allowing us to understand fully the contradictions and impasses they inevitably confront (5). Whereas Smith asserts that the neoliberal subject "reconciles the contradictory commitments of democratic citizenship and capitalist competition," I suggest that behavioral economics, born of the economic contradictions that have characterized a regime of credit-fueled consumption, can in fact provide no such reconciliation: it produces instead a fractured, incoherent subject, at once valued for its particularity and flattened into genericity (5). In this sense, behavioral economics' account of the emotions shares much more with Smith's "impersonal feelings" than with the "personal feelings" she suggests are typically associated with the novel.

40. McPhee, *Dear Money*, 192 (hereafter cited by page number in the text).
41. Zimmerman, *Panic!*, 130.
42. Ibid.
43. See Andrei Shleifer and Lawrence Summers, "The Noise Trader Approach to Finance," *Journal of Economic Perspectives* 4.2 (1990): 19–33.
44. Walter Benn Michaels, *The Gold Standard and the Logic of Naturalism* (Berkeley: University of California Press, 1987), 33–34.
45. De Goede, "Mastering 'Lady Credit,'" 58–81, 63.
46. John Lanchester, *IOU: Why Everyone Owes Everyone and No One Can Pay* (New York: Simon and Schuster, 2010), 211 (emphasis mine).
47. Ibid., 9.
48. Shiller, *Subprime Solution*, 43.
49. Leigh Claire la Berge, "The Rules of Abstraction: Methods and Discourses of Finance," *Radical History Review* 118 (Winter 2014): 105.
50. Christopher Nealon, "Value, Theory, Crisis," *PMLA* 127.1 (January 2012): 102.
51. Haslett, *Union Atlantic*, 261–62 (hereafter cited by page number in the text).
52. Adam Smith, *An Inquiry into the Nature and Causes of the Wealth of Nations*, Project Gutenberg ebook, book 5, chap. 2, accessed May 27, 2016, http://www.gutenberg.org/ebooks/3300.
53. Adam Smith, *The Theory of Moral Sentiments*, Library of Economics and Liberty, accessed May 27, 2016, http://www.econlib.org/library/Smith/smMS.htm.
54. Smith, *An Inquiry*, book 1, chap. 2.
55. John Maynard Keynes, *The General Theory of Employment, Interest, and Money* (New York: BN Publishing, 2008), 155.
56. "Remarks by the President on Financial Rescue and Reform at Federal Hall," September 14, 2009, New York, https://www.whitehouse.gov/the-press-office/remarks-president-financial-rescue-and-reform-federal-hall.
57. Shiller, *Subprime Solution*, 175.
58. Akerlof and Shiller, *Animal Spirits*, 4.
59. Shiller, *Subprime Solution*, 175.

60. Karl Marx, "The Power of Money," in *Economic and Philosophical Manuscripts of 1844*, trans. Martin Mulligan (Moscow: Progress Publishers, 1959), https://www.marxists.org/archive/marx/works/1844/manuscripts/preface.htm.

61. Dee, *The Privileges*, 41 (hereafter cited by page number in the text).

62. Roth, "Credit Crisis and the Novel."

63. James Wood, "The Very Rich Hours," *New Yorker*, February 15, 2010, http://www.newyorker.com/magazine/2010/02/15/the-very-rich-hours-2.

64. On money, figuration, and the bildungsroman, see Anna Kornbluh, "On Marx's Victorian Novel," *Mediations* 25.1 (Fall 2010): 15–37.

65. Steven Shaviro, *Post Cinematic Affect* (London: Zero Books, 2010), 62.

66. Brian Richardson, *Unnatural Voices: Extreme Narration in Modern and Contemporary Fiction* (Columbus.: Ohio State University Press, 2006), 95–96.

67. Ibid., 96–97.

68. Wendy Brown, *Undoing the Demos: Neoliberalism's Stealth Revolution* (Cambridge, MA: Zone Books/MIT Press, 2015), 31.

69. Aristotle, *The Politics* (Oxford: Oxford University Press, 1998), 1258a35.

70. Walter Benn Michaels, "Going Boom," *Bookforum* (February/March 2009), http://www.bookforum.com/inprint/015_05/3274.

71. Qtd. in Zadie Smith, "Two Paths for the Novel," *New York Review of Books*, November 20, 2008, http://www.nybooks.com/articles/archives/2008/nov/20/two-paths-for-the-novel/.

Chapter 2

1. A portion of this chapter originally appeared as "Bad Credit: The Character of Credit Scoring," *Representations* 126. 1 (Spring 2014) © 2014 by the Regents of the University of California. Published by University of California Press.

2. Lauren Berlant, "Slow Death (Sovereignty, Obesity, Lateral Agency)," *Critical Inquiry* 33 (Summer 2007): 758.

3. "What Is a Credit Score," Experian Corporation, accessed May 23, 2016, http://www.familysecure.com/CreditScore.aspx.

4. Gary Shteyngart, *Super Sad True Love Story* (New York: Random House, 2010).

5. Marcel Mauss, "A Category of the Human Mind: The Notion of Person; the Notion of Self," trans. W. D. Halls, in *The Category of the Person: Anthropology, Philosophy, History*, ed. Michael Carrithers, Steven Collins, and Steven Lukes (Cambridge: Cambridge University Press, 1985), 6.

6. Elizabeth Fowler, *Literary Character: The Human Figure in Early English Writing* (Ithaca, NY: Cornell University Press, 2003), 5.

7. See Ian Baucom, *Specters of the Atlantic: Finance Capital, Slavery, and the Philosophy of History* (Durham, NC: Duke University Press, 2003); Carl Wennerlind, *Causalities of Credit: The English Financial Revolution* (Cambridge, MA: Harvard University

Press, 2011); Doncha Marron, *Consumer Credit in the United States: A Sociological Perspective from the 19th Century to the Present* (London: Palgrave Macmillan, 2009); John Greville Agard Pocock, *Virtue, Commerce, and History* (Cambridge: Cambridge University Press, 1985).

8. See Marron, *Consumer Credit in the United States*; Martha Poon, "From New Deal Institutions to Capital Markets: Commercial Consumer Risk Scores and the Making of Subprime Mortgage Finance," *Accounting, Organizations, and Society* 34 (2009): 654–74; Lendol Calder, *Financing the American Dream: A Cultural History of Consumer Credit* (Princeton, NJ: Princeton University Press, 1999); Louis Hyman, *Debtor Nation: The History of America in Red Ink* (Princeton, NJ: Princeton University Press, 2011).

9. See Margot Finn, *The Character of Credit: Personal Debt in English Culture, 1740–1914* (Cambridge: Cambridge University Press, 2003), 278–316; Rowena Olegario, *A Culture of Credit: Embedding Trust and Transparency in American Business* (Cambridge, MA: Harvard University Press, 2006), 180–218.

10. Kenneth Lipartito, "The Narrative and the Algorithm: Genres of Credit Reporting from the Nineteenth Century to Today," paper presented at the fall 2010 Harvard Business School Business History seminar, 1. Used with author's permission.

11. Qtd. in ibid., 19, 12.

12. See Donncha Marron, "'Lending by Numbers': Credit Scoring and the Constitution of Risk within American Consumer Credit," *Economy and Society* 36 (2007): 108–9.

13. Ingrid Jeacle and Eamonn Walsh, "From Moral Evaluation to Rationalization: Accounting and the Shifting Technologies of Credit," *Accounting, Organizations, and Society* 27 (2002): 743.

14. Finn, *The Character of Credit*; Deidre Lynch, *The Economy of Character: Novels, Market Culture, and the Business of Inner Meaning* (Chicago: University of Chicago Press, 1998). See also Baucom, *Specters of the Atlantic*.

15. See Lynch, *The Economy of Character*, 63–66.

16. Fredric Jameson, *Marxism and Form: Twentieth-Century Dialectical Theories of Literature* (Princeton, NJ: Princeton University Press, 1971), 191. Jameson's account of the character type who is "representative" of his moment or his social class derives from Georg Lukács, especially in *The Historical Novel* (Lincoln, NE: Merlin Press, 1983).

17. On the relationship between psychological interiority and democratic social space, see Alex Woloch, *The One vs. the Many: Minor Characters and the Space of the Protagonist in the Novel* (Princeton, NJ: Princeton University Press, 2003), esp. 30–32.

18. My use of the masculine pronoun here is intentional, since women in this period were more likely to use a kind of shadow or "fringe" lending system, especially pawnbrokers. See Marron, *Consumer Credit*.

19. Quoted in Jeacle and Walsh, "From Moral Evaluation to Rationalization," 743.

20. See Hyman, *Debtor Nation*, 10–44.

21. For another incisive history of this transformation, see Daniel Boorstin, *The Americans: The Democratic Experience* (New York: Knopf Doubleday, 2010).

22. On revolvers vs. non-revolvers, see Hyman, *Debtor Nation*, 220–80.

23. See Louis Hyman, *Borrow: The American Way of Debt* (New York: Vintage, 2012): 148–79.

24. See Andrew Leyshon and Nigel Thrift, "Lists Come Alive: Electronic Systems of Knowledge and the Rise of Credit-Scoring in Retail Banking," *Economy and Society* 28 (August 1999): 434–66.

25. David Hsia, "Credit Scoring and the Equal Credit Opportunity Act," *Hastings Law Journal* 30 (1978–79): 371.

26. "How Credit Scoring Helps Me," myFICO, Fair Isaac Corporation, accessed May 23, 2016, http://www.myfico.com/crediteducation/scoringhelps.aspx.

27. Marron, "Lending by Numbers," 104.

28. Martha Poon, "From New Deal Institutions to Capital Markets: Commercial Consumer Risk Scores and the Making of Subprime Mortgage Finance," *Accounting, Organizations, and Society* 35.5 (2009), 656, passim.

29. Ibid., 659.

30. Ibid., 656.

31. Charles Duhigg, "What Does Your Credit-Card Company Know about You?," *New York Times Magazine*, May 12, 2009, http://www.nytimes.com/2009/05/17/magazine/17credit-t.html?pagewanted=all&_r=0.

32. Ron Lieber, "American Express Kept a (Very) Watchful Eye on Charges," *New York Times*, January 30, 2009, http://www.nytimes.com/2009/01/31/your-money/credit-and-debit-cards/31money.html?pagewanted=all.

33. Federal Trade Commission, Plaintiff, v. CompuCredit Corporation and Jefferson Capital Systems, LLC, Defendants, December 19, 2008, http://www.ftc.gov/os/caselist/0623212/080610compucreditcmplt.pdf, 30.

34. Marron, "Lending by the Numbers," 108–9.

35. Jeacle and Walsh, "From Moral Evaluation to Rationalization," 755.

36. Lipartito, "The Narrative and the Algorithm," 34.

37. Patrick Brockett and Linda Golden, "Biological and Psychobehavioral Correlates of Credit Scores and Automobile Insurance Losses," *Journal of Risk and Insurance* 74.1 (March 2007): 26, 35.

38. Fowler, *Literary Character*, 5.

39. Raymond Williams, *Marxism and Literature* (Oxford: Oxford University Press, 1977), 209.

40. Shteyngart, *Super Sad*, 54–55 (hereafter cited by page number in the text).

41. Rayyan Al-Shawaf, "Äppärät-chic: Gary Shteyngart's *Super Sad True Love Story*," *The Millions*, July 30, 2010, http://www.themillions.com/2010/07/apparat-chic-gary-shteyngart's-super-sad-true-love-story.html.

42. Lynch, *The Economy of Character*, 58, 56.

43. Ibid., 64.

44. Michael Curry, "The Digital Individual and the Private Realm," *Annals of the Association of American Geographers* 87.4 (December 1997): 694.

45. On the "vulgar bookkeeping" of character, see Roland Barthes, *S/Z*, trans. Richard Miller (New York: Hill and Wang, 1991), 190–92.

46. Gilles Deleuze, "Postscript on the Societies of Control," *October* 59 (Winter 1992): 5.

47. See Stephen Ross and John Yinger, *The Color of Credit: Mortgage Discrimination, Research Methodology, and Fair Lending Enforcement* (Cambridge, MA: MIT Press, 2002).

48. National Community Reinvestment Coalition, "The Broken Credit System: Discrimination and Unequal Access to Affordable Loans by Race and Age: Subprime Lending in Ten Large Metropolitan Areas," 2003, http://www.ncrc.org/media-a-resources-main menu-118/-reports-a-research-library-mainmenu-76/345-the-broken-credit-system -discrimination-and-unequal-access-to-affordable-loans-by-race-and-age.

49. Frank Pasquale, "The Emperor's New Codes: Reputation and Search Algorithms in the Finance Sector," paper presented at the NYU "Governing Algorithms" conference, May 17, 2013, http://governingalgorithms.org/wp-content/uploads/2013/05/2-paper-pas quale.pdf, 21.

50. We might thus discern an intimate relationship between typification and stereotypification. As Colleen Lye suggests, "Preoccupation with difference at the level of the typical rather than the individual" corresponds with a "tendency towards racialization, or the reification of social relations into . . . types." Colleen Lye, *America's Asia: Racial Form and American Literature, 1893–1945* (Princeton, NJ: Princeton University Press, 2004), 8. For a seminal account of the relationship between typicality, race, and credit, see Baucom, *Specters of the Atlantic*, 3–34, 80–112.

51. See Poon, "From New Deal Institutions to Capital Markets," passim.

52. Fred Moten, "The Subprime and the Beautiful," *African Identities* 11.2 (2013): 240.

53. Sianne Ngai, *Our Aesthetic Categories: Zany, Cute, Interesting* (Cambridge, MA: Harvard University Press, 2012), 193. I refer to Ngai's "zany" not only because it shares the caricature's prerealist origins and contemporary return but also because her description of a figure whose affect veers between comedy and pathos, perpetually "wanting too much and trying too hard," equally describes Shteyngart's Lenny Abramov. Moreover, Lenny's job in the "Creative" sector resonates with Ngai's description of zaniness as the affective style of a post-Fordist economy, the result of a mode of production that "'put[s] to work' affect and subjectivity" and demands of its zany characters that they labor primarily at "amusing/educating/servicing the rich" (188–89).

54. From Cassie Thornton, "Give Me Credit" artist statement, courtesy of author. For more on this project, see http://givemecred.com/.

55. Walter Benn Michaels, "The Beauty of a Social Problem," *Brooklyn Rail* (October 3, 2011), http://www.brooklynrail.org/2011/10/art/the-beauty-of-a-social-problem.

56. David Graeber, *DEBT: The First 5000 Years* (Brooklyn: Melville House, 2011); Richard Dienst, *The Bonds of Debt: Borrowing against the Common Good* (London: Verso, 2011); Miranda Joseph, *Debt to Society: Accounting for Life under Capitalism* (Minneapolis: University of Minnesota Press, 2014); Angela Mitropoulos, *Contract and Contagion: From Biopolitics to Oikonomia* (Wivenhoe, NY: Minor Compositions Press, 2012); Maurizio Lazzarato, *The Making of the Indebted Man*, trans. Joshua David Jordan (Cambridge, MA: MIT Press, 2012); [Jason Read], "Debt Collectors: The Economics, Politics, and Morality of Debt," *Unemployed Negativity* (blog), November 13, 2011, http://www.unemployednegativity.com/2011/11/debt-collectors-economics-politics-and.html; Jussi Parikka, "On Borrowed Time: Lazzarato and Debt," *Machinology* (blog), November 29, 2011, http://jussiparikka.net/2011/11/29/on-borrowed-time-lazzarato-and-debt/; Brett Neilson, "The Magic of Debt, or Amortise This!," *Mute* 2.6 (July 5, 2007), http://www.metamute.org/editorial/articles/magic-debt-or-amortise; Melinda Cooper, "Life, Autopoiesis, Debt," *Distinktion: Journal of Social Theory* 8.1 (2007): 25–43; Simon Wortham, "Time of Debt: On the Nietzschean Origins of Lazzarato's Indebted Man," *Radical Philosophy* 180 (July/August 2013), http://www.radicalphilosophy.com/article/time-of-debt-on-nietzschean-origins-of-lazzarato.

57. Karl Marx, "Comments on James Mill," in *Éléments d'economie politique* [1844], trans. Clemens Dutt, in *Collected Works*, http://www.marxists.org/archive/marx/works/1844/james-mill/index.htm.

58. Friedrich Nietzsche, *On the Genealogy of Morality*, trans. Carol Diethe, Cambridge Texts in the History of Political Thought (Cambridge: Cambridge University Press, 2006), 45–46.

59. Lazzarato, *Making of the Indebted Man*, 30–31, 42, 49.

60. Hyman, *Debtor Nation*, 219.

61. See Heidi Shierholz and Lawrence Mishel, "A Decade of Flat Wages," Economic Policy Institute, Briefing Paper 365, August 2013, http://www.epi.org/publication/a-decade-of-flat-wages-the-key-barrier-to-shared-prosperity-and-a-rising-middle-class/; Harriet Komisar, "The Effects of Rising Health Care Costs on Middle-Class Economic Security," AARP Public Policy Institute Middle Class Security Project, January 2013, http://www.aarp.org/content/dam/aarp/research/public_policy_institute/security/2013/impact-of-rising-healthcare-costs-AARP-ppi-sec.pdf, 1.

62. John Bellamy Foster, "The Household Debt Bubble," *Monthly Review* 58.1 (May 2006), http://monthlyreview.org/2006/05/01/the-household-debt-bubble/.

63. The question of whether higher bankruptcy rates are due to "less stigma or more financial distress," as the title of one article puts it, has been hotly debated by economists, with behavioralists arguing the former and economic historians like Elizabeth Warren claiming the latter. See Teresa A. Sullivan, Elizabeth Warren, and Jay Lawrence Westbrook, "Less Stigma or More Financial Distress: An Empirical Analysis of the Extraordinary Increase in Bankruptcy Filings," *Stanford Law Review* 59.2 (November 2006): 213–56. My argument here is that while Warren and her colleagues are clearly

right that the cause of bankruptcy is the material circumstances of "financial distress," the behavioralists are also right to observe a "change in consumer attitude from the abhorrence of debt to its general acceptance as part of modern life" such that "the normalisation of debt . . . signals a pattern of attitude tolerance." Deidre O'Loughlin and Isabelle Szmigin, "'I'll Always Be in Debt': Irish and UK Student Behavior in a Credit Led Environment," *Journal of Consumer Marketing* 23.6 (2006): 340, 336.

64. Adrienne Roberts, "Doing Borrowed Time: The State, the Law, and the Coercive Governance of 'Undeserving' Debtors," *Critical Sociology* 40 (2014): 672. The use of debt peonage to enslave African Americans, however, remained a common practice in the post-bellum South well into the twentieth century. See Douglas Blackmon, *Slavery by Another Name* (New York: Knopf, 2008).

65. "Credit History," Think Glink, accessed May 23, 2016, http://www.thinkglink.com/category/credit-history/.

66. [Read], "Debt Collectors"; Tiziana Terranova, "Debt and Autonomy: Lazzarato and the Constituent Powers of the Social," *New Reader* 1 (2014), http://thenewreader.org/Issues/1/DebtAndAutonomy; David Palumbo-Liu, "Reframing Debt, Acting on Debt," *Oc.Ca.Sion* 7 (November 2014), http://arcade.stanford.edu/occasion/introduction-reframing-debt-acting-debt.

67. John Protevi, "Semantic, Pragmatic, and Affective Enactment at OWS," *Theory & Event* 14.4 (2011), http://muse.jhu.edu/journals/theory_and_event/v014/14.4S.protevi.html.

68. Melinda Cooper and Angela Mitropoulos, "In Praise of Usura," *Mute* 2.13 (May 27, 2009), http://www.metamute.org/editorial/articles/praise-usura.

69. Ibid.

70. Moten, "The Subprime and the Beautiful," 243.

71. Ngai, *Our Aesthetic Categories*, 193.

72. Alberto Toscano, "Alien Mediations: Critical Remarks on *The Making of the Indebted Man*," *New Reader* 1 (2014), http://thenewreader.org/Issues/1/AlienMediations.

73. Claire Bishop, *Artificial Hells: Participatory Art and the Politics of Spectatorship* (London: Verso, 2010), 25.

74. Cassie Thornton, *Our Bundles Our Selves* (San Francisco: Blurb Press, 2012).

75. On conceptual poetry, poetic subjectivity, and data aesthetics, see Paul Stephens, "From the Personal to the Proprietary: Conceptual Writing's Critique of Metadata," *Digital Humanities Quarterly* 6.2 (2012), http://www.digitalhumanities.org/dhq/vol/6/2/000124/000124.html. For a very different take on conceptual poetry's historicity, see Joshua Clover, "The Technical Composition of Conceptualism," *Mute* (April 2014), http://www.metamute.org/editorial/articles/technical-composition-conceptualism.

76. Mathew Timmons, *The A, D, O's and 1, 6, 10's of CREDIT* (Los Angeles: Insert Blanc Press, 2010). As this citation already suggests, I should note that I do not actually own—nor have I seen in person—the eight hundred–page version of *CREDIT*, which costs $199 in a physical copy and $299 to download. Rather, I own *The A, D, O's and*

1, 6, 10's of CREDIT, "a shortened, condensed, more affordable version of *CREDIT!*" Obviously, the high price of the full version is part of the point of the project—the press website selling both books notes that *CREDIT* is "the most expensive book publishable through the online service lulu.com" and describes it, cheekily, as "a book the author himself lacks the cash or credit to buy." The condensed version, from which all quotations here are taken, comprises 140 pages taken from the original. For the source of the quotations about the book, see http://www.insertblancpress.net/products/credit-by-mathew-timmons.

77. Stephen Voyce, "Reading the Redacted," presented at Post45 Conference, University of Iowa, November 2015, quoted with author's permission.

78. Ibid.

79. For a further account of conceptual poetry and the digital, see Kenneth Goldsmith, *Uncreative Writing: Managing Language in the Digital Age* (New York: Columbia University Press, 2011).

80. By willingly disclosing apparently private information, the text also insists that, in the words of the Experian website, "who you are as a person" has nothing to do with your ability to repay debt responsibly. It suggests that the "depersonalization" of credit—the anachronism of any language of moral responsibility or personal character in an age of impersonal lending agreements and algorithmic risk assessment—can be turned around on the lending institutions themselves, transforming the so-called ethics of responsibility into the politics of a refusal to repay one's debts or even simply the material condition of an inability to do so. See "What Is a Credit Score."

81. On conceptualism and information, see Ngai, *Our Aesthetic Categories*, 144–70.

82. Theodor Adorno, "Lyric Poetry and Society," in *The Lyric Theory Reader*, ed. Virginia Jackson and Yopie Prins (Baltimore: Johns Hopkins University Press, 2013), 340.

83. Craig Dworkin and Kenneth Goldsmith, eds., *Against Expression: An Anthology of Conceptual Writing* (Evanston, IL: Northwestern University Press, 2011), xlv.

84. Virginia Jackson, "Who Reads Poetry?," *PMLA* 123.2 (January 2008): 186.

85. Adorno, "Lyric Poetry and Society," 344.

86. Mary Poovey, *A History of the Modern Fact: Problems of Knowledge in the Sciences of Wealth* (Chicago: University of Chicago Press, 1998), 57–58.

87. Paul de Man, *The Rhetoric of Romanticism* (New York: Columbia University Press, 1984), 75–76.

88. Timothy Donnelly, *The Cloud Corporation* (Seattle: Wave Books, 2010), 7–9.

89. De Man, *The Rhetoric of Romanticism*, 75.

90. See Friedrich Engels, *Herr Eugen Duhring's Revolution in Science* (London: Forgotten Books, 2015).

91. Karl Marx, *Capital, Volume 1*, trans. Ben Fowkes (New York: Penguin Classics, 1976), 163–64.

92. Qtd. in Jonathan Flatley, "Warhol Gives Good Face: Publicity and the Politics of

Prosopopoeia," in *Pop Out: Queer Warhol*, ed. Jennifer Doyle, Jonathan Flatley, and Jose Esteban Munoz (Durham, NC: Duke University Press, 1996), 117. I am more generally indebted to Flatley's account of prosopopoeia as well.

93. It thus renders the particular strangeness of a commodity that "speaks to others for us, and speaks for others to us," as Jasper Bernes states in an eloquent essay on the relationship between the lyric voice and class relation. Jasper Bernes, "John Ashbery's Free Indirect Labor," *Modern Language Quarterly* 74.4 (December 2013): 532.

94. Ronda situates Donnelly's work among other contemporary poetic texts, including Timmons's, that demonstrate "how crisis produces defaulted or foreclosed forms of personhood." I want here to extend Ronda's compelling and urgent account but also to argue that the relationship between debt and the subject is more complicated than her framing (via Lazzarato) of the relationship between indebtedness and personality allows. I argue that in fact Donnelly's prosopopoeia conveys precisely this more complicated relationship between the apparent personality of credit and the coercive, material impersonality of debt. Margaret Ronda, "'Not *One*': The Poetics of Multitude in Great Recession-Era America," in *Class and the Making of American Literature*, ed. Andrew Lawson (London: Routledge, 2014), 246.

95. De Man, *The Rhetoric of Romanticism*, 81.

96. Lazzarato, *Making of the Indebted Man*, 59.

97. Marx, "Comments on James Mill."

98. Lazzarato, *Making of the Indebted Man*, 49.

Chapter 3

1. Calculated using Compound Annual Growth Rate Calculator for inflation-adjusted stock market returns, including dividends, between 1900 and 2000. Calculator accessed May 23, 2106, http://www.moneychimp.com/features/market_cagr.htm. See also Robert Shiller, "Why Home Prices Change (or Don't)," *New York Times*, April 13, 2013, http://www.nytimes.com/2013/04/14/business/why-home-prices-change-or-dont.html?pagewanted=all.

2. S&P Case-Shiller Home Price Indices, accessed May 23, 2016, http://us.spindices.com/index-family/real-estate/sp-case-shiller.

3. Karl Marx, *Capital, Volume 1* (New York: Penguin Classics, 1990), 919.

4. See Shane Sherlund, "The Past, Present, and Future of Subprime Mortgages," Finance and Economics Discussion Series, Divisions of Research and Statistics and Monetary Affairs, Federal Reserve Board, Washington, DC, November 2008, http://www.federalreserve.gov/pubs/feds/2008/200863/200863pap.pdf.

5. See Yuliya Demyanyk and Otto Van Hemert, "Understanding the Subprime Mortgage Crisis," Social Science Research Network, December 5, 2008, http://papers.ssrn.com/sol3/papers.cfm?abstract_id=1020396, 2; Samantha Parks, "Recent Foreclosure Statistics," Foreclosure Data Online, October 2012, http://www.foreclosuredataonline.com/blog/foreclosure-rate/recent-foreclosure-statistics/.

6. See CoreLogic, "Negative Equity Report," March 8, 2011, http://www.corelogic.com/downloadable-docs/corelogic-q4-2010-negative-equity-report.pdf; New York Federal Reserve, "Quarterly Report on Household Debt and Credit," February 2011, https://www.newyorkfed.org/medialibrary/media/newsevents/events/regional_outreach/2011/DistrictReport_Q4_2010.pdf, 9.

7. Pam Bennett, "The Aftermath of the Great Recession: Financially Fragile Families and How Professionals Can Help," *Forum for Family and Consumer Issues* 17.1 (Spring/Summer 2012), http://ncsu.edu/ffci/publications/2012/v17-n1-2012-spring/bennett.php.

8. For an overview of the data on losses in wealth among African American households in the wake of the crisis of 2008, see Charles Nier and Maureen R. St. Cyr, "A Racial Financial Crisis," *Temple Law Review* 83 (2011): 941–78.

9. Richard Dienst, *The Bonds of Debt: Borrowing against the Common Good* (London: Verso, 2011), 119.

10. Ben Hallman, "In Widely Published Photo, a House That Illustrates the Foreclosure Crisis," *HuffPost Business*, April 24, 2012, http://www.huffingtonpost.com/2012/04/24/mortgage-settlement-foreclosure-crisis-islip-brentwood-new-york_n_1444157.html.

11. Paul Reyes, "Picturing the Crisis," *New York Times*, October 12, 2010, http://opinionator.blogs.nytimes.com/2010/10/12/picturing-the-crisis/.

12. Ibid.

13. Siegfried Kracauer, "Photography," trans. Thomas Y. Levin, *Critical Inquiry* 19 (Spring 1993): 425, 429; See also Allan Sekula, "The Traffic in Photographs," *Art Journal* 41.1 (Spring 1985): 15–25.

14. Rosler, qtd. in Paula Rabinowitz, "Voyeurism and Class Consciousness: James Agee and Walker Evans, 'Let Us Now Praise Famous Men,'" *Cultural Critique* 21 (Spring 1992): 147.

15. Ariella Azoulay, "What Is a Photograph? What Is Photography?," *Philosophy of Photography* 1.1 (2010): 10.

16. Geoffrey Batchen, "Phantasm: Digital Imaging and the Death of Photography," *Aperture* 136 (Summer 1994): 48.

17. Walter Benjamin, "Paris, Capital of the Nineteenth Century," *New Left Review* 48 (March–April 1968): 85.

18. Sarah Safransky, "Greening the Urban Frontier: Race, Property, and Resettlement in Detroit," *Geoforum* 56 (2014): 238.

19. Rachel Hughes, "Race, Colonialism, and Vegetative Life," *Cultural Studies Review* 10.2 (September 2004): 200.

20. Richard Norton, "Feral Cities," *Naval War College Review* 56.4 (Autumn 2003): 98.

21. James Griffioen, "Feral Houses," *Sweet Juniper!* (blog), July 23, 2009, http://www.sweet-juniper.com/2009/07/feral-houses.html.

22. Bruce Gilden, "Detroit," accessed May 23, 2016, http://www.brucegilden.com/portfolio/detroit-michigan/.

23. "Remarks by the President on the Mortgage Crisis," The White House, February 18, 2009, speech at Mesa, AZ, https://www.whitehouse.gov/the-press-office/remarks-president-mortgage-crisis.

24. Brent White, "Underwater and Not Walking Away: Shame, Fear, and the Social Management of the Housing Crisis," *Arizona Legal Studies*, Discussion Paper No. 09-35 (October 2010): 999–1000.

25. Michael Lewis, "California *and* Bust," *Vanity Fair*, November 2011, http://www.vanityfair.com/news/2011/11/michael-lewis-201111.

26. Lauren Berlant, "Slow Death (Sovereignty, Obesity, Lateral Agency)," *Critical Inquiry* 33 (Summer 2007): 758.

27. See Charles Cunningham, "To Watch the Faces of the Poor: *LIFE* Magazine and the Mythology of Rural Poverty," *Journal of Narrative Theory* 29.3 (Fall 1999): 278–302.

28. Fredric Jameson, *The Seeds of Time* (New York: Columbia University Press, 1996), 151.

29. Jordan Weissmann, "The Recession's Toll: How Middle Class Wealth Collapsed to a 40-Year Low," *The Atlantic*, December 4, 2012, http://www.theatlantic.com/business/archive/2012/12/the-recessions-toll-how-middle-class-wealth-collapsed-to-a-40-year-low/265743/.

30. James Agee and Walker Evans, *Let Us Now Praise Famous Men* (New York: Mariner Books, 2013), 5, 164.

31. Susan Sontag, *Regarding the Pain of Others* (New York: Picador, 2003), 55.

32. Thus, according to Paula Rabinowitz, images like Evans's paradoxically "indicat[e] middle-class normality through absence. The photograph, revealing the lack of material objects in the lives of the poor, affirms by contrast the abundance of the viewer." Rabinowitz, "Voyeurism and Class Consciousness," 143.

33. See Cara A. Finnegan, *Picturing Poverty: Print Culture and FSA Photographs* (Washington, DC: Smithsonian Books, 2003); Cunningham, "To Watch the Faces of the Poor."

34. Shawn Shimpach, "Realty Reality: HGTV and the Housing Crisis," *American Quarterly* 64.3 (September 2012): 529, 520. See also Fiona Allon, "Speculating on Everyday Life: The Cultural Economy of the Quotidian," *Journal of Communication Inquiry* 34.4 (2010): 366–81.

35. In this sense they are very different from the post-crisis genre of reality-TV "poverty porn," which likewise centers around the house and domestic property but turns its prurient fascination to the depredations of financial insecurity, economic pathology, and the desire to turn a profit on others' losses: TLC's *Hoarding: Buried Alive* and A&E's *Hoarders*; Spike's *Auction Hunters* and A&E's *Storage Wars*; and Spike's *Flip Men* and HGTV's *Flip or Flop* (both specifically about flipping foreclosed properties) all were produced in the post-crisis period.

36. This ideological shape shifting has origins in genres prior to reality television. As Ian Watt points out in *The Rise of the Novel*, the realist novel's interest in *psychic*

interiority went hand in hand with a historical interest in the interior spaces of domestic life—thus, he observes, "we get inside the characters' minds as well as inside their houses." Watt historicizes this turn by observing that the rise of domestic fiction was concomitant with the rise of the suburb, that quintessentially removed sphere of domestic life that finds its apotheosis in Orange County's gated communities. Ian Watt, *The Rise of the Novel: Studies in Defoe, Richardson, Fielding* (Berkeley: University of California Press, 2001), 175.

37. Allen Sekula, "The Body and the Archive," *October* 39 (Winter 1986): 7.

38. See Linda Coco, "Debtor's Prison in the Neoliberal State: 'Debtfare' and the Cultural Logics of the Bankruptcy Prevention and Consumer Protection Act of 2005," April 2012, http://works.bepress.com/linda_coco/2.

39. Creola Johnson, "Renters Evicted en Masse: Collateral Damage Arising from the Subprime Foreclosure Crisis," *Florida Law Review* 62 (January 2010): 977–78.

40. See Kevin Valine, "Calif. LODD Shows Dangers of Serving Evictions," Officer.com, April 13, 2012, http://www.officer.com/news/10695653/calif-lodd-shows-dangers-of-serving-evictions.

41. Laura Gottesdiener, "The Great Eviction: The Landscape of Wall Street's Creative Destruction," TomDispatch.com, August 1, 2013, http://www.tomdispatch.com/post/175731/tomgram%3A_laura_gottesdiener,_the_backyard_shock_doctrine/.

42. Mike King, "The Vacancies of Capitalism," *CounterPunch* (November 30, 2011), http://www.counterpunch.org/2011/11/30/the-vacancies-of-capitalism/.

43. Adrienne Roberts, "Doing Borrowed Time: The State, the Law, and the Coercive Governance of 'Undeserving' Debtors," *Critical Sociology* 40 (2014): 672.

44. My thinking on this issue was helped by e-mail conversations with Bill McClanahan and Tyler Wall.

45. Anne Carson, *Economy of the Unlost: Reading Simonides of Keos with Paul Celan* (Princeton, NJ: Princeton University Press, 2009), 59.

46. Sigmund Freud, "The Uncanny," trans. James Strachey (1955), *New Literary History* 7.3 (Spring 1976): 619–45, 621.

47. Anthony Vidler, *The Architectural Uncanny: Essays in the Modern Unhomely* (Cambridge, MA: MIT Press, 1992), 4.

48. Freud, "The Uncanny," 624. As Nicholas Royle notes in his book-length study of Freud's uncanny, the uncanny unleashes "a crisis of the proper . . . a disturbance of the very idea of personal or private property." Nicholas Royle, *The Uncanny* (Manchester, UK: Manchester University Press, 2003), 1.

49. Melinda Cooper and Angela Mitropoulos, "Household Frontier," *ephemera* 9.4 (2009): 367.

50. Theodor Adorno, *Minima Moralia* (London: Verso, 2006), 39.

51. On Marx and Freud's shared concern with "the vexed subject-object relations created by commodity fetishism," see John Marx, *The Modernist Novel and the Decline of Empire* (Cambridge: Cambridge University Press, 2005), 125.

52. Karl Marx, "Comments on James Mill," *Éléments d'économie politique* [1844], trans. Clemens Dutt, in *Collected Works*, http://www.marxists.org/archive/marx/works/1844/james-mill/index.htm.

53. Dienst, *Bonds of Debt*, 119.

54. Curiously, Marx himself was also interested in Hoffman's stories and, according to his daughter Eleanor, often told versions of them to his children. Richard Dienst has an extended reading of these stories in *The Bonds of Debt*. For Dienst, Marx's early analysis of debt evinces a kind of nostalgia for "an originary . . . plenitude." However, I suggest that by reading Marx on debt through Freud on the uncanny, we can see that this residue of the past made manifest by debt is not a symptom of nostalgia but of an uncanny return of the repressed. And in so doing, I think we are able to see that debt functions not so much as an apparent absence concealing a surplus of potential social wealth but rather as the total absence around which capital's constitutive antisocial violence circulates. Ibid., 137–53.

55. Freud, "The Uncanny," 636.

56. Evan Calder Williams, "Hostile Object Theory," *Mute* (February 1, 2011), http://www.metamute.org/editorial/articles/hostile-object-theory. For Williams, the "hostile objects of capitalism aren't just indifferent to us or darkly coherent behind our intentions" but "indicat[e] an impersonal, total enmity." Williams's hostility echoes what I describe in the Coda as the uncanny of sabotage.

57. Freud, "The Uncanny," 624.

58. Fred Moten and Stefano Harney, "Debt and Study," *E-Flux* 14 (March 2010), http://www.e-flux.com/journal/debt-and-study/.

59. For a discussion of the fascination with Detroit in the immediate aftermath of the financial crisis, see Thomas Morton, "Something, Something, Something Detroit," *VICE*, August 1, 2009, http://www.vice.com/read/something-something-something-detroit-994-v16n8.

60. See Detroiturbex, "Fischer Body Plant 21," accessed May 23, 2016, http://www.detroiturbex.com/content/industry/fisher/index.html.

61. John Patrick Leary, "Detroitism," *Guernica*, January 15, 2011, https://www.guernicamag.com/features/leary_1_15_11/.

62. Ibid.

63. Leary also discusses Detroit as metonymy but again sees the metonymic as the obverse of the historical.

64. Robert Brenner, "What Is Good for Goldman Sachs Is Good for America: The Origins of the Current Crisis," April 2009, http://www.escholarship.org/uc/item/0sg0782h, 5.

65. Gopal Balakrishnan, "Speculations on a Stationary State," *New Left Review* 59 (September–October 2009): 11.

66. Leary, "Detroitism."

67. Balakrishnan, "Speculations on a Stationary State," 15.

68. As Georg Lukács argues, crisis "makes manifest the unity of processes which had become individually independent." Georg Lukács, "Realism in the Balance," in *Aesthetics and Politics* (London: Verso, 1980), 32.

69. For a powerful account of this process as it appears in representations of Detroit in particular, see Morgan Adamson, "Labor, Finance, and Counterrevolution," *South Atlantic Quarterly* 111.4 (2012): 803–23. As Adamson puts it, a theorization of historical transition would account for a logic of cyclical continuity "between industrial capitalism and our financialized present," allowing us to read the "short American century through the crisis in its capital: Detroit" (804).

70. See Helene Cixous, "Fiction and Its Phantoms: A Reading of Freud's *Das Unheimliche*," *New Literary History* 7.3 (Spring 1976): 525–48.

71. Freud, "The Uncanny," 635.

72. Karl Marx, *Capital, Volume 3*, trans. David Fernbach (New York: Penguin Classics, 1993), 463, 523.

73. Detroiturbex, *Packard Automobile Plant*, accessed May 23, 2016, http://www.detroiturbex.com/content/industry/packard/index.html.

74. Leary, "Detroitism."

75. Michael Alexander Ulfstjerne, "Creative Land Grabs: The Ordos 100 Spectacle Revisited," Creative Transformations Asia, October 2012, http://www.creativetransformations.asia/2012/10/creative-land-grabs-the-ordos-100-spectacle-revisited/.

76. Ibid.

77. Yang, qtd. in Kate McKenzie, "China's Ubiquitous Ghost Cities," *Financial Times*, November 26, 2012, http://ftalphaville.ft.com/2012/11/26/1279513/chinas-ubiquitous-ghost-cities/.

78. "Time for a Property Tax," *The Economist*, February 4, 2012, http://www.economist.com/node/21546014; Vitaliy Katsenelson, "Why China Is Really in Big Trouble," *Forbes*, October 18, 2010, http://www.forbes.com/sites/greatspeculations/2010/10/18/why-china-is-really-in-big-trouble/.

79. See Eric Hayot, "Chinese Bodies, Chinese Futures," *Representations* 99.1 (Summer 2007): 99–129.

80. Colleen Lye, "The Literary Case of Wen-Ho Lee," *Journal of Asian American Studies* 14.2 (June 2011): 272.

81. Rachel Lee, *The Exquisite Corpse of Asian America: Biopolitics, Biosociality, and Posthuman Ecologies* (New York: New York University Press, 2014), 14.

82. Chandni Rathod and Gus Lubin, "And Now Presenting: Amazing Satellite Images of the Ghost Cities of China," *Business Insider*, December 14, 2010, http://www.businessinsider.com/pictures-chinese-ghost-cities-2010-12.

83. Karl Marx, *A Contribution to the Critique of Political Economy*, ed. Maurice Dobbs (New York: International Publishers, 1970), 88–89.

84. Balakrishnan, "Speculations on a Stationary State," 26.

85. Marx, *Capital, Volume 3*, 524, 573.

86. Freud, "The Uncanny," 635.

87. Marx, *Capital, Volume 3*, chap. 27, https://www.marxists.org/archive/marx/works/1894-c3/ch27.htm. I selected this source over the Penguin edition previously cited because of the power of this particular way of translating the phrase.

88. Theodor Adorno, *Prisms*, trans. Samuel Weber and Shierry Weber Nicholsen (Cambridge, MA: MIT Press, 1981), 233.

89. Benjamin, "Paris, Capital of the Nineteenth Century," 88.

Chapter 4

1. Part of this chapter originally appeared as "Dead Pledges: Debt, Horror, and the Credit Crisis," *Post45 Peer Reviewed* (May 7, 2012), http://post45.research.yale.edu/2012/05/dead-pledges-debt-horror-and-the-credit-crisis/.

2. "House of Horrors, Part 2," *The Economist*, November 26, 2011, http://www.economist.com/node/21540231.

3. *Drag Me to Hell*, dir. Sam Raimi (Universal City, CA: Universal Studios, 2009), DVD; *Dream Home* (*Wai dor lei ah yut ho*), dir. Pang Ho-cheung (Orlando Park, IL: MPI Home Video, 2010), DVD; *Mother's Day*, dir. Darren Lynn Bousman (Beverly Hills, CA: Anchor Bay Entertainment, 2010), DVD; *Crawlspace*, dir. Josh Stolberg (Beverly Hills, CA: Vuguru, 2013), https://play.google.com/store/movies/details?id=rjYUacke87k.

4. See Douglas W. Arner, "The Global Credit Crisis of 2008: Causes and Consequences," *International Lawyer* 43.1 (Spring 2009): 91–136.

5. See Robert Brenner, "What Is Good for Goldman Sachs Is Good for America: The Origins of the Present Crisis," October 2, 2009, http://www.escholarship.org/uc/item/0sg0782h.

6. See Robin Blackburn, "The Subprime Crisis," *New Left Review* 50 (March–April 2008): 63–106.

7. See Souphala Chomsisengphet and Anthony Pennington-Cross, "The Evolution of the Subprime Mortgage Market," *Federal Reserve Bank of St. Louis Review* 88.1 (January–February 2006): 31–56; Dan Immergluck, *Foreclosed: High Risk Lending, Deregulation, and the Undermining of America's Mortgage Market* (Ithaca, NY: Cornell University Press, 2009).

8. Macleod, qtd. in Vinod Kothari, *Securitization: The Financial Instrument of the Future* (New York: Wiley, 2006), 4.

9. See Louis Hyman, *Debtor Nation: The History of America in Red Ink* (Princeton, NJ: Princeton University Press, 2011), esp. 251–78.

10. On the relationship between the US government and the deregulation of this market, see Peter Gowan, "Crisis in the Heartland," *New Left Review* 55 (January–February 2009): 5–29.

11. See Blackburn, "The Subprime Crisis."

12. Whereas the collateral of an asset-backed security is the asset itself (in the case

of MBSs, the house), the collateral of a CMO is another structured product (all of the pooled MBSs). Thus, CMOs and CDOs (collateralized debt obligations, securities backed by a range of debt types) are highly diversified investments since they can include securities backed by everything from houses to small businesses to exotic assets like litigation settlements.

13. Ben Bernanke, "Housing, Housing Finance, and Monetary Policy," Federal Reserve Board speech, August 31, 2007, Jackson Hole, WY, http://www.federalreserve.gov/newsevents/speech/bernanke20070831a.htm. See also Kevin Fox Gotham, "Creating Liquidity out of Spatial Fixity: The Secondary Circuit of Capital and the Subprime Mortgage Crisis," *International Journal of Urban and Regional Research* 33.2 (June 2009): 355–71.

14. See Vincenzo Bavoso, "Financial Innovation, Structured Finance, and Off Balance Sheet Financing: The Case of Securitization," Social Science Research Network, January 1, 2010, http://papers.ssrn.com/sol3/papers.cfm?abstract_id=1746109.

15. On risk, leverage, and the CDO crisis, see Gowan, "Crisis in the Heartland"; Blackburn, "The Subprime Crisis"; Brenner, "What Is Good for Goldman Sachs."

16. Karen McCormack and Iyar Mazar, "Foreclosure Risk: The Role of Nativity and Gender," *Critical Sociology* 4.1 (February 2013), passim. One way to understand this form of lived risk is as the intensification of the "everyday" risk that Randy Martin influentially describes in *The Financialization of Daily Life* (Philadelphia: Temple University Press, 2002). Martin attends to the discourse and affects of risk that entered both the consciousness and the domestic economies of middle- and working-class families during the financial boom; McCormack and Mazar's idea of radical risk extends Martin's account to describe the risk that transformed the material circumstances of those same economic subjects during the collapse.

17. See Yuliya Demyanyk and Otto Van Hemert, "Understanding the Subprime Mortgage Crisis," Social Science Research Network, January 2009, http://papers.ssrn.com/sol3/papers.cfm?abstract_id=1020396; Samantha Parks, "Recent Foreclosure Statistics," Foreclosure Data Online, October, 2012, http://www.foreclosuredataonline.com/blog/foreclosure-rate/recent-foreclosure-statistics/.

18. Shadi Houshyar, Julia Isaacs, and Phillip Lovell, "The Impact of the Mortgage Crisis on Children," First Focus, May 2008, http://firstfocus.org/resources/report/impact-mortgage-crisis-children/.

19. See Elvin Wyly, C. S. Ponder, Pierson Nettling, Bosco Ho, Sophie Ellen Fung, Zachary Liebowitz, and Dan Hammel, "New Racial Meanings of Housing in America," *American Quarterly* 64.3 (September 2012): 571–604; Jesus Hernandez, "Redlining Revisited: Mortgage Lending Patterns in Sacramento 1930–2004," *International Journal of Urban and Regional Research* 33.2 (June 2009): 291–313.

20. John Gittelsohn, "Blackstone to Get 2.1 Billion Loan for Home Purchases," Bloomberg, March 13, 2013, http://www.bloomberg.com/news/2013-03-13/blackstone-said-to-get-2-1-billion-bank-loan-for-home-purchases.html. See also Motoko Rich, "Investors Looking to Buy Homes by the Thousands," *New York Times*, April 2, 2012,

http://www.nytimes.com/2012/04/03/business/investors-are-looking-to-buy-homes-by-the-thousands.html?pagewanted=all.

21. Aaron Glantz, "Report: Investors Buy Nearly Half of Oakland's Foreclosed Homes," *Bay Citizen*, June 28, 2012, http://californiawatch.org/dailyreport/report-investors-buy-nearly-half-oaklands-foreclosed-homes-16863.

22. David Dayen, "Your New Landlord Works on Wall Street," *New Republic*, February 12, 2013, http://www.newrepublic.com/article/112395/wall-street-hedge-funds-buy-rental-properties.

23. Laura Gottesdiener, "Wall Street's Hot New Financial Product: Your Rent Check," *Mother Jones*, March/April 2014, http://www.motherjones.com/politics/2014/01/blackstone-rental-homes-bundled-derivatives; Yves Smith, "New Real Estate Train Wreck Coming: Securitized Rentals," Naked Capitalism, August 27, 2012, http://www.nakedcapitalism.com/2012/08/new-real-estate-train-wreck-coming-securitized-rentals.html.

24. See Aaron Unterman, "Exporting Risk: Global Implications of the Securitization of U.S. Housing Debt," *Hastings Business Law Journal* 90–91 (Winter 2008): 77–134.

25. The gothic fiction of the Victorian era was also often a response specifically to financial panic: critic Gail Houston argues that just as Victorian capitalism "normalized economic panic" and made it seem necessary to healthy economic function, gothic literature used horror as a way to "register, manage, and assess the intense panic produced and elided by the unstable Victorian economy" and even taught its readers how to "sublimat[e] panic in order to achieve financial success." However, for Houston as for Moretti, gothic "crisis fiction" ultimately serves to naturalize crisis and fear by literally "domesticating" it. Gail Turley Houston, *From Dickens to Dracula: Gothic, Economics, and Victorian Fiction* (Cambridge: Cambridge University Press, 2005), 10–11, 3.

26. Stephen King, *Danse Macabre* (New York: Simon and Schuster, 2010), 13.

27. Ibid.

28. Franco Moretti, *Signs Taken for Wonders: On the Sociology of Literary Forms* (London: Verso, 2005), 84–108.

29. Isabella Christina Pinedo, *Recreational Terror: Women and the Pleasures of Horror Film Viewing* (Albany: State University of New York Press, 1997),15; King, *Danse Macabre*, 13.

30. Bruce Kawin, "The Mummy's Pool," in *Planks of Reason: Essays on the Horror Film*, ed. Barry Grant and Christopher Sharrett (Lanham, MD: Scarecrow Press, 2004), 7; Barry Brummett, "Electric Literature as Equipment for Living: Haunted House Films," *Critical Studies in Mass Communication* 2.3 (1985): 253; Houston, *From Dickens to Dracula*, 10–11.

31. There are of course critics who see horror as having a much more critical function. Recent work by Peter Paik on the relationship between zombies and neoliberalism, for instance, refuses to see Moretti's "restoration of order" in horror, but the end result is more baleful than critical, since Paik reads contemporary zombie culture as symptomatic of neoliberalism and consumer culture. Paik, "The Gnostic Zombie and the State

of Nature: On Robert Kirkman's *The Walking Dead*," Social Science Research Network, August 18, 2011, http://papers.ssrn.com/sol3/papers.cfm?abstract_id=1912203, 20.

32. Moretti, *Signs Taken for Wonders*, 84–108.

33. Fredric Jameson, *The Political Unconscious* (Ithaca, NY: Cornell University Press, 1981), 79.

34. See James Swallow, *Dark Eye: The Films of David Fincher* (Surrey, UK: Reynolds and Hearn, 2003).

35. A list on Wikipedia includes seventeen home-invasion films released just between 2008 and 2012 (and as a very incomplete list, it doesn't even include *Mother's Day* or *Crawlspace*)—compared with the approximately ten per decade listed for the previous fifty years; this suggests a growing fascination with the home-invasion plot. Indeed, a number of the post-2008 home-invasion films are remakes of 1970s classics, most notably *Straw Dogs* and *Last House on the Left*.

36. Scott Hallam, "Director Josh Stolberg Gets into the Crawlspace," dreadcentral.com, July 2014, http://www.dreadcentral.com/news/55076/director-josh-stolberg-gets-into-the-crawlspace/.

37. *Mother's Day*, dir. Charles Kaufman (Long Island City, NY: Troma Retro, 1980), DVD.

38. Carol Clover, *Men, Women, and Chainsaws* (Princeton, NJ: Princeton University Press, 1993), 134.

39. "President Calls for Expanding Opportunities for Home Ownership," remarks by George W. Bush, AME Church, June 2002, Atlanta, http://georgewbush-whitehouse.archives.gov/news/releases/2002/06/20020617-2.html.

40. Tom Palmer, "An Ownership Society Fosters Responsibility, Liberty, Prosperity," Cato Institute, January 13, 2004, http://www.cato.org/publications/commentary/ownership-society-fosters-responsibility-liberty-prosperity.

41. Greenspan, qtd. in Edmund Andrews, "Fed Shrugged as Subprime Crisis Spread," *New York Times*, December 18, 2007, http://www.nytimes.com/2007/12/18/business/18subprime.html?pagewanted=print&_r=.

42. Palmer, "An Ownership Society."

43. Paula Marantz Cohen, "Conceptual Suspense in Hitchcock's Films," in *A Companion to Alfred Hitchcock*, ed. Thomas Leitch (London: Wiley Blackwell, 2011), 136.

44. John Locke, *Second Treatise of Government* (Cambridge: Cambridge University Press, 1988), 286.

45. Margaret Jane Radin, "Property and Personhood," *Stanford Law Review* 34.5 (May 1982): 957–1015.

46. See Jacques Derrida and Anne Dufourmantelle, *Of Hospitality*, trans. Rachel Bowlby (Stanford, CA: Stanford University Press, 2000).

47. See Dan Immergluck and Jonathan Law, "Speculating in Crisis: The Metropolitan Geography of Investing in Foreclosed Homes in Atlanta," *Urban Geography* 35.1 (2014): 1–24.

48. Qtd. in Lee Anne Fennell, "Efficient Trespass: The Case for 'Bad Faith' Adverse Possession," *Northwestern University Law Review* (2006): 1048.

49. Fennell, "Efficient Trespass," 1040.

50. Hannah Dobbz, *Nine-Tenths of the Law: Property and Resistance in the United States* (New York: AK Press, 2012), 114–15.

51. See Alan Weinberger, "Let the Buyer Be Well Informed? Doubting the Demise of Caveat Emptor," *Maryland Law Review* 55.2 (1996): 387–424.

52. See David Chapman and Marty Ludlum, "Stigmatized Property: You Don't Have a Ghost of a Chance," *Journal of Business Cases and Applications* 11 (July 2014), http://www.aabri.com/manuscripts/131758.pdf.

53. See Colin Dayan, *The Law Is a White Dog: How Legal Rituals Make and Unmake Persons* (Princeton, NJ: Princeton University Press, 2011), 3–5.

54. Bruce Carruthers and Arthur Stinchcombe, "The Social Structure of Liquidity: Flexibility, Markets, and States," *Theory and Society* 28.3 (June 1999): 353.

55. Adam Smith, *An Inquiry into the Nature and Causes of the Wealth of Nations*, Project Gutenberg ebook, book 4, chap. 7, accessed May 27, 2016, http://www.gutenberg.org/ebooks/3300.

56. See Richard Sennet, *Flesh and Stone: The Body and the City in Western Civilization* (New York: W.W. Norton, 1996), 256.

57. See Brad Pasanek and Simone Polillo, "Guest Editors' Introduction," *Journal of Cultural Economy* 4.3 (2011): 231–38.

58. Gotham, "Creating Liquidity," 359.

59. Hyman, *Borrow*, 213.

60. Pasanek and Polillo, "Guest Editors' Introduction," 237.

61. John Maynard Keynes, *The General Theory of Employment, Interest, and Money* (New York: BN Publishing, 2008), 155.

62. Deidre Lynch, *The Economy of Character: Novels, Market Culture, and the Business of Inner Meaning* (Chicago: University of Chicago Press, 1998), 96–98.

63. Dick Bryan, Michael Rafferty, and Randy Martin, "Financialization and Marx: Giving Labor and Capital a Financial Makeover," *Review of Radical Political Economics* 41.4 (September 2009): 465.

64. Matt Taibbi, "The American Bubble Machine," *Rolling Stone*, April 5, 2010, http://www.rollingstone.com/politics/news/the-great-american-bubble-machine-20100405.

65. Keynes, *General Theory*, 155.

66. The original Cantonese title, *Wai dor lei ah yut ho*, translates literally as "No. 1 Victoria Bay," the address of the apartment building in which the killings take place. The Mandarin title translates to the slightly less subtle "Bloody Real Estate." Thanks to Chenhao Tan and Hu Fu for the translation.

67. The Arrow, "Interview: Dream Home Director Ho-Cheung Pang Drops By!," March 18, 2011, http://www.joblo.com/horror-movies/news/interview-dream-home-director-ho-cheung-pang-drops-by.

68. See Hung Ho-fung, "Paper Tiger Finance?," *New Left Review* 72 (November–December 2011): 138–44.

69. See Chan Kam Wah, "Prosperity or Inequality: Deconstructing the Myth of Home Ownership in Hong Kong," *Housing Studies* 15.1 (2000): 28–43.

70. Kwok Kin Fung and Ray Forrest, "Securitization, the Global Financial Crisis, and Residential Capitalisms in an East Asian Context," *Housing Studies* 26.7–8 (2011): 1235.

71. Comparatively, during the US housing boom the median down payment was 2 percent, with more than 40 percent of borrowers paying 0 percent. Even in the post-subprime crisis United States, most buyers borrow about 80 percent of a home's value, and FHA-sponsored loans can cover up to 96.5 percent.

72. Fung and Forrest, "Securitization," 1243. See also Alan Smart and James Lee, "Financialisation and the Role of Real Estate in Hong Kong's Regime of Accumulation," *Economic Geography* 79.2 (2003): 153–71.

73. See Wah, "Prosperity or Inequality," 38.

74. Helen Hau-ling Cheng, "Consuming a Dream: Homes in Advertisements and Imagination in Contemporary Hong Kong," in *Consuming Hong Kong*, ed. Gordon Matthews (Hong Kong: University of Hong Kong Press, 2001), 221.

75. Bhaskar Sarkar, "Hong Kong Hysteria: Martial Arts Tales from a Mutating World," in *At Full Speed: Hong Kong Cinema in a Borderless World*, ed. Esther Yau (Minneapolis: University of Minnesota Press, 2001), 159–76.

76. As critic Audrey Jaffe has suggested, irrational exuberance forces us to "register the identification of the economic with emotional well-being," to acknowledge that market values—volatile, temporary—index feeling as much as fact. *Dream Home*, like the real estate market itself, thus consistently fails to differentiate between the quantitative and the qualitative, reason and madness. Audrey Jaffe, "Trollope in the Stock Market: Irrational Exuberance and *The Prime Minister*," *Victorian Studies* 45.1 (Autumn 2001): 48.

77. Chris Hogg, "Hong Kong's 'Sandwich Class' Face Housing Woes," BBC News, Hong Kong, May 15, 2011, http://www.bbc.com/news/business-13385794; Eunice Yoon, "Living in a Cage in Hong Kong," CNN News, October 2009, http://edition.cnn.com/2009/WORLD/asiapcf/10/28/cage.homes/index.html.

78. See David McNally, "From Financial Crisis to World-Slump: Accumulation, Financialisation, and the Global Slowdown," *Historical Materialism* 17 (2009): 35–83.

79. See Anne Haila, "Real Estate in Global Cities: Singapore and Hong Kong as Property States," *Urban Studies* 37.12 (July 2000): 2241–56; Grace Wong Bucchianeri, "The Anatomy of a Housing Bubble: Overconfidence, Media and Politics," Social Science Research Network, April 2011, http://papers.ssrn.com/sol3/papers.cfm?abstract_id=1877204.

80. "Hong Kong Properties: Mid-Levels They Ain't," *The Economist*, April 28, 2012, http://www.economist.com/node/21553462.

81. Tyler Durden, "Hong Kong Housing Bubble Suffers Spectacular Collapse as

Sales Plunge 42% to Record Low," Zero Hedge, December 3, 2015, http://www.zero hedge.com/news/2015-12-03/hong-kong-housing-bubble-suffers-spectacular-collapse-sales-plunge-42-record-low.

82. Moretti, *Signs Taken for Wonders*, 84–108.

83. According to linguist Carole Hough, a linguistic association between repayment and revenge occurs in many languages, suggesting a powerful "metonymic connection" between these two semantic fields. Carole Hough, "Repayment and Revenge," *English Historical Linguistics* (2012): 85–98.

84. Amanda Bailey, "*Timon of Athens*, Forms of Payback, and the Genre of Debt," *English Literary Renaissance* 41.2 (Spring 2011): 382.

85. Clover, *Men, Women, and Chainsaws*, 21–64.

86. Fredric Jameson, "The Brick and the Balloon: Architecture and Land Speculation," *New Left Review* 1.228 (March–April 1998): 46.

87. Mike Davis, *Planet of Slums* (London: Verso, 2006), 26.

88. Bishnupriya Ghosh, "The Security Aesthetic in Bollywood's High-Rise Horror," *Representations* 126.1 (Spring 2014): 60–63.

89. Clover, *Men, Women, and Chainsaws*, 115.

90. Ibid., 163.

91. Ibid., 135–37. The Koffins even appear to be among what policy makers call the "unbanked," foolishly sending cash by mail rather than by virtual bank transfer and insisting on being paid their ransom in bills (when Ike holds up two women at an ATM machine and one offers to write him a check, he refuses, saying, "Sorry, sweetheart, I don't have time for the check to clear").

92. Ibid., 124.

93. Alex Schafran, "Discourse and Dystopia, American Style: The Rise of 'Slumburbia' in a Time of Crisis," *City: An Analysis of Urban Trends, Culture, Theory, Policy, Action* 17.2 (2013): 130–31.

94. Locke, *Second Treatise of Government*, 350.

Coda

1. An early version of this Coda appeared as "The Living Indebted: Student Militancy and the Financialization of Debt," *Qui Parle* 20.1 (Fall/Winter 2011). Published by University of Nebraska Press.

2. For reports on these incidents, see Michael Phillips, "Buyers' Revenge: Trash the House after Foreclosure," *Wall Street Journal*, March 28, 2008, http://www.wsj.com/articles/SB120665586676569881; "8 Insane Ways People Destroyed Their Foreclosed Homes," InvestingAnswers, August 30, 2012, http://www.investinganswers.com/personal-finance/homes-mortgages/8-insane-ways-people-destroyed-their-foreclosed-homes-4603.

3. Jasper Bernes, "The Double Barricade and the Glass Floor," in *Communication and Its Discontents: Contestation, Critique, and Contemporary Struggles*, ed. Benjamin Noyes (Brooklyn: Minor Compositions, n.d.), 161–62.

4. For a useful and powerful account of sabotage as "the mirrored moment of exchange," see Evan Calder Williams, "Hostile Object Theory," *Mute* (February 1, 2011), http://www.metamute.org/editorial/articles/hostile-object-theory.

5. Morgan Adamson, "Accounting for Ashes: The Art of Sabotage in the Chilean Student Movement," *Minnesota Review* 85 (2015): 162, 163.

6. See the City Life/Vida Urbana website, accessed May 23, 2016, http://www.clvu.org/.

7. Final Straw, "History of the Foreclosure Defense Group: An Interview with Brooke on Race, Class, and Housing," Fireworks: Anarchist Counterinformation Project for the Bay Area, January 15, 2016, https://fireworksbayarea.com/featured/history-of-the-foreclosure-defense-group-an-interview-with-brooke-on-race-class-and-housing/.

8. See Federal Reserve Bank of New York, "Household Debt Continues Upward Climb While Student Loan Delinquencies Worsen," February 17, 2015, https://www.newyorkfed.org/newsevents/news/research/2015/rp150217.html; Juan Sánchez and Lijun Zhu, "Student Loan Delinquency: A Big Problem Getting Worse?," Federal Reserve Bank of St. Louis Economic Research Department, April 10, 2015, https://research.stlouisfed.org/publications/economic-synopses/2015/04/10/student-loan-delinquency-a-big-problem-getting-worse/; Meta Brown, Andrew Haughwout, Donghoon Lee, Joelle Scally, and Wilbert van der Klaauw, "Looking at Student Loan Defaults through a Larger Window," Federal Reserve Bank of New York *Liberty Street Economics* (blog), February 19, 2015, http://libertystreeteconomics.newyorkfed.org/2015/02/looking_at_student_loan_defaults_through_a_larger_window.html#.Vx5Qa3qgqNM.

9. Catherine Dunn, "America's Private Student Loan Debt Rising, Despite Risks, Costs That Exceed Government Loans," *International Business Times*, June 13, 2014, http://www.ibtimes.com/americas-private-student-loan-debt-load-rising-despite-risks-costs-exceed-government-1600860.

10. Thomas Harnisch, "The Public Realities of Private Student Loans: A Higher Education Policy Brief," American Association of State Colleges and Universities, April 2008, http://www.aascu.org/policy/publications/policymatters/2008/privatestudentloans.pdf, 2; The Institute for College Access & Success, "Private Loans: Facts and Trends in 2008," May 2014, http://ticas.org/sites/default/files/legacy/files/pub/private_loan_facts_trends_08.pdf.

11. Congressional Budget Office, "Baseline Projections for the Student Loan Program," April 2014, https://www.cbo.gov/sites/default/files/51310-2014-04-StudentLoan.pdf.

12. Jonathan Marino, "Startups Are Going to Make Billions Doing a (Safer) Version of What Wall Street Did with Home Loans," *Business Insider*, June 10, 2015, http://www.businessinsider.com/startups-are-securitizing-student-loans-2015-6.

13. Terri Harris, "Student Loan Default Could Result in License Revocation," Tennessee Bar Association, July 21, 2010, http://www.tba.org/journal/student-loan-default-could-result-in-license-revocation.

14. Doug Lederman, "Inside the Cuomo Probe," *Inside Higher Ed*, July 30, 2007, https://www.insidehighered.com/news/2007/07/30/cuomo.

15. Jeffrey Sparshott, "Congratulations, Class of 2015. You're the Most Indebted Ever (for Now)," *Wall Street Journal*, May 8, 2015, http://blogs.wsj.com/economics/2015/05/08/congratulations-class-of-2015-youre-the-most-indebted-ever-for-now/.

16. College Board, "Tuition and Fees and Room and Board over Time, 1975–76 to 2015–16, Selected Years," December 2015, http://trends.collegeboard.org/college-pricing/figures-tables/tuition-and-fees-and-room-and-board-over-time-1975-76-2015-16-selected-years.

17. Bob Meister, "Debt and Taxes: Can the Financial Industry Save Public Universities?," *Representations* 116 (Fall 2011): 128.

18. Posted by Steven, "We Are the Crisis," *After the Fall: Communiqués from Occupied California*, February 26, 2011, http://libcom.org/library/after-fall-communiques-occupied-california.

19. From a January 8, 2011, conference presentation at the "MLA Sub-Conference," an alternative to the 2011 Modern Language Association. Courtesy of the author.

20. See the Debt Collective, accessed May 23, 2016, https://debtcollective.org/.

21. Lynn O'Shaughnessy, "More Students Working (a Lot) in College," CBS Money Watch, February 5, 2013, http://www.cbsnews.com/news/more-students-working-a-lot-in-college/.

22. Adamson, "Accounting for Ashes," 164.

23. For the most influential of these criticisms, see Martha Nussbaum, *Not for Profit: Why Democracy Needs the Humanities* (Princeton, NJ: Princeton University Press, 2010); Henry Giroux, *Neoliberalism's War on Higher Education* (Chicago: Haymarket Books, 2014); and Wendy Brown, *Undoing the Demos: Neoliberalism's Stealth Revolution* (Cambridge, MA: MIT Press, 2015).

24. See Pedro Nuno Teixeira, "Gary Becker's Early Work on Human Capital—Collaborations and Distinctiveness," *Journal of Labor Economics* 3.12 (2014): 1–20.

25. James Galbraith, *Created Unequal: The Crisis in American Pay* (Chicago: University of Chicago Press, 2000), 25.

26. See Diana Carew, "Young College Grads: Real Earnings Fell in 2011," Progressive Policy Institute, September 20, 2012, http://www.progressivepolicy.org/issues/economy/young-college-grads-real-earnings-fell-in-2011/; Jared Bernstein and Lawrence Mishel, "Education and the Inequality Debate," Economic Policy Institute, February 8, 2007, http://www.epi.org/publication/ib232/; John Cassidy, "College Calculus: What's the Real Value of Higher Education?," *New Yorker*, September 7, 2015, http://www.newyorker.com/magazine/2015/09/07/college-calculus.

27. Sánchez and Zhu, "Student Loan Delinquency."

28. Lauren Berlant, *Cruel Optimism* (Durham, NC: Duke University Press, 2011), 2. Later in the book, Berlant deals explicitly with the effects of the crisis on "cruel optimism," arguing that "a recession grimace has appeared, somewhere between a frown, a

smile, and a tight lip. As more people . . . are seen watching their dreams become foreclosed on in material and fantasmatic ways, the grimace produces another layer of face to create a space of delay while subject and world adjust to how profoundly fantasmatic the good-life dreams were, after all" (196). I find this a helpful account, yet I think the subjectivity I am describing differs from Berlant's "grimace" in two ways. First, historically/generationally, I am suggesting that the students I am describing aren't forced to "adjust" to the loss of the good-life fantasy because they never had a very strong attachment to it in the first place—not necessarily because they don't want it but because they have never felt entirely confident they would achieve it; for many of them, after all, the dream of upward mobility was already foreclosed for their parents. Second, politically, I am suggesting that these students (perhaps unlike their parents) do not find it necessary to produce a stoic front—although they are not deluded, they are very angry, and they are willing to share their anger with one another.

29. Chris Nealon, "Value/Theory/Crisis," *PMLA* 127.1 (January 2012): 106.

Index

Adamson, Morgan, 187, 192–93, 220n69
Adorno, Theodor, 89–90, 125–26, 141
affect: collective, 36, 195; consumer, 26–28; and debt, 57–58, 76–77, 80–81, 83–86, 95, 195–96; and credit relations, 79; and irrational exuberance, 172; relationship to the home, 149; and realism, 206n39
Agee, James, 114, 116
Ai, Weiwei, 135–36
Akerlof, George, 22, 26
Al-Shawaf, Rayyan, 69
American Insurance Group (AIG), 21–22
Amityville Horror, The, 149–50, 160
Ariely, Dan, 26
Aristotle, 34, 52
Arrighi, Giovanni, 13–14
Azoulay, Ariella, 104

Bailey, Amanda, 176
Baker, Jennifer, 4
Balakrishnan, Gopal, 13–14, 131–32, 140, 203n53
Bank of America, 72
Batchen, Geoffrey, 104
Baucom, Ian, 3–4, 211n50
behavioral economics, 16, 22–24, 25–30, 31–33, 36, 38, 40–41, 46, 47–48, 50–51, 53–54, 55, 206n38, 206–07n39; psychological foundations of, 28–29, 205n20
Benjamin, Walter, 93, 105, 141–42
Berlant, Lauren, 55, 194–95, 229–30n28
Bernanke, Ben, 146, 162–63
Bernes, Jasper, 186–87, 215n93
Bishop, Claire, 86
Blackstone (hedge fund), 147–48
Bourke-White, Margaret, 112–13
Brenner, Robert, 131
Brown, Michael Christopher, 137–40
Brown, Wendy, 52
Bryan, Dick, 167
Bush, George W., 153–54

capital: accumulation, 12–15, 131, 179, 187; circulation of, 46, 163, 169, 186; creation/destruction, 42; finance, 29, 52, 143, 187, 190; global, 51–52, 141, 148; human, 52, 192–93; and labor, 150,186; speculative, 137, 173–74
capitalism, 2–4, 10–12, 13–16, 42, 127, 136; crisis of 13–14, 17–18, 103, 132, 135, 140, 142, 187; late, 47, 71, 74, 105, 142; and subjectivity, 54, 95
caricature, 58, 68, 69–71; and the zany, 74–76, 211n53
Carruthers, Bruce, 162
Carson, Ann, 123
Cassidy, John, 27
Cato Institute, 154–57, 183
caveat emptor, doctrine of, 18, 152, 160–61
Cayne, Jimmy, 22
character/characterization: and credit, 58, 60; moral, 2, 18, 23, 40; novelistic, 2, 4, 16–17, 58–61, 66–67, 69, 75–77; psychology of, 30, 51; racialization of, 67–68; rich, 33, 54; and type, 58, 60–61, 67–68, 76
China, ghost cities of, 102, 135–42
City Life/Vida Urbana, 187–88
Clover, Carol, 153, 177, 179–80
Clover, Joshua, 191
Cohen, Paula, 155
collateralized debt obligation (CDO), 49, 221–22n12
collateralized mortgage obligation (CMO), 146, 221–22n12
consumer: debt, 4, 7–8, 10, 54, 79, 112, 120, 136–37, 187–89, 194; demand, 41, 54, 62; desire, 25, 38–39; irresponsibility of, 23, 38
consumption, 1, 5, 10, 25, 37–38, 46, 62, 112, 115–16, 154
Cooper, Melinda, 78, 84, 125, 129
Corinthian Colleges, 192
Countrywide Mortgage, 22, 72
Crawlspace (dir. Josh Stolberg, 2013), 143–44, 151, 152–53, 155, 157–61, 182–83

credibility: and character, 61; epistemology of, 58; fiscal, 55, 64; narrative, 76; social, 61
credit, 39, 54; bureaus, 56–57, 63–65, 76; consumer, 55, 59–62, 67–68; cost of, 21; crisis, 16; depersonalization of, 214n80; economy, 1–2, 58, 59–62, 65, 74; feminization of, 38; market, 21, 23; and personal responsibility, 2, 55, 57, 65; relationships, 56, 78; and subjectivity, 16; supply of, 11–13
credit-crisis novel, 16, 22–25, 30, 31–33, 40, 43, 53, 54, 67
credit evaluation: and moral character, 58, 59–61, 63, 65; and narrative, 59–60, 62–63, 65–66, 75–76, 79; and novel reading, 60; and novelistic character, 60–61, 65, 66–67; objectivity of, 56–57, 63, 64–65; and personal data, 65–66, 86–90; quantitative turn in, 58, 62–65, 67, 72; and typification, 59, 60–61, 65–68
credit monitoring/reporting, 55–56, 59–60, 63, 75–76, 80
credit scoring, 2, 16–17, 55–58, 63, 65–66, 79; and character/characterization, 58–59, 69; personal nature of, 56–57, 75–76, 214n80; personification of, 55–57; racialization of, 17, 55, 63–64, 66–68, 71–74; and risk, 61–62
Creedon, Kelly, 102
Crippens, Kirk, 101
crisis: capitalist, 13–16, 42, 103; credit, 22; and culture, 13–16; economic, 22, 26; financial, 21–22, 25, 28, 45–46; housing, 38; market, 26, 29; subjectivity, 18, 196–97; subprime, 47–48; terminal, 15, 105, 141–42, 203n53
Curry, Michael, 69

Davis, Mike, 178
dead pledge, 1–2, 16, 18, 126–27, 150, 183, 189, 197
De Boever, Arne, 31
debt: and anti-debt politics, 18; collection, 120; consumer, 7–8; consumerism and, 23, 54; critical study of, 2, 57, 77–79, 80–81; culture of, 2–4; default, 1–2; domestic, 24; economy, 5–15; in fiction, 23; impersonality of, 77, 80, 82, 86–95; invisibility of, 113; market in, 24; and moral obligation, 144, 159, 195; mortgage, 38–39, 148; personal nature of, 58, 77–79, 80–86; punishment for, 120; securitization of, 2, 5–7, 10, 17, 21, 29, 38–39, 62, 144–48; strike, 18, 192, 197; and subjectivity, 16; unpayable, 1, 25, 76, 100, 144, 146. See also indebtedness
Debt Collective, 192
Dee, Jonathan: *The Privileges*, 16, 22, 24, 30, 31, 32, 49–54
Defoe, Daniel, 29

Deleuze, Gilles, 71
de Man, Paul, 91–92, 94
deregulation: banking, 6, 12–13, 62; of mortgage industry, 145–46, 153, 221n10
Derrida, Jacques, 156–57
Detroit, photography of, 102, 104, 105–13, 129–35, 137, 141–42; as uncanny spectacle, 131–32, 220n69
Dienst, Richard, 3, 77–78, 100, 102, 113, 126, 219n54
Dobbz, Hannah, 159
domestic life/domesticity, 23–24, 47, 105, 115–16, 125, 217–18n36
Donnelly, Timothy, 17; "To His Debt," 58, 77, 91–95, 215n94
Drag Me To Hell (dir. Sam Raimi, 2009), 143–44, 151, 161–69, 182–83
Dream Home (dir. Pang Ho-cheung, 2010), 143–44, 148, 151, 161–63, 169–76, 182–83, 226n76
Dreiser, Theodor, 34–35, 37
Dworkin, Greg, 90

economic rationality/irrationality, 2, 25–30, 34, 36, 38–40, 46, 48, 54, 55
Engels, Friedrich, 93
Equal Credit Opportunity Act (1974), 63
Equifax (credit bureau), 63
Equal Credit Opportunity Act (1974), 5, 63–64
Evans, Walker, 114–16
Eviction, 9, 16; action against, 2, 187–88; photography of, 17, 101–03, 113–21, 146–47, 154; and the police, 118–21; spectacle of, 100; violence of, 148
Experian (credit bureau), 56–57, 63, 147, 214n80

Fair Isaac Corporation (FICO), 56, 63, 65
Fannie Mae, 6, 145
Federal Trade Commission (FTC), 64
Federal Reserve, 7, 21, 43–45, 146, 194
feral houses, 103, 105–113; and racialization, 109–10
financial crisis (2008), 1–2, 5, 14–16, 18, 21–24, 25–30, 38, 41–42, 43, 46, 47–48, 49–50, 102, 105, 130–32; humanization of, 31–33, 40
financialization, 1–2, 13–14, 52, 135, 143,148–49, 166, 168
Finn, Margot, 3–4, 60
foreclosure, 2, 16–18, 100, 147, 153; and the anti-foreclosure movement, 186–88; crisis, 152, 154–55, 158; photography of, 101–04, 105–113, 121–24, 127–29; and the police, 186–88; risk of, 18, 143–44, 222n16; violence of, 155
Foreclosure Defense Group, 188
Fowler, Elizabeth, 59, 66
Fox, Justin, 27

Franzen, Jonathan, 32
FreeScore.com, 63; "Three Score Guys, The," 55–57, 66–67, 72–73, 112
Freud, Sigmund, 103, 123, 125–27, 129, 133, 141, 219n54

Gaddis, William, 32
Gagnier, Regina, 25
Ghosh, Bishnupriya, 178
Gilden, Bruce, 102, 105–13, 140
Glass Steagall Act (1933), repeal of, 145, 167
Goede, Marieke de, 38
Goldman Sachs, 18, 24, 168
Goldsmith, Kenneth, 90
Gotham, Kevin Fox, 163
gothic genre, 143, 149–50, 156, 223n25; and the gothic economy, 18, 144
Gowan, Peter, 13, 221n10
Graeber, David, 2–3, 77–78
Great Depression, 1, 6, 145
Greenspan, Alan, 23, 154, 172
Griffioen, James, 102, 105–13

Harney, Stefano, 3, 129
Harvey, David, 12
Harvey, William, 162
Haslett, Adam: *Union Atlantic*, 16, 22, 24, 30, 31, 32, 42–49
Hido, Todd, 102, 123–25
Holmes, Oliver Wendell, 158–59
homo economicus, 25–27, 38, 54, 79
homelessness, 9, 100, 147, 180, 182
Hong Kong, housing bubble in, 170–76
horror film genre, 18, 143–44, 149–53, 160–61, 167–68, 177–83, 223–24n31; and the final girl, 177, 182; and the home-invasion thriller, 18, 143, 151–53, 155, 179, 224n35
hospitality, 156–57
housing bubble, 99–101, 115, 143, 153, 170
housing crisis, 16–18, 38, 100–102, 105–10, 113, 118, 147, 159, 180, 192
Hughes, Rachel, 109
Hyman, Louis, 7, 10, 79, 163

indebtedness, condition of, 2, 54, 58, 83, 113, 185–197, 201n26; experience of, 77–86; persistence of, 195–97; political action against, 185–88, 191–92, 196–96. *See also* debt
individual: as economic actor, 24–25, 27–29, 32, 35–49, 53–54, 57, 61, 63, 65; and moral obligation, 45; psychology, 22, 43, 48, 51, 54, 57, 61, 63–64; self-interest, 45–46
irrational exuberance, 26, 30, 38, 76, 172–73, 226n76; from below, 84, 162, 197. *See also* economic rationality/irrationality

Jackson, Virginia, 90
Jameson, Fredric, 61, 113–14, 132, 151, 178
Jeacle, Ingrid, 65
Joseph, Miranda, 3, 77–78

Kahneman, Daniel, 26
Kennerk, Emily, 102
Keynes, John Maynard, 47, 163–64, 169
King, Stephen, 149–50
Koumoundourous, Olga, 102
Kracauer, Siegfried, 103–04

La Berge, Leigh, 41–42, 204n3
Lady Credit, figure of, 29, 38
Lancaster, John, 31, 32, 40
Lazzarato, Mauricio, 2–3, 78–80, 94
Leary, John Patrick, 131
Lee, Rachel, 136–37
Levi-Strauss, Claude, 15–16
Lewis, Michael, 112
Lipartito, Kenneth, 59–60, 65
liquidity, 21, 29, 47, 51, 148–49, 161–170; crisis of, 5–7
Lo, Andrew, 28
Locke, John, 155–56
Lorentzen, Christian, 31
Lye, Colleen, 136, 211n50
Lynch, Deirdre, 3–4, 60, 69, 164–65
Lypsyte, Sam: *The Ask*, 22–23, 30

Macleod, Henry Dunning, 145
macroeconomics, 24–25, 28–29, 40, 44
Marchand, Yves, 102, 129–35, 140
markets, financial, 29, 35–36, 39–42, 47–48; regulation of, 28–29, 37, 45–46; public faith/trust in, 44–49; and sociality, 46–49
Marron, Donncha, 63, 65
Martin, Randy, 167, 222n16
Marx, Karl, 12, 49, 54, 78–79, 93–94, 103, 126, 133, 140–41, 186, 219n54
Mauss, Marcel, 58–59
Mazar, Iyar, 147, 222n16
McCormack, Karen, 147, 222n16
McPhee, Martha: *Dear Money*, 16, 23, 24, 30, 31, 32, 33–42, 48
mediation: cultural, 4, 17, 30, 39–41, 58, 85, 116, 141–42; economic, 45, 54, 182; photographic, 103–04, 116; problem of, 33, 42–43; through credit evaluation/scoring, 16, 65–66, 68, 76; through personification, 57, 77; through prosopopoeia, 95; through typification, 61, 104
Meffre, Romain, 102, 129–35, 140
Meister, Robert, 190
Merrill Lynch, 21

Index

Michaels, Walter Benn, 37, 53, 77
microeconomics, 2, 16, 24–25, 29, 32, 37–38, 40, 44, 48, 65, 206n30, 206–07n39
Mirowski, Philip, 26
Mitropoulos, Angela, 3, 78, 84, 125, 129
money, 2, 37, 39, 40, 46–49; agency of, 50–54, 133; circulation of, 43–45, 54, 162–64, 167–68; liquidity of, 10, 164–68, 173, 182; and the talking coin, 164–65
Moore, John, 102, 114–18, 121
Moretti, Franco, 150, 167–68, 176
mortgage, 6–9, 16–17, 35, 41, 72, 101; adjustable-rate, 6; contract, 1, 18, 144, 150; as debt, 8–10, 38–39, 100; industry deregulation, 153–54; holders, 23–24, 154, 177, 189; lending, 143–48, 189; subprime, 6–7, 9, 21–22, 72, 100, 145–48, 174, 186–87, 189, 191, 196; title to, 159–60. *See also* dead pledge
mortgage-backed security (MBS), 6–7, 21, 34, 37–38, 48–49, 120, 146, 163, 221–22n12
Moten, Fred, 3, 74, 84
Mother's Day (dir. Darren Lynn Bousman, 2010), 143–44, 148, 151, 152–53, 156–61, 179–83
Mother's Day (dir. Charles Kaufman, 1980), 152–53, 179–82
Mozilo, Angelo, 22–23

narrative: and credit evaluation, 59–60, 62–63, 65; form, 17, 24–25, 35–36, 54; focalization, 31–33, 44–45, 50; and free indirect style, 51–53; omniscience, 45, 51; perspective/voice, 40, 52
naturalism, 32, 34–35, 41–42
Nealon, Christopher, 42, 196
Neilson, Brett, 78
Ngai, Sianne, 74–75, 84, 211n53
Nietzsche, Friedrich, 78–80, 125–26
Norris, Frank, 29, 35–36
Norton, Richard, 109

Obama, Barack, 47, 110
Occupy Wall Street, 58, 81
Ortlieb, Claus Peter, 14–15

Parikka, Jussi, 78
Pasanek, Brad, 163
Pasquale, Frank, 72
Paulson, Henry, 24
payback (retribution), 18, 144, 164, 176–83
personhood, 2, 53–54; debt and, 16, 25, 57, 93; economic, 57; fictions of, 17, 53, 67; legal, 91; and property, 156; social, 59, 75–78, 80, 95; subjective, 65–66. *See also* social person
personification, 17, 55, 57–58, 75–80, 82–84, 90–95

Peschel, Joseph, 31
Peters, John Francis, 102, 121–25
photography: aerial, 137–38; documentary, 101–05; of eviction, 17, 101–03, 113–21, 146–47, 154; of foreclosure, 101–04, 105–113, 121–24, 127–29; indexicality of, 103–04; as mediation, 103–04, 141–42
photojournalism, 101–03; and collusion with police, 118–21
Platt, Spencer, 101, 105
Pocock, J.G., 29, 36
Polillo, Simone, 163
political economy, 14–15, 25, 38
Poon, Martha, 64
Poovey, Mary, 3, 90–91
portraiture, 58, 77, 80–86
Proechel, T.J., 102, 127–29
property, 1–2, 15, 34, 41; adverse possession of, 158–59; domestic, 99, 114–16, 123, 126; property ownership, 18, 39–40, 99, 144, 148–50, 153–60, 183; and privacy, 102–03, 114–16; private, 125–26; rights of, 109, 118, 125, 144, 154–55, 158–59; and sentiment, 144, 154, 156–58; stigmatized, 160–61, 172, 175, 178–79; violence against, 186–88
prosopopoeia, 58, 77, 80
psychology: behavioral, 26, 63; collective/mass, 32, 36, 205n20; economic, 26–29, 47, 51; individual, 22, 30, 32–33, 48, 50–52, 54, 205n20
Puchner, Eric: *Model Home*, 22–23, 30

Radin, Margaret Jane, 156
Rafferty, Michael, 167
Ranieri, Lewis, 147
Read, Jason, 78
Reagan, Ronald, 8
real estate, 34, 37, 38–39; and horror film, 149–51; and liquidity, 148–49, 161–70, 173; and the rental market, 147–48; and risk, 144–49, 161–63; and securitization, 161–63, 167, 174
reality television, 115, 217n35, 217–18n36
realist novel, 3–4, 16–17, 22, 23, 24, 30, 32, 33, 36, 58, 59–61, 67, 68, 69, 151
reverse redlining, 72, 148, 180, 182
Reyes, Paul, 102–04
Rich, Damon, 101–02
Richardson, Brian, 52
risk, 18, 21, 34, 40; assessment of, 56, 59–60, 61–62, 65, 74–75; control by, 64, 74, 144–45; financialization of, 143–44; prediction of, 63–64; pricing of, 5–6, 62–63, 145; radical, 147, 222n16
Roberts, Adrienne, 79–80, 121
Rogers, Daniel, 25
Ronda, Margaret, 94, 219n54

Rosler, Martha, 104–05
Ross, Andrew, 3
Roth, Marco, 31, 49–51
Rothko, Mark, 123

sabotage, politics of, 186–88, 197
Safransky, Sarah, 107–09
Sarkar, Bhaskar, 171–72, 173
Schafran, Alex, 180
Schillinger, Liesl, 30–31
Securities and Exchange Commission (SEC), 21–22
Sekula, Alan, 103–04, 118
Shaviro, Steven, 51
Shaw, George Bernard, 34
Shell, Marc, 3
Shelley, Mary, 150
Shiller, Robert, 22, 26, 27–28, 29, 31, 40, 41, 47–48, 99, 172
Shimpach, Shawn, 115
Shteyngart, Gary: *Super Sad True Love Story*, 17, 58, 67–75, 84, 95, 211n53
Skinner, B.F., 28
Smith, Adam, 45–46, 48, 162–63, 165
Smith, Douglas, 102
Smith, Rachel Greenwald, 206–07n39
social person, 57, 58–59, 65–67, 69–70, 75–81. *See also* personhood
social reproduction, 10–11, 54, 82, 93, 195, 197; sites of, 186–87
Sontag, Susan, 114–15
speculation, economic, 29, 34, 36, 38; and risk, 24, 28
squatters' rights, 158–59
stereotype, 58, 68, 71–75; racial, 71–74, 211n50
Stinchcombe, Arthur, 162
Stoker, Bram, 150, 167–68, 176
student loan asset backed securities (SLABS), 189
student loan debt, 2, 8–9, 188–97; and default, 194, 196–97; and human capital, 192–93; and race, 189; and student militancy, 191–92
Suau, Anthony, 102, 114, 118–21
subprime: class/population, 74, 84, 95, 121, 148; crisis, 29, 47–48; lending, 6–7, 9, 21–22, 58, 66, 72, 100, 145–48, 174, 176–77, 180, 186–87, 189, 191, 196
sympathy, 31, 47, 49–50, 113–14, 116, 159

Taibbi, Matt, 168
Taleb, Nassim, 41
Tapia, Francisco, 187

Thaler, Richard, 26
Thatcher, Margaret, 53
Thornton, Cassie, 17, 58, 75–77, 83–86, 95
Time (magazine), 21–23, 28, 38
Timmons, Mathew, 17; *CREDIT*, 58, 77, 86–91, 95, 213–14n76, 215n94
Toscano, Alberto, 84–85
totality, economic, 44, 174; historical, 42; social, 16, 24–25, 32–33, 38, 40, 42–46, 66, 95
toxic assets, 7
Toyoshima, Tak, 72–73
TransUnion (credit bureau), 63
Trenkle, Norbert, 12
Tversky, Amos, 26
type/typification, 58–61, 104–05; and racialization, 67–68, 211n50; and social class, 61, 66–67

Ulfstjerne, Michael Alexander, 135
uncanny: and finance capital, 143; homes, 103, 123–29; and horror film, 151; landscapes, 103, 135–42; and nostalgia, 125, 219n54; postindustrial, 129–35; temporality of, 17–18, 132–33, 140–41
universities: and the financial economy, 188–93; political action against, 191; and student debt 189–90; and the tuition bubble, 190

vandalism: against foreclosed property, 185–86
VantageScore (credit scoring), 63
Vidler, Anthony, 125
Voyce, Stephen, 86–87

Walsh, Eamonn, 65
Walter, Jess: *Financial Lives of the Poets, The*, 22–23, 30, 41
Watt, Ian, 217–18n36
"We Are the 99%" tumblr, 77, 81–83
Wharton, Edith, 35
Wells, David, 102
White, Brent, 110
Williams, Raymond, 67
Wood, James, 22, 49–50
Woolf, Edward, 113
World Bank, 5
Wortham, Simon, 78

Yang, Anne Stephenson, 136

Zajonc, Robert, 27
Zimmerman, David, 35
Žižek, Slavoj, 54

Amy Hungerford, *Making Literature Now*

J.D. Connor, *The Studios After the Studios: Neoclassical Hollywood, 1970–2010*

Michael Trask, *Camp Sites: Sex, Politics, and Academic Style in Postwar America*

Loren Glass, *Counter-Culture Colophon: Grove Press, the* Evergreen Review, *and the Incorporation of the Avant-Garde*

Michael Szalay, *Hip Figures: A Literary History of the Democratic Party*

Jared Gardner, *Projections: Comics and the History of Twenty-First-Century Storytelling*

Jerome Christensen, *America's Corporate Art: The Studio Authorship of Hollywood Motion Pictures*

The authorized representative in the EU for product safety and compliance is:
Mare Nostrum Group
B.V Doelen 72
4831 GR Breda
The Netherlands

www.ingramcontent.com/pod-product-compliance
Lightning Source LLC
Chambersburg PA
CBHW031808220426
43662CB00007B/575